CHINA'S ECONOMIC DEVELOPMENT
AND DEMOCRATIZATION

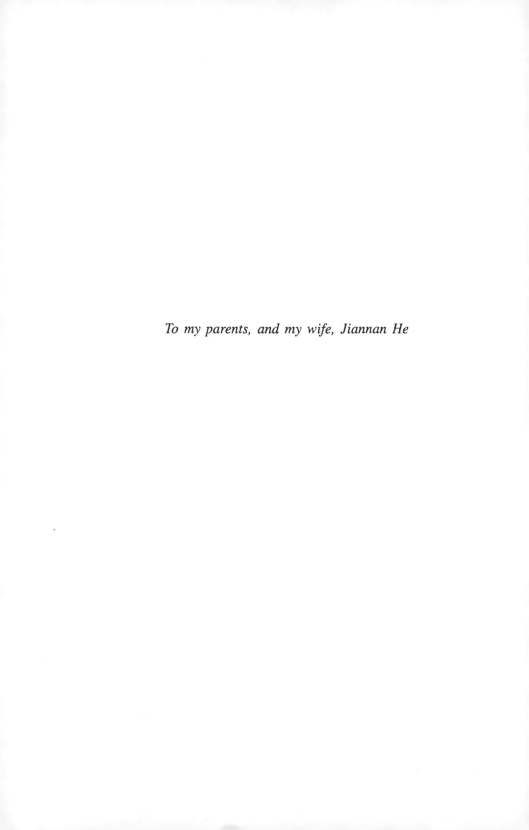

To my parents, and my wife, Jiannan He

China's Economic Development and Democratization

YANLAI WANG
University of Limerick, Ireland

Routledge
Taylor & Francis Group

LONDON AND NEW YORK

First published 2003 by Ashgate Publishing

2 Park Square, Milton Park, Abingdon, Oxon OX14 4RN
711 Third Avenue, New York, NY 10017, USA

Routledge is an imprint of the Taylor & Francis Group, an informa business

First issued in paperback 2016

British Library Cataloguing in Publication Data
Wang, Yanlai
    China's economic development and democratization. - (The
    Chinese economy series)
    1. Democratization - China 2. China - Economic policy -
    1976-2000 3. China - Economic policy - 2000- 4. China -
    Economic conditions - 1976-2000 5. China - Economic
    conditions - 2000- 6. China - Politics and government -
    1976 -
    I. Title
    338.9'51

Library of Congress Cataloging-in-Publication Data
Wang, Yanlai, 1953 -
    China's economic development and democratization / Yanlai Wang.
        p. cm. -- (The Chinese economy series)
    Includes bibliographical references and index.
    ISBN 978-0-7546-3620-5
    1. China--Economic policy--1976-2000. 2. China--Economic conditions--1976-2000. 3. China--Politics and government--1976- 4. Democratization--China. I. Title. II. Series.

    HC427.92.W388 2003
    330.951--dc21

                                 2003056075

ISBN 978-0-7546-3620-5 (hbk)
ISBN 978-1-138-25867-9 (pbk)

Transfered to Digital Printing in 2009

Contents

List of Figures

List of Tables

Preface

Two decades of economic reforms and opening up to the outside world have transformed China tremendously, bringing economic development and modernization to China as expected by the ruling elite who inaugurated the reforms in 1978. However, the economic reforms and open-door policy have also brought some economic, social and political transformations that were unexpected by the ruling elite. The market economy has been accepted as the economic system to replace the command economy in China. Private ownership has been restored and the private sector has become an indispensable component of the economy. The Communist Party of China (CPC) has changed from a proletariat revolutionary party that vowed to eliminate haves to a party that opens its door to haves. Although the CPC's ultimate goal – communism – remains the same, the route to reach the end – common prosperity – has changed from eliminating haves and reaching common prosperity among the whole population at the same time in the unforeseeable future, to creating and multiplying haves among sections of the population and gradually reaching common prosperity among the whole population.

What would China look like two decades later when the market economy has replaced the command economy in every aspect of the Chinese economy, when the middle and upper classes have become the majority among the population, and when the private sector has become the backbone of the economy? China would become a democratic country with basic features of a democratic polity, such as free press, independent judiciary, and multi-party competition for government office, as some analysts predict. China would maintain the present political system with the CPC dominating the political power, as the CPC hopes. China might either turn into a military dictatorship or become disintegrated into several states, the worst scenario of the Chinese transformations as worried by analysts. Or, China might become something between these scenarios.

A safer way to predict the outcomes of the Chinese transition is to investigate the economic, social and political transformations China has undergone since 1978, find out the nature of the Chinese transition, and predict its future transition route based on an analysis of these transformations. As the case of China's transition is unique and demands new approaches to these unfolding transformations, this book proposes an institutional approach and applies it to the Chinese transitional case. Based on transitional theories and the new institutionalism, this book suggests an institutional analytic framework that comprises political actors, institutions, and six policy institutional environments: international environment, ideological environment, domestic political environment, domestic economic environment, constitutional environment, and domestic civil-social environment. Since it is impossible to apply the institutional analytic framework to all the cases of the Chinese transformations within the limited space of this book, the new framework is applied to three selected cases: (1) agricultural reform and open-door policy, (2) the restoration of private enterprises and property rights, and (3) the political and cultural orientations of the mass public. The first two case studies are devoted to examining the dynamic interactions between political actors, institutions and policy institutional environments in institutionalizing China's major economic reforms and open-door measures that have led to China's economic, social and political transformations since 1978. The third case study is a public opinion survey, employing the same questionnaire that Andrew J. Nathan and Tianjian Shi used in their 1990 survey.[1] The survey will help us find out what changes have occurred in the orientations of the mass public who have experienced such dramatic social, economic and political transformations since 1978.

The author has selected the three cases as the first case is the origination of the Chinese transition, the second case is the confirmation of freedom of pursuing wealth and holding private assets, and the third case is a review of the mass public political and cultural orientations. Although the book has an inherent limitation of three case studies, the author believes that these studies will add to the understanding of the Chinese transition and help to answer these difficult questions: will economic freedom lead to political freedom? Will social and economic development and transformations lead to democratization? Is China moving closer towards democracy? The major findings from the case studies on the dynamic interactions between political actors, institutions and policy institutional environments indicate that changes in one institutional environment often lead to changes in other institutional environments. With the help of the case studies, we have also found that changes in the institutional environments have an influence on the institutional behavior of the post-Mao ruling elite, who tend to be less authoritarian, more pragmatic, and more responsive to the institutional environments. The evidence of the case studies suggests that China is moving closer, on the continuum of regime change, towards democracy, as institutional building in the economic arena or environment has been spreading into the ideological, civil-social, constitutional and political environments.

This book has many limitations but it attempts to find a new approach to the study of the Chinese transition. The author welcomes researchers of China to refine or refute his arguments in order to find a better approach to the Chinese transition, which is taking a country of over 20 per cent of the world population towards modernization and economic prosperity in the first half of the 21st century, an exciting economic and social development prospect for mankind and an exciting transitional event that economists and political and social scientists would not want to miss. May we join forces to find a better way to understand the Chinese transition and help it to move towards not only economic prosperity, but also social stability and political democracy!

---

[1] Andrew J. Nathan is Professor of Political Science at Columbia University and Tianjian Shi, Assistant Professor of Political Science, at the University of Iowa.

Acknowledgements

I owe the publication of this book to those institutions and people who have offered me their generous help, while any mistakes and omissions in the book remain mine. My sincere thanks go to Professor Nicholas Rees, Professor Bernadette Andreosso-O'Callaghan, and Dr. Neil Robinson for their excellent academic supervision and unwavering encouragement during the process of my Ph.D. research and thesis writing, on which the present book is based.[1] I am particularly grateful to Professor Nicholas Rees and Professor Bernadette Andreosso-O'Callaghan for offering me invaluable suggestions and comments on revising the original manuscript.

I would very much like to thank the University of Limerick for granting generous financial assistance, including the CCP Scholarship and the Seed Funding, for carrying out the Ph.D. research, conducting an opinion survey in China, and attending conferences, which has made it financially possible for the Ph.D. research to be completed as planned.

I would also like to express sincere thanks to Professor Andrew J. Nathan and Professor Tianjian Shi for offering their 1990 survey questionnaire to be used in the 2000 survey.

I am deeply grateful to Professor Yongzheng Wei of Journalism Institute, Shanghai Academy of Social Sciences, Professor Weizhi Deng of Shanghai University, and Professor Gongyun Gu of East China University of Politics and Law for offering me their inspirational suggestions and comments on the research proposal. I would also like to thank Professor Guangchu Ren and Ms. Xin Ye for their cooperation in the 2000 survey.

I would like to thank Brendan George, Mary Savigar, Anne Keirby, Carolyn Court, Donna Hamer, Amanda Richardson, and Adrian Shanks for their professional assistance in having this book published by Ashgate. I would also very much like to thank Margaret O'Reilly and Mrs. Pam Bertram for their excellent editing that has made this book quite a readable one.

My special thanks go to my parents, Yongqing Wang and Ronghua Shui, and my wife, Jiannan He, who have provided me with their continual emotional support and encouragement, without which I could not possibly have gone so far as to turn the research into a book.

---

[1] Dr. Robinson was my supervisor when I spent the first year of my Ph.D. research at the University of Essex; Professor Rees and Professor Andreosso-O'Callaghan were my supervisors when I spent the next two years at the University of Limerick.

List of Abbreviations

CASS	Chinese Academy of Social Sciences
CIPE	Center for International Private Enterprise
CPC	Communist Party of China
CPPCC	Chinese People's Political Consultative Conference
EC	European Community
EU	European Union
FDI	Foreign Direct Investment
GDP	Gross Domestic Product
GNP	Gross National Product
IMF	International Monetary Fund
ISSP	International Social Survey Program
KMT	Kuomintang (Nationalist Party)
MOFTEC	Ministry of Foreign Trade and Economic Cooperation, PRC
NATO	North Atlantic Treaty Organization
NGO	Non-governmental Organizations
NPC	National People's Congress
PLA	People's Liberation Army
PRC	People's Republic of China
RMB	Renminbi (Chinese Currency)
SEZ	Special Economic Zone
SOE	State-owned Enterprises
UK	United Kingdom
UN	United Nations
UNCTAD	United Nations Conference on Trade and Development
USA	United States of America
WTO	World Trade Organization

PART I
UNDERSTANDING THE CHINESE TRANSITION

Chapter 1

Introduction

This chapter examines the achievements of China's economic reforms and the opening up of its economy to the outside world, reviews scholarship on China's social, economic and political transformations, suggests a need to develop a new analytical framework in order to capture the dynamics of the Chinese transition, outlines assumptions and hypotheses, and lays out the structure of the book.

China's Economic Reforms and Opening Up

At the start of the 21st century, China has left behind a century that was marked by a persistent search for independence, modernity, and revolutions to achieve independence and modernization.[1] In the first half of the 20th century China witnessed successive chaotic periods of warlords, civil wars between the Kuomintang (KMT, the Nationalist Party) and the Communist Party of China (CPC), the Japanese invasion, and civil wars again between the KMT and the CPC. Under the CPC rule, China started its industrialization first based on the Soviet model in the 1950s and then on Mao's self-reliance model in the 1960s. Only in the late 1960s and the early 1970s did China find an opportunity to look towards the West for ideas, technology, and investment for its modernization.[2] Deng Xiaoping seized the opportunity and launched economic reforms and open-door programs in 1978. Deng Xiaoping called his reform 'The Second Revolution' (Deng, 1993, p.113). The first revolution was initiated by Mao Zedong in the countryside. Mao organized peasants into an armed struggle against the KMT rule, circling the cities under the KMT control and eventually winning the civil war by driving the KMT troops out of the mainland. Ironically, Deng Xiaoping initiated the second revolution also in the countryside, encouraging peasants to dismantle the agricultural collective institution: the people's commune, one of the achievements of Mao's first revolution, spreading the reform momentum into urban areas, eventually leading to the abandonment of the socialist economic system: the command economy, another achievement of Mao's first revolution. China's economic reforms and open-door policy were thus described as the restoration of capitalism (Chossudovsky, 1986, pp.201-21).

Nevertheless, more than twenty years of economic reforms and opening up to the outside world have produced significant social, economic and political changes. According to international standards, China is still a poor, developing country.[3] However, its economic development has been a success in the last two decades.

China's GDP and per capita GDP grew, between 1978 and 2001, by an average yearly rate of 9.5 per cent and 8.1 per cent, respectively. China's economy has been increasingly integrated into the world economy. Its exports and imports' share of the GDP has increased from 4.6 per cent and 5.2 per cent in 1978 to 22.9 per cent and 21.0 per cent in 2001, respectively.[4] Among the developing countries, China has been the most attractive destination for foreign direct investment (FDI).[5] For example, in 2001 China attracted 46.846 billion USD dollars of FDI, accounting for 22.87 per cent of the total FDI flow into the developing countries.[6] China was actively seeking WTO membership and has joined WTO in December 2001. China's WTO membership has boosted its external economic integration dramatically.[7] Besides the economic integration, China is seeking social and political integration with the world community, signing the International Covenant on Economic, Social and Cultural Rights in June 1998 and the International Covenant on Civil and Political Rights in October 1998.

The Communist Party of China (CPC) is developing into a party embracing not only the working class, cadres, and intellectuals, but also private entrepreneurs – the bourgeoisie that was eliminated in the 1950s.[8]

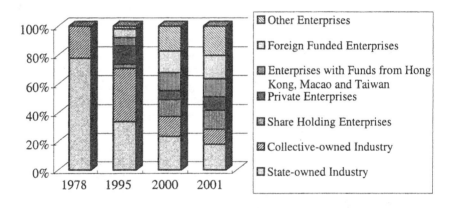

Figure 1.1 Industrial Output Value by Ownership, 1978-2001

a. Other Enterprises refer to cooperative enterprises, joint ownership enterprises, limited liability corporations, and other types of enterprises.

b. State-holding enterprises cannot be isolated from the data as they are among the non-state-owned enterprises. Their share of the industrial output value is 20,398.08 million RMB yuan in 2000 and 25,179.3 million RMB yuan in 2001.

c. The non-state-owned industrial enterprises with an annual sales income of less than five million RMB yuan have not been included since 2000.

Source : China Statistical Yearbook 1996, 1999, 2002 .

China has experienced a structural change in its economy, with its primary industry shrinking and its tertiary industry expanding[9] and with its economy diversifying into a mixture of state-owned, collective, private, foreign-funded, and share-holding economic entities (see Figures 1.1 and 1.2). China's economic freedom ranking on the *Fraser Institute Economic Freedom Index* has risen from zero in 1975 to 5.3 points in 2000 while its political rights and civil liberties rankings has shown little improvement, remaining stagnant at 7 and 6 respectively since 1998 on the *Freedom House Political Rights and Civil Liberties Freedom Index*.[10]

Market-oriented economic reforms have led to a differentiation of social classes. One research reported that there are four major social classes in China: the political and economic elites, representing one per cent of the total workforce; a new middle-class, 15.8 per cent of the total workforce; the working class, rural-urban migrants, and the peasantry, about 69 per cent of the total workforce; and the 'off-post' group: unemployed and pauperized rural population, about 14 per cent of the total workforce (He, 2000). Another research showed that there are ten social classes: Managers of State and Society (2.1 per cent of the total workforce), Managers of Enterprises (1.5 per cent), Private Enterprise Owners (0.6 per cent), Professional Specialists and Engineers (5.1 per cent), Clerks (4.8 per cent), Individual Businessmen (4.2 per cent), Commercial and Service Sector Staff (12 per cent), Industrial Workers (22.6 per cent), Agricultural Workers (44 per cent), and Urban and Rural Jobless, Unemployed, and Semi-unemployed People (3.1 per cent) (Lu, 2002)

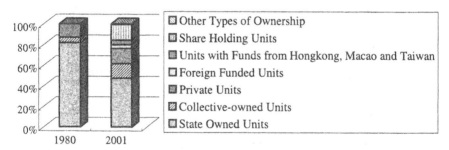

Figure 1.2 Total Investment in Fixed Assets by Ownership, 1980, 2001

Source: China Statistical Yearbook 1996, 1999, 2002.

To a large degree, two decades of China's economic reform and open-door policy have been a process of decentralization in an attempt to readjust and regulate the relations among the state, local governments, enterprises, individuals, and private businessmen, and to mobilize their enthusiasm for the four-modernization[11] drive. The main features of the decentralization are summarized as follows:

- Granting freedom to pursue wealth and to own private assets to Chinese people;

- Granting production autonomy to peasants;
- Granting production autonomy to state owned enterprises;
- Granting regulation formulating power to people's congresses of provinces, autonomous regions, municipalities directly under Central Government, cities of the provincial government seats, and other cities approved by the State Council;
- Division of administrative responsibilities between the central and local governments through a taxation and expenditure reform of 1994 that demarcates tax revenues and responsibilities for expenditures between the central and local governments (see Table 1.1).[12]

Table 1.1 Tax Revenues and Expenditures, by the Central and Local Governments

Central Revenue
- Tariffs;
- Consumption and value-added taxes collected by the Customs;
- Consumption tax;
- Income tax paid by the enterprises under the control of the central government;
- Income tax paid by local domestic banks, foreign banks, and non-bank financial institutions;
- Earnings submitted by the railway company, domestic bank head offices, and insurance central offices;
- Profits of the enterprises under the control of the central government.

Local Revenue
- Operation tax (excluding that paid by the railway company, domestic bank head offices, and insurance central offices);
- Income tax paid by local enterprises (excluding that paid by local domestic banks, foreign banks, and non-bank financial institutions);
- Individual income tax;
- Urban land use tax;
- Fixed asset investment orientation adjustment tax;
- Tax on city construction and maintenance;
- Property tax;
- Vehicle and ship tax;
- Stamp tax;
- Animal slaughter tax;
- Land value-added tax;
- Proceeds from transfer of state-owned land;
- Other miscellaneous taxes.

Revenues shared by the central and local governments
- Value-added tax: 75 per cent goes to the central government and 25 per cent to local governments;
- Tax on resources: tax on ocean oil resources goes to the central government while tax on other resources to local governments;
- Stamp tax on securities transaction: a 50-50 split between the central and local governments.

Expenditures of the central government
- For national defence;
- For the armed police troops;
- For key construction projects;
- For government administration;
- Operating expenses of government agencies;
- Payment for the debts.

Expenditures of local government
- For local government administration;
- Operating expenses of local government agencies;
- For local capital construction and technology innovation;
- For supporting agricultural production;
- For city construction and maintenance;
- For price subsidies;
- Other miscellaneous expenses.

Source: adapted from Feng and Hong (1999, pp.316-28).

Since 1978 the distribution of the GDP has been in favor of the society, indicating a wider distribution of economic resources in the society (see Figure 1.3). However, the disparity between the rich and the poor has been growing. It took less than 20 years for China to change from a society of equal poverty into one with a high disparity of income distribution. China's Gini Index rose from 0.16 in 1978 to 0.415 in 1995 and to 0.456 in 1998, higher than that of the United States.[13]

In spite of an increasing disparity of income distribution, the living standard of the general public has been improved. Its rural per capita annual net income and urban per capita annual disposable income rose from 78.6 and 185.9 US dollars in 1978 to 285.7 and 828.5 US dollars in 2001, respectively. And the people's material and cultural life has also been upgraded (see Table 1.2). Only on two fronts, the pre-reform-era ruling elite had a relatively satisfactory record of performance, namely, 95.5 per cent of children received primary education and 81 per cent of urban residents had access to tap water. On the other fronts, the reform-era ruling elite have delivered a marked improvement, narrowing down the deficiencies left over by their predecessors.

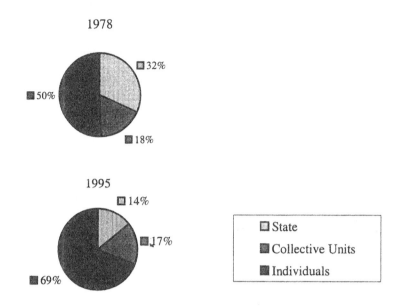

Figure 1.3 Distribution of GDP, 1978, 1995

Source: Yang and et al., (1997); *China Financial Yearbook 1996*.

Table 1.2 Improvement in People's Material and Cultural Life

Items	1978	2001
Urbanization, urban population (% of the total population)	17.9	30.4
Rural Annual Per Capita Net Income (US dollars)[14]	78.6	285.7
Urban Annual Per Capita Disposable Income (US dollars)	185.9	828.5
Rural Annual Per Capita Consumption (US dollars)	81.2	335.7
Urban Annual Per Capita Consumption (US dollars)	238.2	641.2
Balance of Savings Deposit of All Residents (year-end) (in 100 million US dollars)	123.9	8908.5
Per Capita Balance of Savings Deposit (US dollars)	12.9	698
Rural Per Capita Net Space of Residential Buildings (sqm)	8.1	25.7
Urban Per Capita Floor Space of Residential Buildings (sqm)	3.6	20.8
Rate of Access to Tap Water in Urban Areas (%) *	81	72.3
Rate of Access to Gas and Liquefied Gas in Urban Areas (%)	13.9	60.4
Number of TV Sets in Rural Areas (per 100 households)	0	105.2

Number of Color TV Sets in Urban Areas (per 100 households)	0	120.5
Enrolment Ratio of School-age Children (%)	95.5	99.1
Number of University Students (per 10,000 persons)	8.9	56.3
Number of Hospital Beds (per 10,000 persons)	19.28	23.9
Number of Doctors (per 10,000 persons)	10.73	16.9
Number of Personal Computers (per 1,000 persons in 2000)	0	15.9
Number of Internet Hosts (per 1,000 persons)	0	9.8
Access to Mobile Phones (sets per 100 persons)	0	11.4
Access to Telephones (sets per 100 persons)	0.45	14.5

* Data on the public utilities of city are based on the non-agricultural population in urban areas before 2000, but based on the total urban population in 2001.

Source: *China Statistical Yearbook 1999 and 2002*; *World Development Indicators* database, World Bank, 2002; *Semi Annual Survey Report on Internet Development in China* (January 2002).

The differentiation of social classes and the decentralization have led to a rapid development of various associations.[15] Before 1978 there were about a hundred national associations and some 6,000 regional ones. By 1996 there had been over 1,800 registered national associations and more than 200,000 regional associations, which are classified, in terms of degrees of autonomy, into three types: government-run associations, civilian-run associations, and semi-official and semi-civilian associations (Li, 1998a: pp.250-84).

Scholarship on China's Transformation

Compared to Russia's political-reform-first strategy and economic reform 'Shock therapy' which has left Russia in chronic economic disarray, China's two decades of economic reform and open-door policy experiment have been quite successful, attracting the world's attention. Scholars on China have tried, from different perspectives, to explain the process and results of China's reform experiment. Although it is widely accepted by both Chinese and Western scholars that the chaos and destruction caused by the Cultural Revolution 1966-1977 led to the initiation of China's economic reforms, Dali Yang (Yang, 1996a, and 1996b) argues that China's agricultural reform may be attributed to the Great Leap Famine of 1959-1961.[16]

Barry Naughton (Naughton, 1995, p.311) suggests that China's economic reform success did not derive from step-by-step empiricism, but rather, to a large extent, relied on the interplay of the traditional plan and the new market mechanisms. In other words, the old institutions are employed to resolve immediate economic problems while the policy-makers are committed to opening markets as rapidly as possible. He believes this gradual reform is not merely feasible but also a resilient, natural way to transform a command economy, a transformation process of 'growing out of the plan'. Susan Shirk (1993: pp.144-5) considers that the Chinese transition is a second-best and gradual two-track approach, which is creating a dynamic non-state sector while keeping the state sector afloat. It is this second best approach, Shirk argues, that successfully raises living standards and sustains the momentum of the reform drive.

Other researchers (e.g., Pei, 1995), however, argue that China's initial success owes much to the advantages of its backward state socialism. When China started the reform, it was predominantly an agricultural economy, with over 70 per cent of its labor force working in the agricultural sector without any state–paid social security. Therefore, it was much easier for China to implement an agricultural reform than an industrial reform (White, 1993, p.82).

Another group of scholars attribute China's success to its deliberately delaying of political reform, because empirical studies have shown that a sharp political discontinuity tends to be counterproductive to economic reform (Nelson, 1994). The economic-reform-first strategy is considered pragmatic, plausible, and applicable especially in poor countries (Lipset, 1994; Armijo, Biersteker and Lowenthal, 1995, pp.227-37). And recent empirical studies have shown that authoritarian regimes might be another route to modernity (Diamond and Plattner, 1995, p. xi, Haggard and Kaufman, 1992, pp.270-315).

There is no indication that the ruling elite of the Communist Party of China (CPC) and the government will reverse the market-oriented economic reform. Instead, they are trying to maintain the growth momentum through further economic and political reforms and opening up of China to the world.[17] It is conceivable that China will complete its modernity journey, covering the five stages of economic development, envisioned by Rostow (1971), in the first half of the 21st century.[18] The prospects of China emerging as a world superpower in terms of its aggregate economic power have already caused concern in the industrialized camp and its Asian neighbors. The prospects of China's modernity with mass consumption available to a population of over 1.2 billion people is not only making environment conscious people concerned of its damaging effect on the global environment,[19] but also making industrialized nations perceive China more as a potential competitor than as a developing country,[20] and even leaving some researchers and some US policy-makers worried about the 'China threat' to US security (Bernstein and Munro, 1997; McGeary, 1999).

China's prospective emergence in the 21st century as an economic superpower has triggered waves of readjustments in the world community's posture towards China. Behind the perceived 'China threat' is a deep-rooted liberal assumption that war is less likely to develop among democratic countries (Segal, 1997; Huntington, 1991a, pp.28-30). What is more, China is the largest developing country under communist rule and is developing remarkably fast. Whether China will emerge at the end of its modernity journey as a liberal democracy, military dictatorship, or something between the two extreme scenarios, therefore, is of particular importance to the world community, a lingering concern of Western policy makers, who are trying to engage China to ensure that the world's next superpower turns out more like America than like the former Soviet Union (Pellegrini, 1999).

Will economic freedom lead to political freedom? Will social and economic development and transformations lead to democratization? Is China moving closer towards democracy?

Theoretically and empirically speaking, there is little consensus among scholars on whether economic development leads to political democratization. Modernization theorists strongly believe in the eventual transition from economic development to political democracy (Lipset, 1959; Inglehart, 1997; Diamond, 1992.). Some scholars, however, offer arguments against the automatic transition from economic development to political democratization suggested by the modernization assumption, arguing that 'the emergence of democracy is not a by-product of economic development' and that 'it can be initiated at any level of development' (Przeworski and Limongi, 1997, pp.155-83). Some scholars stress both the importance of socio-economic conditions for democratization and the significant role of the leadership in the political process of democratization (Huntington, 1984, pp.193-218; 1991, p.65, p.310). After a statistical analysis of seventeen Latin American countries, Landman (1999) observed that there was no positive relationship between economic development and democracy in Latin America, while in another empirical study of 125 countries, Helliwell (1994) found a robust positive relationship between the level of per capita income and the adoption of democracy.

Scholars on China are also divided about the prospects of democratization in China. Some of them are pessimistic about the prospects of democratization in China. They argue that although the Communist Party of China (CPC) allows economic liberalization and some limited public participation in policy making process, such as village committee elections, and may even eventually accept some limited power sharing with other power groups, it is unlikely in the next decade that the CPC will relax its tight control over these democratization processes. The most likely future polity of China is one-party authoritarian regime with economic liberalization and limited political pluralism (Zhao, 1998, pp.54-9; Harding, 1998, pp.11-7).

Some are less pessimistic. Since the economic development will further the development of socio-economic pluralism based upon growing international communications and exchanges, certain kinds of significant discontinuity in the character of China's political system is more likely. In the end, the CPC will be pressed to make the necessary accommodations for political liberalism, sharing power with other new power centers. It is more likely, therefore, that China will adopt a East-Asian-style capitalist economy with a high degree of authoritarian features, or in other words, a 'gray' or quasi–democratization (White, 1993, p.256; Brzezinski, 1998, pp.4-5; Scalapino, 1998, pp.35-41; Wang, 1998, pp.48-53).

Others show some reserved optimism about China's democratic prospects. Although there exist many obstacles to democratization, such as the party leaders' determination to maintain their power through authoritarian rule, unwillingness to revisit the crackdown of the 1989 student demonstrations, reluctance to separate the party and the government, and failure to redefine its fundamental ideology in accordance with the building of a market economy in China, some encouraging democratization developments such as village committee free elections, the formation of non-governmental organizations, and the development of a legal system, are transforming China into a more democratic society than most analysts think likely. By introducing free elections at the grass root level organizations such as the village committee, the democratization momentum has been initiated and will grow in force and eventually expand upward into higher-level organizations. Although the CPC dominance will be maintained in these democratization processes by its status quo monopoly of power at early stages, its dominance will certainly be challenged and marginalized with the deepening of democratization. Since such a democratization process will contribute to China's stability, raise the leaders' international profile, consolidate their power, enhance their governance of China, and generate public support – a new source of legitimacy, it seems more likely in the next decade that democratic polity will be the best option to the Chinese policy makers (Oksenberg, 1998, pp.27-34; Chen, 1998, pp.7-10).

Still others sound more optimistic about China's democratization. While the present Chinese economy already depends, to a large extent, on the workings of a free market, the current political institutions have not been adapted quickly enough to meet the challenges created through a swift economic liberalization throughout China. China's rapid economic growth and people's rising living standards have thus made a 'revolution of rising expectations' more and more likely with the prosperity growing among its people. It is most likely, therefore, that Chinese Communism will come to an end in the next decade. After a period of turbulence in China, perhaps, two kinds of polities might evolve, one is more authoritarian when the center (the elite of the Central Government) has controlled the transition process, and the other might be more democratic when the regional powers (provinces and municipalities) have a larger say in determining the formation of the future polity (Waldron, 1998, pp.41-7)

Some researchers are more concerned about the manner of the regime's transformation. They argue that, based on the CPC intolerance of the formation of any types of legal and moderate opposition, the one-party authoritarian regime excludes the possibility of a peaceful transition and looks for a violent transformation (Nathan, 1998b).

It seems that there is a consensus among China scholars and researchers that China's market oriented reform and open policy have not only brought economic prosperity but also generated certain degrees of political liberalization and pluralism and openness to China. However, they differ with each other about the nature, manner and speed of the political change in China. In terms of the nature of the prospective polity in China, opinions vary from the authoritarian rule with limited pluralism to a liberal democracy. In terms of the manner of the change, predictions differ from an evolution to a big bang. And in terms of the time frame of the change, researchers seem to agree more on a long-term prediction than on a short-term guess.

The divergence of opinions among scholars regarding the future political development in China may be due to a number of reasons: (1) their inquiry starting points are different, ranging from origins of economic reforms to the nature of the CPC; (2) their analyses focus on different social, economic and political changes and the effects of these changes on different political aspects of the regime; and (3) their predictions mainly derive from reading into intentions of the ruling elite, or in other words, what the regime is capable of imposing on the society.

The variety of research has certainly provided insights into the social, economic and political changes since 1978 and the nature and capability of the regime. However, the conclusions are so diverse that they cannot offer a reliable prediction as to the political future of China. To explore the dynamic changes in the Chinese economic and political systems needs a new analytical framework specifically devised for the Chinese transition.

This book proposes an institutional approach to the study of the social, economic and political transformations in China. The institutional analytic framework, to be discussed in the next chapter, is intended to examine the dynamic interactions between political actors and institutions[21] in the context of six macro institutional environments: international environment, ideological environment, domestic political environment, domestic economic environment, domestic constitutional environment, and domestic civil-social environment. Its analysis focuses both on the constrains of the institutions on policy choices of political actors and on the policy preferences and the capability of political actors to revise or abandon existing institutions, or to create new institutions to serve their specific purposes.

The inquiry starting point of this new approach is the general institutionalization environments in which the ruling elite are making policy choices rather than specific characteristics of the economic and political system. The analysis focuses on a series of policy decisions and their effects on the future policy preferences of political actors rather than on one specific change and one specific effect. Its conclusions are derived from the 'intentions' of the general institutionalization environments, that is, the constraints of the general institutionalization environments on political actors, while the intentions and purposes of political actors are taken into consideration. This new strategy of studying China's politics may provide a more reliable and testable prediction on the future development of China.

The institutional analytic framework should be based upon democratic transition theories and new institutionalism rather than upon theories of totalitarianism. The totalitarian model views communist politics exclusively in terms of its essential continuity, rather than its real or potential change and depicts such a monopolistic party-state as a near absolute autocracy maintaining a tight control over allocation of resources, over the society, and over the life of its people, preventing non-party independent groups and special interests from developing into organized opposition and thus preventing them from challenging the party's monopoly of power. (Manning 1990, p.3; Baum 1989, p.111). Manning (1990, p.11) observes that because of the predominance of the totalitarian model in the field of academic studies in communism, it is very difficult for researchers to overcome the bias in conceptualizing communist regimes as politically static and frozen; its predominant focus on the essential continuity of communist political systems make researchers 'literally incapable of contemplating their potential change'. Manning (1990, p.13) argues that communist systems are, rather, ever changing, in a constant state of transformation, which 'we are not particularly well-trained to comprehend'.

In a similar vein, Baum (1989, pp.111-3) ironically points out while profound systemic changes are taking place in such communist countries as China, the Soviet Union, Hungary, Poland, and Yugoslavia, over the past decade, Brzezinski and Huntington's prognosis of unbroken 'continuity in the pattern of political control and indoctrination on the basis of growing collectivist consensus', which was designed to explain the static nature of communist systems, now seems itself overly static and conservative and may no longer suffice to explain these dynamic changes. In other words, with communist systems under constant transition there is a need to have a new conceptualization of post-totalitarian evolution.

The analytical framework is to be formulated in the next chapter and the author intends to examine the institutionalization of China's reform policies in the context of the ruling elite's decision making, focusing on when, why, and how some old institutions, but not others, are discarded or maintained while some new ones are being crafted.

Areas of Analysis, Assumptions and Hypotheses

After studying the transitional cases of two Leninist systems, China and the Soviet Union, Stephen Dale Manning found a market-oriented economic system and an independent and autonomous civil society to be 'absolutely critical for a democratic transition' (Manning, 1990, p.383). His projection failed to explain the actual political development of the former Soviet Union, where the nationalism and regionalism are driving forces behind the democratic transition, but it does not mean his findings may not apply to the Chinese transition. As Huntington argues that causes of democratization differ substantially from one place to another and from one time to another (Huntington, 1991a, p.30, p.38), the causes of democratization in China may differ from those of the former Soviet Union.

Based on the analysis of the social, economic and political changes in the previous sections, I assume that three interrelated transformations may be important for the development of democratization in China: (1) the institutionalization of agricultural reform and open-door policy, inaugurating a market economy in China; (2) the institutionalization of private enterprises and property rights, leading to a rapid development of the private sector;[22] and (3) an emerging new political culture. The first assumption is that a market economy presupposes the rule of law; therefore, to install a market economy in China is a process of establishing the rule of law and phasing out the authoritarian rule. The second assumption is that the driving force behind the market and legal building is the restoration of private property rights, which result in redistribution of economic and political power resources in favor of the society, eroding the authoritarian forces and promoting liberal and pro-democratic forces. The third assumption is that mass public orientations[23] in China have been changing towards liberal and pro-democratic values in the context of these social, economic and political transformations, especially, with respect to individual economic freedom and private property rights.

The null hypothesis, or scenario, is that China is not moving closer to democracy in spite of all these social, economic and political changes. The alternative hypothesis is that China is moving closer towards democracy or has already embarked on a transition towards democracy. The objective of the book is to apply the institutional analytic framework to the three cases of policy institutionalization in order to examine these hypotheses.

The institutional case studies explore, among other things, the following particular questions: (1) whether the market economy has been established, pressing for the establishment of the rule of law and the phasing out of the rule of party, which represents a new important aspect of the economic institutional environment conducive to democratization, (2) whether the private sector based on private property rights has become an important and indispensable component of the economy with an increasing share of the economic power resources, representing another new important aspect of the economic institutional environment conducive to democratization, and (3) whether mass public orientations have shifted towards liberal and democratic values, representing a fundamental change in the civil-social environment conducive to democratization. If the institutional case studies have produced evidence to reject the null hypothesis and support the alternative hypothesis, China is moving closer to the democratization of its political system, or China may have already embarked on a transition towards democracy, although it is not a democratic transition conventionally recognized by transitional theorists because it lacks an immediate regime change.

Research Methodology and Structure of the Book

The institutional analysis will rely on both primary and secondary information sources. The primary source consists of documents, reports, and opinion surveys. Some of the documents published in the late 1990s reveal deep divisions among the CPC ruling elite over policy choices, which used to be inconceivable in the past but now are available. In the summer of 2000, Professor Nicholas Rees, Professor Bernadette Andreosso-O'Callaghan and Yanlai Wang replicated the opinion survey conducted in 1990 by Professor Andrews J. Nathan and Tianjian Shi, collecting data on approximately fifty political-cultural variables and providing a glimpse of changes in the Chinese mass orientations. The writer of this book went to Shanghai twice to supervise the survey, including organizing a training session for student interviewers. The 2000 survey assessed some fifty political-cultural variables and offered first-hand data on Chinese people's attitudes towards economic, social and political issues. Secondary-source literature on general theories of democratic transition and country case studies are numerous but very few of them consider China's democratic transition because China's transition has never been treated by transitional theorists as a case of democratic transition.

Therefore, there is a need to devise an institutional analytic framework to study the Chinese transitional case.

This book comprises eight chapters. The first chapter is an introduction, laying out a framework of the book and formulating theoretical assumptions and hypotheses. The second chapter is devoted to devising an institutional analytic framework based on a critical review of the literature on democratic transitions and new institutionalism, providing an institutional analytic tool for the institutional case studies in the following chapters. The third chapter summaries the institutional legacies of Mao's Era: constraints or opportunities to his successors. The fourth chapter examines Deng's revising Mao's ideological institutions, a strategic change in the ideological environment, justifying for the takeoff of the economic reform and opening to the outside world. The fifth chapter investigates the institutionalization of agricultural reform and open-door policy, inaugurating a market economy in China, a meaningful change in the economic institutional environment. The sixth chapter concerns the institutionalization of private enterprises and property rights, leading to a rapid development of the private sector, another meaningful change in the economic institutional environment. The seventh chapter is devoted to the analysis of the findings of two opinion surveys, indicating shifts in the political-cultural orientations of the general public – a meaningful change in the civil-social environment. The last chapter, Chapter 8, provides an aggregate picture of these changes in the institutional environments, assessing their significance in terms of the development of democracy in China.

Notes

1   For a discussion of the three themes of the Chinese contemporary history up to 1977, see Wang Gungwu, *China and the World Since 1949*, Macmillan, London and Basingstoke (1977).

2   Before China began to normalize relations with the United States in the early 1970s, Western European countries and Japan had been the main sources of China's imports of capital goods and technology, although on a small scale, for its economic development and industrialization.   For more discussion, see Taylor, 1996, pp.1-5; Andreosso-O'Callaghan and Qian, 1999, p.123.

3   In 2001, China's GNI per capita (Atlas method and PPP) is 890 and 4,260 US dollars respectively, below that of the low and middle-income group (1,240 and 5,020 US dollars). *Data source: World Development Indicators*, World Bank, August 2002.

4   *Data source: China Statistical Yearbook 2002.*

5   Foreign direct investment and collaborative ventures are considered as important channels for technology transfer but they are not necessarily symmetrically connected. For instance, although the total FDI from the EU countries only accounted for less than 5 per cent of the total FDI in China by the end of 1998, the EU-15 is China's major supplier of advanced technology and equipment. In 1994, for example, the EU represented 43.8 per cent of China's total imports of technology (US$764.4 million). For a further discussion on this, see Andreosso-O'Callaghan and Qian, 1999.

6   This figure excludes the FDI flow into Hong Kong. *Data source*: UNCTAD, *World Investment Report* 2002.

7   In 2002, its import and export value reached 620.785 billion US dollars, a 21.77 per cent increase over 2001; its foreign direct investment amounted to 52.743 billion US dollars, 12.51 per cent higher than the previous year. *Data source*: MOFTEC.

8   For a discussion of the intellectuals' recruitment, see Dickson, 2000; and also see Zhang, Xiaowei, 1998.

9   The composition of its gross domestic product: in 1978, the primary sector represented 28.1 per cent of the GDP, the secondary industry 48.2 per cent and the tertiary industry 23.7 per cent; and in 2001, the respective figures were 15.2 per cent, 51.1 per cent and 33.6 per cent. *Data source: China Statistical Yearbook 2002.*

10 Summary Economic Freedom rating is sorted from the highest '1.0' to the lowest '10.0'. Countries whose combined averages for political rights and for civil liberties fall between 1.0 and 2.5 are designated 'free'; between 3.0 and 5.5 'partly free'; and between 5.5 and 7.0 'not free'.

11 Modernization of agriculture, industry, defense, and science and technology. The modernization program was officially endorsed at the Fourth National People's Congress in January 1975.

12 For a discussion of taxation reform, see Taylor, 1996, pp. 33-6. For a discussion of the policy bargaining between the center and the periphery over the fiscal decentralization, see Shirk, 1993; and also see Li, 1997. For a discussion of the grabbing of the financial resources by the periphery through diverting budgetary funds into extra-budgetary funds, see Huang and Cheng, 1996. For a discussion of modes of decentralization since 1978, see Hu, 1996.

13 *World Development Indicators*, World Bank, 1998; Li and Hou, 2000.

14 1 USD=1.7 RMB *Yuan* in 1978, and 1 USD=8.28 RMB *Yuan* in 2001.

15 For a discussion of regional associations in China, see White, 1993. For a discussion of business associations, see Unger, 1996; Pearson, 1997, pp.116-35. For a discussion of associations in China, see Li, 1998a.

16 His cross-sectional data analysis informed by cognitive psychology suggests that the enthusiasm with which a province pursued rural reform in the late 1970s and early 1980s was in direct proportion to the pain it had experienced during the Great leap Famine, which resulted directly from the push for people's communes during the Great Leap Forward (1958-1961). Out of the ruins of the Great Leap Famine arose the incentives for rural institutional change, eventuating in rural de-collectivization in the early 1980s.

17 Speaking at the Fortune Global Forum (27th - 29th September 1999) in Shanghai on 27th September, Jiang Zemin promised to push ahead with economic reforms. He said: 'The Chinese people will firmly and unswervingly follow the path of reform and opening up'. For the full text of Jiang's speech, see http://forum.shanghai-china.org/English/NewsAnd Report/9909/. The three-day forum had gathered together chief executives from more than 300 multinational corporations, including such luminaries as former Singapore PM Lee Kuan Yew and former U.S. Secretary of State Henry Kissinger. For more discussion, see Crowell and Mooney, 1999. Jiang Zemin reiterated China's economic and political reforms and opening up in the report he delivered to the CPC 16th National Congress on the 8th November 2002.

18 It was estimated that if China maintains an annual growth rate of 6.4 per cent in the next twenty years, China's per capita GDP might reach 2,500 US dollars in 2020, the present average level of middle-income countries. For more discussion, see Wang, Xiaolu, 2000. If China maintains an annual growth rate of 7.2 per cent, its per capita GDP might reach 3000 US dollars in 2020 (*China Economic Times*, 15th November 2002).

19   Anderson and Chao (1998) and Sims (1999) believe that China will become a net fuels importer before long. More consumption of fuels means more air pollution.

20   Industrialized nations are trying to attach special safeguard measures against Chinese exports to China accession to the WTO. For more discussion, see Wall, 1996.

21   Political actors are defined here and thereafter as those who have the political power to initiate and institutionalize a policy. Political institutions are defined here and thereafter in this book as specific laws, regulations, rules, or policies derived from the six macro arenas or environments.

22   The private sector here and thereafter refers to economic units and enterprises other than the collective, state-owned and state holding economic units and enterprises.

23   'Orientations' here and thereafter refers to a broad range of beliefs, values, and assumptions that people hold about social and political life. Such orientations may be cognitive, affective, or evaluative. They are general in the sense that they may structure many more specific attitudes or opinions.

Chapter 2

Towards an Institutional Analytic Framework

This chapter reviews the literature on democratic transitions and new institutionalism with two objectives. First, a critical review of the scholarship on democratic transitions gives a general view of the developments of transitional theories and offers an outline of useful concepts that can be adapted in the institutional analytic framework. Second, it devises, based on the literature review, an institutional analytic framework specifically for the Chinese transition. Third, it classifies institutions, actors, dynamic interactions between institutions and actors. And lastly, it identifies the level of institutions and actors for analysis in this book. The new framework needs to be, on the one hand, sufficiently robust to account for institutional statics and dynamics, and on the other hand, it should be simple but adequate enough to give a detailed examination of the institutional changes at the national level.

Theories of Democratic Transition

This section briefly examines developments of some single-dimensional models and emergence of multi-dimensional models of transitional theories, focusing on the areas of their inquiry and methods of their analyses. First of all, a definition of democracy is outlined below.

Definition of Liberal Democracy

It seems necessary to outline a definition of democracy that is employed in this book since there is a proliferation of categories of democracy, such as direct democracy and indirect democracy, pluralist democracy, radical democracy, liberal representative democracy, socialist democracy, one-party democracy, elitist democracy and so on.[1] In this book 'democracy' refers to liberal democracy unless it is defined differently. Liberal democracy is a form of government that is based on popular majority votes, competition between potential political representatives, a separation of powers, minority protection, and freedom of the press, speech and public association. Theorists and researchers sometimes use different typologies to refer to such a government, such as protective democracy (Held, 1987, p.70), liberal or representative democracy (Held, 1995, p.51), or liberal constitutionalism (Weale, 1999, p.34).

Liberal democracy has three basic features: (1) decision-making power is exercised by a political elite, a sub-group of 'representatives' who have been elected by popular majority votes; (2) electorates can turn politicians out of office through the vote; and (3) minority interests are protected through counter-majoritarian devices and a system of checks and balances.[2] Held (1995, p.51) argues that the successful functioning of liberal democracy depends on a cluster of rules and institutions as follows:

- The constitutional entrenchment of control over governmental policy in elected officials;
- The establishment of mechanisms for the choice and peaceful removal of elected officials in frequent, fair and free elections;
- The right to vote for all adults in such elections (unless legitimately disbarred due to severe mental illness or criminal conviction);
- The right to run for public office;
- An effective right for each citizen to freedom of expression, including the freedom to criticize the conduct of government and the socioeconomic system in which it is embedded;
- Accessible sources of information other than those controlled by government or by any other single body or group; and
- An established right to form and join independent associations, whether they be political, social or cultural, that could shape public life through legitimate, peaceful means.

One-dimensional Models

Developing with experiences and practices of democratization in the world, theories of democratic transition may be roughly grouped into three major schools of democratization. They are (1) the modernization school that stresses macro socio-economic prerequisites of democracy,[3] (2) the state-centric approach that emphasizes state political institutions,[4] and (3) the agent-centric approach that focuses on strategic interaction and bargaining among the ruling and opposition elites.[5]

Modernization models The research agendas of democratic transition theorists and scholars have adjusted to comprehend and explain the ever-changing nature and characteristics of regime change and transformation. During the Cold War, modernization theory was quite popular since its assumptions supported the West's economic aid program to encourage the periphery countries to move towards democracy rather than towards communism. The basic assumption of modernization theory, in its various versions, is that economic development helps spread communication and education, enlarge middle classes, raise living standards, promote a gradual differentiation of social structures, and give rise to supportive cultural orientations, which lead to a demand for political tolerance, participation, incorporation, and eventually lay necessary conditions for a society to proceed towards its democratization (Lipset, 1959; Inglehart, 1997). Or it is reformulated tersely by Diamond as: 'The more well-to-do the people of a country, on average, the more likely they will favor, achieve, and maintain a democratic system for their country'.[6]

Tatu Vanhanen (1984; 1997) has produced a universal model of democratic transitions along the line of the modernization approach. He names his evolutionary theory of democratization after the Darwinian theory of evolution by natural selection.[7] His central hypothesis (Vanhanen, 1997, p.5) states that 'democratization is expected to take place under conditions in which power resources have become so widely distributed that no group is any longer able to suppress its competitors or to maintain its hegemony'. He believes that the positive correlation between the level of economic development and democracy could be better explained in terms of the distribution of power resources. His theory has seven basic explanatory variables, three sectional indices of explanatory variables, one structural imbalance index, and two combined indices of explanatory variables.[8] Through regression analysis of these indices, Vanhanen (1997, p.6) claims that countries usually tend to cross the threshold of democracy at about the same level of resource distribution. For this explanatory power, he also calls it a resources distribution theory of democratization.

Agent-centric models The seventies and eighties are a period of dynamics when democracies broke down, such as Chile in 1973, and some dictatorships became democracies, such as Brazil in 1978, Greece in 1974, Portugal in 1975, and Spain in 1976, Uruguay in 1985, and South Korea in 1988. As a result, various versions of the agent-centric transition approach emerged, challenging the basic assumptions of modernization theory. Its analytic focus is on the ruling and the opposition elites, their preferences, and their strategic interaction, since economic interests and political institutions important in the analysis of stable regimes were less relevant during democratic transitions (O'Donnell and Schmitter, 1986). In other words, democracy is the outcome of negotiation and bargaining among rational, self-interested, and strategy-minded politicians and thus has little to do with economic interests and political institutions.[9]

In the early nineties, following the breaking down of communism and a wave of democratization throughout the former communist countries in the Soviet Union and Eastern Europe, there was a revival of the agent-centric scholarship on democratic transition. Among many influential scholars of this school in this period is Adam Przeworski.[10] Following the agent-centric tradition, Przeworski developed a game-theoretic model of authoritarian withdrawal, by which the process of democratic transition from authoritarian regimes could be analyzed through focusing on the strategic interaction among the ruling elite (hardliners and softliners) and the opposition elite (moderate democrats and extreme democrats).

Institutional models   In the late sixties, institutional analysis of democratic transition, which was also critical of modernization theory, was advocated by Samuel P. Huntington (1965) based on his deep observation of the heavy deficit of the newly independent Third World countries in the capacity of their administrative and political organizations, which he argued might lead to autocratic military or one-party regimes.   Like the agent-centric approach, the institutional approach stresses that there is nothing automatic about the translation of socio-economic modernization into political democracy or stability, or vice versa, because modernization and political development might be related positively, negatively, or not at all.   But unlike the agent-centric approach, the institutional approach stresses political institutionalization defined by Huntington (1965, p.394) as 'the process by which organizations and procedures acquire value and stability'.   As socio-economic changes brought about by modernization tend to undermine institutionalization (or stability), three policy options were suggested by Huntington to strengthen the capability of state:

- Slowing down the process of social mobilization;
- Restricting competition among elites for popular support; and
- Constructing new political institutions to mitigate the negative forces of modernization, for example, a highly institutionalized political party.

International dimensions With growing globalization and interdependence among nations, international factors play a vital part[11] in nation states' choice of political institutions, whether to maintain authoritarian rule or to embark on transition from authoritarian rule to democratic government. Whitehead (1991, pp.45-57) points out that the European Community has played a constructive role in influencing the Southern European countries to move towards democratization by offering them EU membership – an elaborate structure of economic and social incentives. Huber, Rueschemeyer, and Stephens (1993, pp.81-3) observe that the British colonial policy to allow the working class to organize unions and middle classes to form political parties made a critical contribution to the emergence of democracy in the West Indies in the 1960s and 1970s, while the U.S. policy to support the military rule in Central America in the same period contributed to the continued failure of pressures for democratization in that region.

Later Whitehead (1996) and Schmitter (1996) identify four international dimensions or sub-contexts for the exercise of international influence over domestic democratization. They are summarized as follows:

- Contagion, or the diffusion of experience through neutral, i.e. non-coercive and often unintentional, channels from one country to another;
- Control, or the promotion of democracy by one country in another through explicit policies backed by positive or negative sanctions;
- Consent, a category involving a complex set of interactions between international processes and domestic groups that generates new democratic

norms and expectations from below. In the extreme, this may lead to an irresistible drive to merge with an already existing democracy (e.g. Germany); in a milder form, it underlies the desire to protect democracy within a given state by joining a regional bloc (e.g. the EU);

- Conditionality, the deliberate use of coercion – by attaching specific conditions to the distribution of benefits to recipient countries – on the part of multilateral institutions, such as the IMF, the European Community, the Council of Europe.

Geoffrey Pridham (1991, pp.29-30) produces a comparative framework to analyze the international factors that may influence democratic transition, which is summarized as below:

International Environment
- Time Context / Geopolitical Situation: significant international events;
- International Economy: socio-economic modernization pressures;
- International Organizations: such as EC, NATO, IMF;
- Bilateral links with other countries.

Operational Environment
- Structures of government in the different phases of democratic transition; how the changing system / distribution of power relates to external linkages;
- Political uncertainties in democratic transition: problems of government stability under the new democracy; external policy continuity.

Domestic Linkage Actors and 'Crossing the Boundary'
- Different elite groups: their motivation, extent to which they developed 'international dimensions' to their strategies in democratic transition or not; and their transnational links;
- Pre-transition phase: role of opposition groups under previous dictatorship and how much dependent on international links;
- Political elites and political parties: strategies, preferences and options.
- Economic elites, business community, economic interest groups;
- Military elites: how their (changing) position during transition is related to external considerations;
- Other elites, where relevant, e.g. bureaucratic.

Domestic Environment
- Internal cohesion & division: political opposition;
- Media / communications;
- Public opinion;
- Expectations of relationship with international powers such as the EC.

The analytic framework of Pridham focuses more on the domestic environments and elements of the recipient country in the context of international democratic pressures while that of Whitehead and Schmitter emphasizes the international influence over domestic democratization in a recipient country. As far as applicability of these two models is concerned, the later one is easier to be applied to a case study with international influence targeted as the priority of analysis.

Expanding the Old Paradigms

In responding to the experiences of new democracies struggling for consolidation in the eighties and early nineties, researchers and scholars have expanded their analytic paradigms to make them more applicable to cases of democratic transitions and consolidation.

Expanding modernization variables   While still regarding economic development as the dominant explanatory factor, proponents of the modernization school observe that historical, cultural, and political factors, behavior of leaders, and other factors such as national idiosyncrasies may also play a role in producing democratization (Lipset, Seong, and Torres, 1993).   The list of relevant factors eventually covers nearly everything one may find relevant for democratization (Diamond, Linz and Lipset, 1990; Lipset, 1994):

- legitimacy and performance;
- political leadership;
- political culture;
- social structure and socio-economic development;
- associational life;
- state and society;
- political institutions;
- ethnic and regional conflicts;
- the military; and
- international factors.

The expansion of modernization variables in transitional studies indicates a tacit acknowledgement of the inadequate analytic power of its economic variables in explaining democratic transitions and the necessity of adding social, political and international institutions to its analytic variables to increase its analytic power. They represent a tendency to move closer to or converge with paradigms of analysis of other transitional approaches.

Expanding institutional variables   Noticing the proliferation of factors relevant for democratization, Huntington (1984) points out that the emergence of democracy is helped by higher levels of economic well-being, the absence of extreme inequalities in wealth and income, greater social pluralism, a market-oriented economy, greater influence vis-à-vis the society of existing democratic states, and a culture that is less monistic and more tolerant diversity and compromise. However, Huntington (1991, p.38) observes that the independent variables (factors) and the combination of causes producing democracy are varying at different times and in different places. He summarizes his arguments in six propositions as follows:

- No single factor is sufficient to explain the development of democracy in all countries or in a single country.
- No single factor is necessary to the development of democracy in all countries.
- Democratization in each country is the result of combination of causes.
- The combination of causes producing democracy varies from country to country.
- The combination of causes generally responsible for one wave of democratization differs from that responsible for other waves.
- The causes responsible for the initial regime changes in a democratization wave are likely to differ from those responsible for later regime changes in that wave.

In other words, the route to democracy is time specific and country specific. As for the third wave of democratization, Huntington suggests that five changes in the independent variables have played significant roles in bringing about the latest wave of democratization (Huntington, 1991a, p.45):

- The deepening legitimacy problems of authoritarian systems that relied on performance legitimacy;
- The unprecedented global economic growth of the sixties – effects of modernization;
- The role of the Catholic Church, changing from defenders to opponents of the authoritarianism;
- The role of the established liberal democracies, changing from their tolerance of authoritarianism to promotion of human rights and democracy in other countries; and the role of Gorbachev, abandoning the Soviet repressive policy towards former Eastern European communist countries;
- 'Snowballing' or demonstration effects, enhanced by new means of international communication.

To list relevant factors is one thing, and to devise an analytic model that can incorporate them, measure them, and weight their relative significance is another. Researchers who attempt to incorporate all these variables in their analytic models face one dilemma. While in theory, more variables should make their models more powerful in interpretation; more variables may certainly make their models less operational and workable. A more sensible way out of the dilemma is to select and include in an analytic model those variables from the paradigms that are assumed to play an important role in moving a country towards democratization. This selective approach is strongly supported by the evidence Huntington (1991) gathered regarding the causes of the three waves of democratization that the causes of democracy and the route to democracy are time specific and country specific. No set paradigms of variables are meaningful to all cases of transitions. The next section will present several such attempts with discussions.

Multi-dimensional Models

As democratic transition theories are expanding the focus of their inquiry from their original single factors or independent variables to multiple factors, new comprehensive models are emerging, which acknowledge not only the importance of macro socio-economic conditions, but also the relationship between state and society, the strategic role of elites, political and economic institutions, and the international environment.

Comprehensive power-balancing model Huber, Rueschemeyer, and Stephens (1993)[12] try to incorporate the arguments of the modernization school and the agent-centric school in their analytic model, which interpret the association of socio-economic developments and democracy in terms of balance of powers. Their analysis focuses on three power clusters: (1) the balance of class power; (2) the balance of power between state and civil society; and (3) transnational structures of power. They believe that it is because capitalist development transforms the class structure, enlarges working and middle classes, and facilitates their self-organization that the level of economic development is causally related to the development of political democracy. Their model makes a significant step forward in expanding its analysis sphere by admitting, in their analysis, modernization factors, and clusters of domestic powers (classes, civil society, and state apparatus), and international powers. Although their model appears more like the historical class analysis tradition of Barrington Moore (1966) than an extension of modernization or agent-centric school, the inclusion of the paradigms of other approaches indicates a development of converging with other approaches.

Comprehensive strategic analysis model Following the tradition of the agent-centric school, Stephan Haggard and Robert R. Kaufman (1997) acknowledge the role of the strategic interactions among the ruling and opposition elites but they criticize the agent-centric school for the following costs:

- taking the relative power, preferences, and agenda of the actors as given;
- neglecting the factors that shape actors' preferences and capabilities in the first place and the conditions under which they might change over time;
- ignoring resources contending parties bring to bear in influencing the terms of the transition and the stability of the outcome in the face of subsequent challenges; and

- paying little attention to economic variables and interests that may shape outcomes of transition.

They propose, instead, a strategic analysis model that focuses on the effects of economic conditions on the preferences, resources, and strategies of key political actors in the transition 'game', while taking into account international diplomatic pressures, the 'contagion effect' of transitions, and structural changes brought about by economic development. Its analytic sphere remains in the framework of the agent-centric school but shows some degrees of converging with modernization and institutional approaches by absorbing in some of their analytic paradigms.

Institutional composite models　Soon after the public euphoria over the collapse of communism in Eastern European countries and the Soviet Union, another tough issue emerged of how to make these fragile new democracies sustain themselves both economically and politically. Scholars and researchers of democratic transition were quick to offer prescriptions and suggestions for democratic consolidation. Some scholars suggested that these new democracies should capitalize on their period of 'extraordinary politics' when both the elite and the general public would be more willing to accept radical reform measures (Balcerowicz, 1994).[13] Some claimed that 'radical systemic change is likely to produce greater accomplishment than gradual reform on every front', and that 'the social costs of transition are likely to be lowest under a radical reform scenario' (Aslund, 1994).

Some researchers, however, have offered a cautious reservation about the radical economic reform program of the new democracies. Philippe C. Schmitter (1994) argued that it is by no means a guarantee of success for the fledgling new democracies to imitate the basic norms and institutions of established liberal democracies. Adam Przeworski and Fernando Limongi (1993) examined 18 statistical studies of the relationship between democracy and economic growth and produced an ambivalent conclusion that 'we do not know whether democracy fosters or hinders economic growth'. Although they believe political institutions matter for growth, they think there is no way to 'find institutions that enable the state to do what it should but disable it from doing what it should not'. John F. Helliwell (1994) did a similar statistical study on democracy and economic growth. He found a robust positive relation between the level of per capita income and the adoption of democracy but failed to identify any systemic net effects of democracy on subsequent economic growth. Joan M. Nelson (1994) offers an explanation on the discrepancy between new democracies and their economic performance after studying economic stabilization cases, arguing that market-oriented reforms generally produce severe costs immediately but benefits only gradually and that reforms take years to implement and usually need still more time before they begin to generate robust investment and growth.

Why market-oriented reforms need time to put into place and still more time before generating benefits has a lot to do with the construction of formal institutions (laws, regulations), informal institutions (social norms, customs), and socialization of people's behavior by these new formal and informal institutions. It is unrealistic and inconceivable to install formal and informal norms of the established liberal democracies within a short period of intensive reform programs because the institutional framework of the established liberal democracies has been established over several centuries.[14]

In response to the central challenge faced by new democracies in the consolidation of democracy and the implementation of market reforms, many researchers return to state institutions and institutional building for answers. Political institutions become the focal point of theoretical analysis as Karen L. Remmer (1997, p.50) summarizes: 'Standing at the intersection of political inputs and outputs, political institutions represent the black box of politics through which societal interests are translated into policies and policy outcomes'. Thus, political democracy may be conceptualized as a 'consensual framework' or 'co-operative equilibrium that may be constructed in a variety of ways, involve varying sets of rules or institutional arrangements, and yield disparate sets of political outcomes' (Remmer, 1997, p.51). Remmer calls for a rigorous, testable, and cumulative institutional theory that can effectively address the linkages between international and domestic systems, the two-way interaction between politics and economics, the role of societal actors, and the sources of institutional change.

The resurgence of academic interests in institutions has produced some comprehensive institutional models of democratic transition and consolidation. In a recent article Robert R. Kaufman (1999) proposes an ambitious institutional model that not only includes the ingredients of the agent-centric approach: actors, preferences, and constraints, but also contains what he calls three broad theoretical perspectives: (1) international political economy; (2) institutional rational choice; and (3) institutional sociology. Each theoretical perspective examines different sets of actors, their preferences, and their constraints. The international political economy perspective explains policy outcomes and institutional change by focusing on the relations among economic interest groups and the way such groups are linked to global trade and capital markets. The institutional rational choice perspective examines the role of politicians as 'suppliers' of state reform, whose preferences for reform will be motivated by the goal of gaining or retaining office. The institutional sociology emphasizes the broad sociocultural context and examines behaviors of individuals and civic associations and the link between state and society by focusing on social norms and institutions, informal networks, formal associations, and other civic groups. Ambitious as it is, Kaufman leaves it to analysts of democratic transitions to apply his model to cases of democratic transition and consolidation.

Linz and Stepan (1996) produce an institutional framework comprising five arenas that a functioning state needs to have before it can consolidate democracy. These five interacting arenas are listed as follows:

- Civil Society. Where self-organizing groups, movements, and individuals, relatively autonomous from the state, attempt to articulate values, create associations and solidarities, and advance their interests.

Primary organizing principle: freedom of association and communication.

- Political Society. Where the polity specifically arranges itself to contest the legitimate right to exercise control over public power and the state apparatus, including such core institutions as political parties.
Primary organizing principle: free and inclusive electoral contestation.

- Rule of Law that is embodied in a spirit of constitutionalism and a clear hierarchy of laws, interpreted by an independent judicial system and supported by a strong legal culture.
Primary organizing principle: constitutionalism.

- A functioning state and a state bureaucracy that should exercise effectively monopoly of the legitimate use of force in the territory and imperative enforcement on civil, political, and economic societies of democratically sanctioned laws and procedures established by political society.
Primary organizing principle: rational-legal bureaucratic norms.

- Economic society that is a set of socio-politically crafted and accepted norms, institutions, and regulations, which mediates between state and market.
Primary organizing principle: an institutionalized market.

Linz and Stepan stress that it is an interacting framework where each arena receives necessary support from other arenas and exerts primary mediation upon other arenas. When they analyze cases of democratic transition and consolidation in Southern Europe, South America, and Post-communist Europe, they focus their analysis on seven factors or explanatory variables summarized as follows:

- Stateness: problematic or not problematic;
- Prior regime type: authoritarianism, totalitarianism, post-totalitarianism, or sultanism;
- Base of leadership: civilian, military, or party; fragmented, hierarchical, or non-hierarchical;
- Initiator of transition: elites, the regime itself, the communist party, the military, civil society, regime collapse;
- International influences: European Community, the United States, European Socialist Parties, Malvinas/Falklands military defeat (Argentina), *Perestroika* and *Glasnost*, disintegration of USSR, Russia and EU;
- Political economy: economic decline, strong economic growth, weak economy, inequality, economic reform or restructuring, debt problem;
- Constitutional environment: consensus, majoritarian, military-dominated, tightly constrained or controlled, dominated by nationalism.

Their interactive institutional framework provides a blue print of institutions a consolidated democracy needs to acquire. What is significant of their approach is that democracy is no longer considered as just a change of regime per se but as a crafting of institutions in the five interacting arenas or macro institutional environments (Linz and Stepan, 1996, pp.3-15). Their explanatory variables are in fact specific institutions derived from the five institutional environments. Different paradigms of explanatory variables can be selected from the macro institutional environments for the purpose of analyzing a specific transitional case. The second significance of their institutional framework is that it allows meaningful inquiries into not only transitions originating from the Political Society where institutions concerning a regime change are crafted or negotiated among the ruling authoritarian and opposition elites, but also transitions originating from the Economic Society where market institutions necessary for a democracy are crafted by the ruling authoritarian elite.

Towards a Framework for the Chinese Transition

This section proposes an institutional analytic framework specific for the Chinese transition, based on a critical summary of the literature review in the previous section. First, it summarizes the theoretical trends of transitional theories and develops an institutional analytic framework after modifying relevant explanatory variables. Second, it examines features of the Chinese transition through comparing it with other cases of transition and specifies the focus of the institutional analysis in this book: what institutions to be examined? And at what level?

New Trends of Transitional Studies

The literature review has suggested three trends in theories of democratic transitions. Analytic interests are shifting (1) from single-dimensional models to multi-dimensional models, (2) from universal models to case-specific models, and (3) from democratization per se to the crafting of state institutions.

One of the trends is that practitioners are shifting from single-dimensional models to multi-dimensional models, absorbing analytic variables from various single-dimensional models, in an attempt to upgrade analytic power of their models. However, facing multitudinous explanatory variables, researchers are advised to be selective because democratization in different countries may be quite different owing to their different history, culture, regime type, and geopolitics. This leads to the second trend that researchers are devising models for specific cases of democratic transition because the route to democracy is time-specific and country-specific. This latest trend is a shift in transitional studies from focusing on the political process of democratization per se – regime change to stressing the crafting of the institutions in what Linz and Stepan (1996) call 'Five Interacting Arenas' or macro institutional environments on which democracy relies for survival and consolidation. Does this new trend signify a new direction in transitional studies?

Theoretically speaking, democratic transition starts with the dismantling of an authoritarian regime, through to the inauguration of a new democracy, and then to its early operation (Pridham, 1991, p.5). In practice, only when the political system of an authoritarian regime is beginning to be replaced by a democratic polity, can it be considered a new case of democratic transition, because whether economic and political liberalization will lead to democratization is uncertain until the authoritarian regime is starting to be dismantled. This mentality of uncertainty derives, to a certain degree, from the theory of totalitarianism that views authoritarian regimes in terms of perpetual continuity and static monolith, unable to change within. But liberalization is a quite vague concept and is often freely applied to almost any market-oriented economic and political changes in an authoritarian regime, ranging from the freedom to open a family business to the systemic market-oriented transformation of the command economy, and from creating a civilian service system to the systemic building of market-oriented legal system (although the ruling elite in many cases are compelled or constrained to do so) and to the emergence of the civil society. The nature and degree of the later systemic changes matter much more than the former. After applying his composite model of democratization[15] to two Leninist systems case studies, China and the Soviet Union, Stephen Dale Manning (1990, p.383) concludes that a market-oriented economic system and an independent and autonomous civil society are 'absolutely critical for a democratic transition'.

John D. Sullivan[16] points out the close connection between the economic and the political institutional building, arguing that 'the institutional structures of a market economy are often intertwined with the institutional structures of a modern democracy' in at least three areas: (1) the concept of property rights, contract law and commercial codes require and at the same time support the rule of law; (2) freedom of economic information enlarges the democratic space in society; and (3) economy policies such as eliminating non-tariff trade barriers and quantitative restrictions on imports or exports create a different pattern of support for the political institutional building. Hernando de Soto also stresses that democracy has a lot to do with securing property rights.[17] Property rights are the foundation of markets that presuppose the rule of law. It is not really possible to build a democracy without those institutions governing the relationship between people and objects that have been properly drafted and set in place in the Economic Arena.

Developing a New Institutional Analytic Framework

Since the link between the institutions of market economy and those of democracy is so strong, could it be reckoned a new case of democratic transition when the command economic system is being dismantled and replaced by a market economy, when a market-oriented legal institutional framework is being built, and when political-cultural orientations[18] of the mass public have been shifting towards liberal and pro-democratic values conducive to democratization?

In reality, an authoritarian regime could be dismantled and replaced by a democratic polity over night, leaving other systems to be built later. Typical cases are the former Soviet Union republics and Eastern European communist countries. This democracy route is a political-reform-first strategy, a sudden change of political regime, followed by the crafting and building of institutions in all the five arenas identified by Linz and Stepan (1996, p.14). Set in the five arenas, it starts from the political society and moves into other arenas. The crafting of institutions in other arenas after Russia completed its democratic transition turns out to be a difficult and prolonged one. Their lessons suggest that the setting up of the political institutions for a democratic polity per se does not necessarily and automatically guarantee the crafting and building of economic institutions, civic institutions, legal institutions, and even capable and effective state bureaucratic institutions. It is political-reform-first strategy. However, it is unrealistic to expect the institutional building in the five arenas within a short period of intensive reform programs because the five-arena institutional framework of the established liberal democracies has been crafted and installed over several centuries.[19]

Authoritarian regimes could also be dismantled and replaced gradually; first their economic system is being transformed, followed by societal fabrics, their legal institutional framework, and in the end, their political system. Typical examples are most established liberal democracies such as the United Kingdom, and new democracies such as South Korea and Taiwan. This democracy route is an economic-reform-first strategy. It is a gradual transformation of economic, social, and legal institutions, accompanied by the gradual distribution of powers in favor of the civil society and the corresponding gradual but consistent erosion of the authoritarian rule, and followed by an orderly or packed transformation of the authoritarian regime into a democratic polity. The Chinese transition clearly resembles the second route, although it is quite different from the Korean and the Taiwanese cases.

Gordon White (1996, pp.210-11) proposes to regard regime changes moving in either direction along a continuum from 'totalitarian' through 'authoritarian' to 'democratic' systems. This theoretical modeling of region changes can explain most regime changes in both directions. The 1999 military coup that toppled the elected government in Pakistan represents a retreat away from the democratic end on the continuum. The coup may be attributed to the institutional weakness of Pakistan in its five arenas in general and its rule of law in particular. In the new institutional analytic framework, White's continuum modeling regime changes is revised and extended to cover the long journey from 'totalitarianism' through 'authoritarianism' to 'democracy' and to 'consolidated democracy' (see Figure 2.1).

Totalitarianism / Authoritarianism - - - - - - - - - - - - - Consolidated Democracy

Figure 2.1 Continuum of Two-Direction Regime Change

On the revised continuum, democracy is defined as the completion of a regime change from an authoritarian rule to a democratic polity with three basic democratic features: (1) free and fair elections of representatives with universal and equal suffrage; (2) responsibility of the state apparatus to the elected parliament; and (3) the freedoms of expression and association as well as the protection of individual rights against arbitrary state action (Rueschemeyer, Stephens, and Stephens, 1992, p.43; Linz and Stepan, 1996, p.13; Held, 1995, p.51). However, the process of completing a democratic transition with the three basic democratic features may start before the formal establishment of a democratic regime, which entails five minimal tasks (Linz and Stepan, 1996, pp.62-5):

- Rule of law and civil society freedom;
- Political society autonomy and trust and legal condition for it;
- Constitutional rules to allocate power democratically;
- State bureaucracy acceptable and serviceable to democratic government;
- Sufficient autonomy for economy and economic actors to assure pluralism of civil society, political society, and economic society.

On this continuum of regime change, democratization is a continual process of transition from authoritarianism towards consolidated democracy, displaying two distinctive dynamic features: (1) the continual building of Linz and Stepan's five arenas towards consolidated democracy, and (2) the initiation of a democratic transition on any point of the continuum. A democratic transition may start on a point closest to the left end of the continuum with few institutions conducive to sustaining a democracy or on a point closest to the right end of the continuum with almost every necessary institution in place for maintaining a democracy. In theory and practice, a democratic regime that appears near the left end of the continuum tends to be less stable while a democratic regime that appears near the right end of the continuum tends to be more sustainable.

For the purpose of analyzing the Chinese transitional case, the new institutional analytic framework comprises six macro institutional environments or independent explanatory variables and one set of dependent variables, which are devised, mainly based on Linz and Stepan's five arenas and explanatory variables and on Pridham's comparative framework of international factors (see Figure 2.2).

The contents of the six macro institutional environments or independent explanatory variables listed below are not exhaustive but sufficient for the present institutional analysis of the Chinese transitional case studies:

International Environment
- Policies of foreign countries and regions;
- Foreign firms' investment and trade objectives;
- Policies and objectives of supra-national organizations, such as the United Nations, WTO, NATO, the European Union, and ASEAN;
- Policies and objectives of non-governmental organizations such as IMF, the World Bank.

Ideological Environment
- Fundamental ideology of the ruling party based on sets of ideas and doctrines initiated by the leadership of the party, defining its purposes and ultimate goal: communism, class and class struggle, and organization principles;
- Operational ideology of the ruling party, specifying sets of political ideas, values and principles initiated by the leadership of the party to guide or justify concrete party policies and specific revolutionary campaigns;
- Ideologies of other political parties, non-governmental organizations, associations, civic groups.

Domestic Political Environment
- political parties and state apparatus, their leadership, and inter-party alliances and state-society relationship;
- Policies and regulations of the ruling party and state apparatuses;
- Political institutions that define such political processes as legislation, elections, or other rules of political games.

Domestic Economic Environment
- Performance of the economy;
- Structures of the economy;
- Living standards;
- Norms and regulations of markets.

Constitutional Environment
- State constitution;
- Laws and legal regulations and rules.

Domestic Civil-Social Environment
- Non-governmental organizations, associations, and civic groups;
- Values and demands of non-governmental organizations, associations and civic groups, which are relatively autonomous from the state and advance their members' interests;
- Attitudes and expectations of the mass public who are not a part of any association and civic group.

Although the above lists of the independent variables do not claim to cover all the categories of the institutional environments, they serve the purpose of analyzing the Chinese transitional case. The set of dependent variables includes two categories: (1) actors, and (2) institutions. Actors are defined in the new institutional analytic framework as representatives of any organizations involved in a negotiation, bargaining, or institution making. Actors are changing constantly according to what institution is in question. Institutions are defined broadly as state constitution and laws; government policies and regulations; market norms and regulations; party ideology, objectives, policies, and regulations; values and demands of organized social groups; attitudes and expectations of the mass public; policies and objectives of foreign states, supra-national organizations, non-governmental organizations, and trans-national companies. Actors and institutions will be classified and examined in an institutional hierarchy to be devised, based on the new institutionalism, in the following sections.

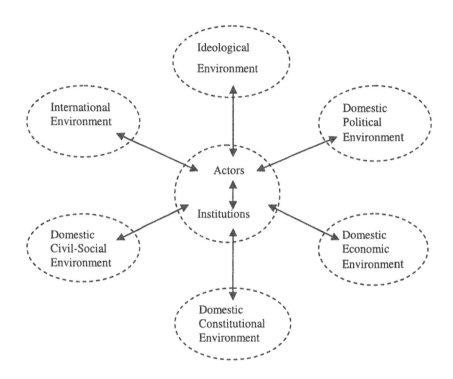

Figure 2.2 An Institutional Analytic Framework

This institutional analytic framework simplifies the interactions among actors, institutions, and macro institutional environments for the sake of highlighting the interactive levels the case study wants to capture. Therefore, it does not show any reciprocal influence between the six institutional environments.

The institutional analytic framework has fewer independent variables and the independent variables will become dependent variables with the changing of the institutions derived from the macro environments in question (see Figure 2.2). Therefore, this model purports to be more dynamic, interactive, and applicable to institutional changes than Linz and Stepan's framework of seven explanatory variables that focuses more on institutions than on institutional changes. The new model covers the major explanatory variables of modernization theory, the agent-centric school, the state-centric approach, and the international dimensions, focusing more on institutional changes than on institutions. It avoids the weakness of the three institutional composite models we have reviewed above in previous section. The power-balancing model of Huber, Rueschemeyer, and Stephens pays too much attention to the balance of power among three clusters of power while neglecting institutional building and constraints. The strategic analysis model of Stephan Haggard and Robert R. Kaufman also overlooks institutional formation and constrains while extending their strategic and interactive analysis of key political actors' preferences, resources, and strategies from the domestic into the international dimensions. Kaufman's three-perspective analytic model offers an institutional analysis of democratic transition in terms of actors' preferences and constraints in three theoretical dimensions: (1) international political economy; (2) institutional rational choice; and (3) institutional sociology. However, Kaufman did not specify how to operationalize the three perspectives within one analytic model, which are widely different in their theoretical frameworks.

The five arenas of Linz and Stepan are originally devised to measure the consolidation of democracies because they believe that 'democracy is more than a regime; it is an interacting system' (Linz and Stepan, 1996, p.13). In the new institutional analytic framework, their five arenas are adopted for explanation of transitions from authoritarian regime through to consolidated democracies and set as an overall guiding map indicating the route of regime transitions, which may start from the political society, the economic society, the rule of law arena, or any combination of them.

The new institutional analytic framework provides the following unique analytic features that are important in examining an authoritarian regime like China in transition towards democracy:

- It offers a detailed account of both historical conditions (origins and causes) and institutional environments (international, social, economic, political, and constitutional) of transitions;
- It gives a dynamic analysis of the actors' preferences that are being shaped by traditional and existing institutions and are at the same time neglecting, revising or abandoning the traditional and existing institutions, or devising new ones; and
- It is dynamic in that it explains transitions originating either from the political arena, the rule of law arena, or the economic arena, or any combination of them in the context of institutional changes.

Institutions, Actors, and Institutionalization Processes

This section and the sections that follow prepare a platform for analyzing the complex interactions between actors and institutions in the context of the six institutional environments identified in the previous section. The objective is divided into three tasks: (1) to prepare definitions of institution and actor that are to be employed throughout this book, (2) to provide hierarchies of institutions and actors and select the hierarchical level on which the institutional analysis will focus, and (3) to summarize the types of institutionalization processes that have been employed by the ruling elite since 1949. First of all, a review of literature on institutionalism is provided as a theoretical background for the analysis of institutions and actors in the chapter.

Institutionalism

The political world is so notoriously complex and multi-faceted that it has kept practitioners of political science trying to offer various theories or approaches one after another to explain, interpret, or predict political phenomena, such as structuralism, functionalism, behaviorism, institutionalism, and rational choice theory. These approaches have usually been developed on the limitations of their predecessors, almost always initially appearing as a brand new approach or a new face out of an old theory, claiming a better analytic power than their predecessors do. In recent years, however, there is a tendency to formulate a mixed or synthetic approach based on two or even several approaches to broaden their analytic scope in explanation, interpretation, and prediction of political phenomena. Practitioners of one approach sometimes draw analytic tools from other approaches to enrich their idioms and to add to their analytic power. Some institutionalists have accommodated ideas of bounded rationality into their institutional approach (March and Olsen, 1989; Taylor, 1989; Krasner, 1984; Thelen & Steinmo, 1992), while some rational choice practitioners accept ideas of institutional constraints in their analyses (Elster, 1989).

If the 'behavioral revolution' in political science in the 1950s and early 1960s, which focused on informal distributions of power, individual attitudes, and political behavior, was a rejection of the old institutionalism, which emphasized formal laws, rules, administrative structures and organizations, the new institutionalism (Rothstein, 1996, pp.133-66) redressed the individualist behavioral tilt by defining institutions as the 'independent variables' which could shape political behavior and constrain policy outcomes.

March and Olsen (1984, p.738) even went one step further, arguing that institutions could be treated as political actors or decision-makers. From this perspective, the state or political institutions can be depicted as making choices on the basis of some collective preferences, goals, and purposes. This treatment gave collective action institutional coherence and autonomy, which turned the role of political institutions from passive mirrors of social forces into active regulators of political behavior. In their political structure, there are collection of institutions, rules of behavior, norms, roles, physical arrangements, buildings, and archives; human action is defined as the fulfillment of duties and obligations; political actors (institutions) associate certain human actions with certain social contexts by rules of appropriateness; and the appropriateness of a particular person in a particular situation is defined by political and social institutions and transmitted through socialization. By political institutions, March and Olsen (1984, p.738; 1989, p.22) meant states, legislatures, and organizations. By rules, they meant the routines, procedures, conventions, roles, strategies, organizational forms, and technologies, and also the beliefs, paradigms, codes, cultures, and knowledge that surround, support, elaborate, and contradict those roles and routines.

Douglas North (North, 1990, p.3) provided another version of institutionalism. He argued that institutions are the rules of the game in a society or the constraints devised by human beings to shape their own interactions. North (1990, p.6-47) divided institutions into formal and informal constraints, with the formal rules including constitution, laws, individual contracts, and any rules that human beings devised and the informal comprising conventions, codes of behavior, customs, and traditions. North made a distinction between institutions and organizations in a different way. By organizations, he meant:

- Political bodies such as political parties, people's congress, city councils, and regulatory agencies;
- Economic bodies such as firms, trade unions, family farms, and co-operatives;
- Social bodies such as churches, clubs, and athletic associations;
- Educational bodies, such as schools, universities, and vocational training centers.

North argued that the institutional framework influences the formation of organizations, which in turn influence the development of the institutional framework. Therefore, the interaction between institutions and organizations is the emphasis in his institutional study.

Organizations, Institutions and Actors

North, and March and Olsen defined institutions differently. North confined his institutions to rules devised by strategic players to shape their behavior, while March and Olsen defined states, legislature, and organizations as institutions. In other words, North treated the rules of March and Olsen as institutions, while the latter treated North's organizations as institutions. Their preference to treat organizations or rules as institutions represents two versions of institutional analysis that have downplayed the influence of personal actors. In March and Olsen's institutional model personal initiatives are minimized to such an extent that personal actors have little space for political maneuverings because human action is defined by political and social organizations. Although organizations are established and run by individual persons, these persons are passive servants rather than active players in March and Olsen's political structure. In their institutional model, therefore, organization may be an over-determinant of political outcomes.

In North's institutional model not only the reciprocal influence between organizations and institutions are acknowledged but also personal contribution to the formation of 'the rules of the game' – institutions are fully acknowledged. His model allows an institutional analysis of the dynamics of the triangular relations between organization, rule, and actor, in particular, the meaningful interactions between actors, decision makers, players, or agents of the organizations in maintaining, redefining, modifying, changing, or manipulating institutions for collective or personal preferences. Therefore, North's model is more suitable for the analytic purposes in this book, although some revisions in the model are needed before it can be applied to the analysis of China's economic and political institutions.

Whenever the rules of the game are institutionalized into formal or informal institutions, institutions stand on their own, capable of shaping human interaction because they ensure rational players the expected outcomes based on limited information and bounded rationality with the expected costs of interaction. In other words, the players are aware of the possible outcomes and the expected cost of their interaction when they enter the procedures of institutions with enough, although not complete, information on the concerned issue and its social context. Normally speaking, when no dispute or anomaly arises, institutions, especially formal institutions, limit choices of actors, players and agents, regulate their behavior, and constrain outcomes of their interaction. In this sense, institutions act as socially and politically accepted conduct standards binding on the behavior of persons in an organization or a society. Whenever any dispute or anomaly occurs, institutions will not act to redress this anomaly until institutional procedures are initiated. For instance, when two businessmen run into a dispute over a business transaction, in most cases, the procedures of informal institutions may be first initiated by one of the businessmen or by a third party to solve the crisis. Several attempts may be made to settle the dispute through informal institutions before one of the businessmen, who is presumably not satisfied with the prospective settlement, initiates the procedures of formal institutions. When the interests of a group of people are at stake, the players or initiators of the procedures will be the agents of an organization rather than individuals. If nobody initiates the procedures of institutions, institutions are blind and dormant to anomalies. One extreme case is that a criminal offender will never be brought to trial until a lawsuit is filed, initiating the lawsuit procedures. From this observation, we can say that institutions matter; whether or not to initiate the procedures of institutions matters; who initiates the procedures matters; what procedures are initiated matters (in case there are different grades of procedures in one institution); the procedures of which institution are initiated also matters. There exists, therefore, a dynamic interplay between institutions, organizations and actors, players, and agents, which shape the outcomes of human interactions.

In order to tackle these complex dynamic interrelations of institutions, organizations and actors, players, and agents, it is proposed to reorganize institutions, organizations and actors, players, and agents, and redefine their roles. In parallel to North's four kinds of organizations: political, economic, social, and educational, formal institutions may be classified as follows:

- Political institutions: constitutions, laws, regulations, decrees, resolutions, and notice;

- Economic institutions: articles of associations, contracts, agreements, and memorandum;
- Social institutions: religious beliefs, welfare regulations, public sanitation rules, public conduct rules, and club regulations;
- Educational institutions: admission regulations, student conduct rules, examination rules, and academic standards.

As actors, players and agents live in a society with specific traditions and culture, which exert influence on their behavior through institutions such as ideology, religious beliefs, conventions, routines, and norms. In modern democracy, ideology also plays a role in mobilizing publics. Erik Asard and W. Lance Bennett (1997, p.30) argue that the health of a polity depends on its marketplace of ideas, which is heavily brokered by elites who hold sway over the formation of interests, the definition of problems, and the production of solutions. This ideological regime consists of the grand visions, or governing ideas, which guide national policy agenda and political alignments for generations, and the rhetoric of everyday politics, which are strategic uses of language and mental images to persuade publics to take positions on policies about particular issues or to make judgments about parties and candidates in elections. Ideology, a type of institution itself, plays an important part in shaping political institutions through mobilizing both political activists and the general public, because ideas are the source material for everyday political discourse.

In China, ideology plays a much more important role in the institutionalization process. Even today, ideology remains the cornerstone on which the CPC has built its power and according to which the policy makers have made their policy decisions. Ideology is treated, therefore, as a special institution in the institutional analytic framework of this book. As the supreme actor of the CPC from 1940s to 1970s, Mao's ideology played a decisive role in shaping China's politics. Strictly speaking, Mao Zedong was not a pure theorist of communism; rather, he was a dedicated practitioner of Marxism and Leninism. Mao accepted ideas of communism wholeheartedly and set it as the maximum program of the CPC, while he was busily engaged in devising, initiating, persuading his colleagues to accept, and implementing a series of specific revolutionary programs – political campaigns, mass movements, and revolutions, to lead China towards socialism and eventually communism. Therefore, the majority of Mao's ideology dealt with the Chinese revolutionary practices rather than pure theoretical issues and may be classified into the second part of the following various versions of the dichotomy of ideology:

- Seliger's fundamental ideology and operative ideology (Seliger, 1976, p.103);
- Moore's ideology of ends and ideology of means / officially promulgated doctrine and operative ideology (Moore, 1950, p.402-3);
- Schurmann's pure ideology and practical ideology (Schurmann, 1968, p.21-45).

The first part of the above dichotomy refers to the end-goal of communism, class and class struggle, public ownership as the base of the proletariat dictatorship, and the historical mission of the proletariat, while the second part refers to political ideas and values advocated by political supreme actors at various stages of revolution and institutionalized and written into their party's resolutions and documents, government policies and regulations, and state laws and constitutions. As the institutional analysis in this book examines national policy institutionalization, it mainly concerns the operative or practical ideology of the CPC.

Hierarchies of Institutions and Actors

Since institutions are created at various levels of organizations, they are classified into the corresponding hierarchical levels of organizations as follows:

- National institutions / State organizations, political parties, people's congress;
- Regional institutions / Provinces, autonomous regions, municipalities;
- Local institutions   / Cities, districts, counties, townships, villages;
- Personal institutions / Family, brotherhood, love, marriage.

Organizations such as churches, clubs, associations, firms, trade unions, co-operatives and their relevant institutions may operate at one level, two levels, or all four levels, depending on the scale of their activities. Institutions are products of the needs to regulate collective actions that culminate in organizations. Organizations are formed of individuals but act collectively through their representatives, who are engaged in constant negotiations and bargaining regarding institutional formation, revision, adaptation, and change. When established, institutions act as rules in shaping human behavior, and they become independent variables. The regulating process may be one in which 'institutions shape politics'. When institutions are being revised, adapted, changed, or created out of conflicts or negotiations, they become dependent variables, which is a process of institutional formation and change when 'politics shape institutions' (Thelen, Steinmo & Longstreth, 1992). To capture the dynamic interplay of institutions, organizations and players, we need to define the roles of individuals in drafting institutions, initiating the institutional procedures, and adapting, modifying, changing, and creating institutions.

Normally speaking, an ordinary individual member can initiate the routine procedures of an institution, but he has little role to play in other acts such as drafting, adopting, modifying, changing, and creating institutions. In our model, such individual members are defined as **players**. To manage daily routines, each organization has its own bureaucrats such as clerks and directors. As human beings, their performance is not only constrained by the institutions they uphold but also influenced by other institutions such as ideology, religious beliefs, conventions, and norms. Their performance in observing and implementing institutions, therefore, may be varying to different issues, situations, and times. Sometimes, they unintentionally deviate from the rules prescribed in the institution, and sometimes, they may deliberately ignore or violate certain rules of the institution.[20] In our hierarchical model, these bureaucrats are classified as **agents**.   There are bureaucrats who are members of party committees, directors of associations, deputies of congresses, who are involved in the process of drafting, adopting, or approving institutions. Our model classifies these bureaucrats as **decision-makers**.

China has a one-party authoritarian regime, which, in most cases, is under the control of a small number of oligarchs, who may be classified as **chief actors**.   In its extreme form, one chief actor tends to place personal will over collective preferences.   This can be traced back to feudal China, when only emperors or empresses had the paramount power. In modern China, both the KMT (Nationalist Party) boss and the CPC boss once enjoyed this power monopoly privilege. Our hierarchical model classifies these powerful authoritarian rulers as **supreme actors**, who play a decisive role in redefining, modifying, changing or discarding old institutions, and in initiating and creating new institutions. These political actors are listed in the following hierarchical order:

Supreme Actors
Chief Actors
Decision-makers
Agents
Players

Lastly, the world seems more and more like a global organism (Todavo, 1997, p.19), and individual states depend on and influence each other in terms of social, economic as well as political developments. Our institutional analytic levels will include not only the domestic institutions: private, local, regional, and national, but also global institutions at the levels of foreign states, international organizations, and foreign corporations. In principle, the higher institutions are in the hierarchy, the more powerful they are. National institutions, for example, have the power of nullifying regional institutions if the later contradict with the former. However, global institutions may usually influence the domestic institutionalization at the domestic national level, although sometimes the influences of the foreign corporations' decisions may penetrate all four domestic levels, depending on their scale of business in China. The revised hierarchical levels of institutional analysis are as follows:

- Global institutions   / Foreign states, international organizations, foreign corporations;
- National institutions   / State organizations, political parties, people's congress;
- Regional institutions   / Provinces, autonomous regions, municipalities;
- Local institutions   / Cities, districts, counties, townships, villages;
- Personal institutions   / Family, brotherhood, love, marriage.

China's Political Institutions and Actors at the Central Level

The institutional analysis in this book focuses on the national policy institutionalization through examining the institutional behavior of the supreme and chief actors, while adequate attention will be given to the influence of the behavior of the decision-makers, actors, and players on the institutionalization of policies. One feature of the Chinese political power structure is that China has two bureaucracies: networks of the CPC organizations and the state organs, with the latter under the leadership of the former. This section gives a general picture of the Chinese political power structure at the national level by detailing China's central powers: the CPC central organizations and the state organs. Against the power structure map, a hierarchy of political actors and institutions are identified and those actors and institutions are selected for detailed analysis whose interactions hold the key to the dramatic social, economic, and political transformations that have occurred since 1978.

A map of China's Central Powers

As soon as the state administrative organs were established in October 1949, the CPC began to install its organizational network in the government at all levels to insure its leadership in the country. In parallel to the central government, provincial governments, local governments, and grass-root units, the CPC has set up corresponding organizations at each level. As the institutional analysis focuses on the national level institutionalization, a map of China's central powers is provided to facilitate the analyses (see Figure 2.3).

Figure 2.3 indicates that the CPC controls the legislature – the National People's Congress (NPC) and the executive – the State Council by default and through organizational means. Firstly, the majority of the NPC representatives are party members[21] and the Head of the State, the Premier of the State Council, and the Chairman of the NPC Standing Committee are also members of the CPC Politburo Standing Committee,[22] the leading core of the CPC. Secondly, through the Working Committee of the State Organs, an agency directly under the CPC Central Committee, the CPC ruling elite enjoy a dual control of the state apparatus. The dual control refers to the practice of the CPC in controlling the state apparatus through both establishing a party committee or branch committee in each state organ and installing a party group in the same state organ. And through the Working Committee of the CPC Central Departments, the CPC ruling elite also have an extra control over the party central organizations beside the normal party administration channel.

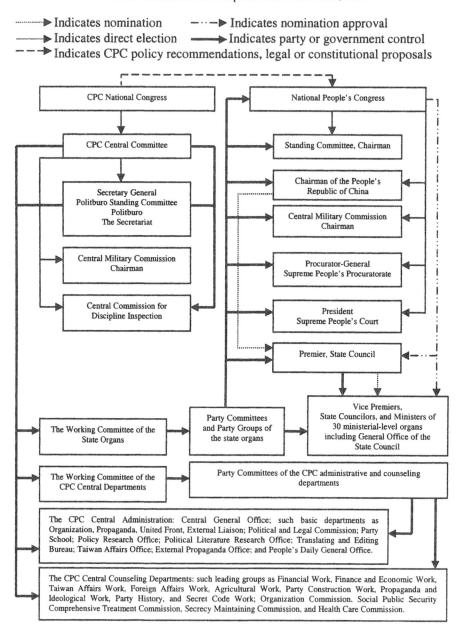

Figure 2.3 Map of China's Central Powers

Source: The map is drawn based on the CPC Constitution and the State Constitution,
showing the present situation of the political power at the central level.

Hierarchy of Legal-bound Institutions, Enacting Bodies, and Actors

According to the State Constitution,[23] the Chinese legal institutions are summarized in a hierarchical order as follows: the Constitution, basic laws,[24] non-basic laws, administrative rules and regulations, and local regulations. The Constitution can only be amended by the NPC; basic laws shall be enacted and amended by the NPC; non-basic laws shall be enacted and amended by the NPC Standing Committee; administrative rules and regulations shall be enacted by the State Council; and local regulations shall be enacted by provincial level[25] people's congresses and their standing committees. Besides, the resolutions and decisions promulgated by the NPC and its Standing Committee, the decisions and orders issued by the State Council, and the standardized decrees, instructions and rules issues by the ministries and commissions under the State Council are also regarded as the state's legal institutions. In addition, since the CPC controls the state apparatus as indicated in Figure 3, the resolutions, decisions, and circulars of the CPC Central Committee, the Politburo and its Standing Committee may as well act as legal-binding institutions; and in some cases, particularly in early stages of the economic reform, they may even override the existing legal institutions when discrepancy arises between the state legal institutions and the party documents. Table 2.1 lists these legal institutions, their enacting bodies, and actors in a hierarchical order.

The National Congress is the highest leading organ of the CPC. Before 1977, it convened at irregular intervals, ranging from once a year at the earliest history of the CPC and once in more than ten years between 1928 and 1969. Since 1977 it has convened once every five years, which has been stipulated in the amendment to the Party Constitution at the CPC Thirteenth National Congress in October 1987. The number of the elected Representatives to the National Congress is varying in different periods of time. Since its Eleventh National Congress, the number ranges from 1,500 to some 2,000. And since its Thirteenth National Congress, about 60 party veterans are invited as Special Representatives to attend the Congress with full rights as the elected Representatives.

The CPC Central Committee is elected by the CPC National Congress, consisting of around 200 full members and 110 to 150 alternate members since its Tenth National Congress. The party boss is usually the Chairman / Secretary General of the Central Committee who also chairs the Central Military Commission. But it may sometimes refer to someone who has the real power in the party and the army. For example, Deng Xiaoping was never made Chairman / Secretary General of the Central Committee but he was the real party boss since China started the economic reform in 1978. There might be two factors underlying Deng's authorities: (1) he produced a renewed ideology for the party members to cope with the economic and political challenges that faced the party following the disastrous Cultural Revolution, and (2) he had the full support of the People's Liberation Army (PLA) and he chaired the Central Military Commission since June 1981.

Table 2.1 Chinese National Legal Institutions, Their Enacting Bodies, and Actors

Legal Institutions	Enacting Bodies	Actors
Party resolutions Decisions Circulars Orders	• The CPC Central Committee • The Politburo Standing Committee • The Politburo	*Supreme Actor*: CPC Boss *Chief Actors*: members of the Politburo Standing Committee *Decision-makers*: • members of the Politburo • members of the Central Committee • representatives of the National Congress
The Constitution Basic laws such as criminal law, civil law, and procedural law	The National People's Congress (NPC)	**Chief** *Actor*: the NPC Presidium *Decision-makers*: • NPC Deputies • NPC Nine Special Committees
Other statutes with the exception of those enacted by the NPC	The NPC Standing Committee	*Chief Actor*: The Council of Chairmen *Decision-makers*: • Members of the NPC Standing Committee • Nine Special Committees
Administrative rules and regulations, decisions, and orders	The State Council	*Chief Actors*: • The Premier • Vice Premiers (from four to a dozen) • The State Councillors (around ten) • The Secretary General of the State Council *Decision-makers*: • The Legal Bureau of the State Council • Ministers of 29 ministerial-level state organs
Ministerial orders, directives, and regulations	Ministries and commissions under the State Council	*Chief Actors*: Ministers *Decision-makers*: Directors of Bureaus

The Politburo was officially introduced at the CPC Fifth National Congress in May 1927. It is elected by the CPC Central Committee, consisting of about 20 full members and two to four alternate members. Although standing members of the Politburo were elected by the CPC Central Committee since the CPC Fifth National Congress in May 1927, the Politburo Standing Committee was officially introduced at the CPC Eighth National Congress in September 1956. It usually comprises five to seven members.

The Chinese People's Political Consultative Conference (CPPCC) used to be the legislature before the National People's Congress was established in September 1954. The number of the NPC deputies used to be fluctuating but has been around 3,000 since its Sixth National Congress in June 1983. The NPC Presidium comprises a chairman and several vice chairmen, and about 160 deputies selected by the outgoing NPC Standing Committee. The Presidium shall decide whether or not to put bills on the agenda of the session.

The NPC has nine special committees, including Law Committee, Nationalities Committee, Internal and Judicial Affairs Committee, Finance and Economic Committee, Education Committee, Science, Culture and Public health Committee, Foreign Affairs Committee, Overseas Chinese Committee, Environment and Resources Protection Committee, and Agricultural and Rural Committee. They work under the direction of the NPC and under the direction of the NPC Standing Committee when the NPC is not in session. Each special committee is composed of a chairman, five to six vice-chairmen, and eight to 27 members, all of whom are nominated by the Presidium from among deputies to the NPC, subject to approval by the NPC. Their chief functions include:

- to examine the bills placed before them by the Presidium or the NPC Standing Committee and prepare reports on the examination;
- to examine rules, regulations, or decisions of the State Council, provincial-level people's congresses, and provincial-level governments, and prepare reports on the examination;
- to make inquiries into specific questions relating to their particular areas of competence and within the scope of the respective functions and powers of the NPC and its Standing Committee, and submit proposals concerning these matters; and
- to assist the NPC and its Standing Committee in, among other things, enacting laws and exercising supervision over the Judiciary and the Executive.

The Council of Chairmen comprises Chairman, 19 Vice Chairmen, and the Secretariat General of the NPC Standing Committee since its Eighth National Congress in March 1993. The Council of Chairmen shall decide whether or not to put bills on the agenda of the meeting of the NPC Standing Committee. The number of The NPC Standing Committee members used to be various but has become quite stable at 155 since its Sixth Congress in June 1983. It can partially supplement and amend basic laws and assumes the NPC powers when the NPC is not in session.

The State Council Legal Bureau is composed of bureaucrats, legal experts and lawyers. It is responsible for (1) drawing up yearly and five-year programs for drafting and enacting administrative rules and regulations, based on the proposals of the ministries; (2) examining the drafts of administrative rules and regulations submitted by various ministries and preparing reports on the examination; and (3) drafting rules, regulations, and implementing regulations that cover functions and powers of several ministries.

The State Council has one general office and 29 ministries and commissions after its 1999 streamlining reform, including ministries of Foreign Affairs, National Defense, Education, Science and Technology, Public Security, State Security, Supervision, Civil Affairs, Justice, Finance, personnel, labor and Social Security, land and Natural Resources, Construction, Railways, Communications, Information Industry, Water Resources, Agriculture, Foreign Trade and Economic Co-operation, Culture, and Health; State Development Planning Commission, State Economic and Trade Commission, State Ethnic Affairs Commission, State Family Planning Commission, and Commission of Science, Technology and Industry for National Defense; The people's Bank of China; and National Audi Office.

As the institutional analysis in this book is investigating the national institutional transformations and changes, it will particularly examine the institutional behavior of the supreme and chief actors and the relevant institutional changes as a result of their efforts. In other words, the institutionalization process that involves important national institutional shifts shall be given special attention.

Conclusion

This chapter has developed an institutional analytic framework and identified the level of institutions and actors and their dynamic interactions to be the focus of the institutional analysis in the case studies in the following chapters.

The case studies intend to show the institutionalization behavior of the supreme and chief actors, with special attention to the policy preference of the supreme leader or actor. The case studies will particularly examine such relevant questions as to why the target policy was initiated. When and where? By whom? Is it the policy preference of the supreme leader? Did he have alternative policy choices? If it is his policy preference, how did he manage to have it endorsed by other ruling elite — through invoking existing or largely dormant institutions, modifying the existing ones, or creating new ones?

The findings of the case studies will be measured on Linz and Stepan's institutional map of democracy and the continuum of two-direction regime change (see Figure 2.1) to determine whether China's social, economic and political changes have moved the country definitively closer to political democratization. After analyzing a series of policy outputs, the institutional analytic framework will also recreate patterns of the policy institutionalization of the ruling elite and indicate what changes have been made in the macro institutional environments. The patterns of the ruling elite's policy institutionalization and changes in the institutional environments will provide reliable insights into what next policy outputs are most likely, providing another indicator of the future political development of Chinese politics.

The next Chapter will examine the political institutionalization in Mao's era, identifying the institutional legacies of Mao, which became the challenges as well as the opportunities for reform-minded Deng Xiaoping.

Notes

1   For a discussion of these typologies, see Held, 1987.
2   For more discussion, see Held, 1987, pp.36-71; 1995, pp.9-12; and also see Weale, 1999, pp.19-39.
3   Seymour Martin Lipset is a strong advocator of this school. Some of his major works on modernization and democracy are: 'Some social requisites for democracy', *American Political Science Review,* 53 (1959), pp.69-105; *Political Man*, Heineman, London, 1960; and 'Social requisites for democracy revisited', *American Sociological Review,* 59 (1994), pp.1-22.
4   Samuel P. Huntington is a pioneer of this school. Some of his major works include 'Political Development and Political Decay', *World Politics*, 17 (April 1965); *The Third Wave*, University of Oklahoma Press, Norman and London, 1991.
5   The agent-centric approach was pioneered by Dankwart A. Rustow in his influential article 'Transitions to Democracy: Towards a Dynamic Model', *Comparative Politics*, 2 (April 1970), pp.337-63.
6   Larry Diamond, 'Economic Development and Democracy Reconsidered', in G. Marks and L. Diamond, eds., *Reexamining Democracy: Essays in Honor of Seymour Martin Lipset*, Sage, London, 1992.
7   Vanhanen (1997, p.22) observes that politics can be interpreted as an expression of the universal struggle for existence in living nature and that politics is a species-specific way to compete for scarce resources and to distribute them among the members of a society.
8   His basic explanatory variables are Urban Population (UP), Non Agricultural Population (NAP), Students (percentage of the population), Literates (the percentage of literates from the adult population), Family Farms (FF), The Degree of Concentration of Non-Agricultural Economic Resources (DC), and The Degree of Decentralization of Non-Agricultural Economic Resources (DD). The Sectional indices of explanatory variables are:
    • Index of Occupational Diversification (IOD), the arithmetic mean of UP and NAP;
    • Index of Knowledge Distribution (IKD), the arithmetic mean of Students (percentage) and Literates;
    • (The above two sectional indices cover the whole period of comparison since the 1850s.)
    • Index of the Distribution of Economic Power Resources (DER). FF and DD are combined by weighting the values of FF and DD by the percentage of agricultural

population (AP) and non-agricultural population (NAP) respectively. DER = (FF x AP) + (DD x NAP). This index covers only the period 1980-1993.

His Index of Structural Imbalance is based on the mean deviation of the three sectional indices: IOD, IKD, and DER. The two combined indices of explanatory variables are:

- Index of Power Resources (IPR). A combination of IOD, IKD, and DER. IPR = (IOD x IKD x DER) / 10,000. In the period 1850-1970, FF is used in place of DER.
- Index of Power Resources and Structural Imbalance (IPRI). IPR is weighted by the value of ISI. IPRI = IPR + ¼ of ISI.

(These two combined indices cover the whole period of comparison since the 1850s.)
For more discussion, see Vanhanen, 1997, pp.42-60.

9 Stehan Haggard and Robert R. Kaufman, 'The Political Economy of Democratic Transitions', *Comparative Politics*, vol.29, no.3, April 27, pp.263-83.

10 Adam Przeworski, *Democracy and the Market: Political and Economic Reforms in Eastern Europe and Latin America*, New York: Cambridge University Press, 1991.

11 There exist different views concerning the degrees of the international influences on domestic democratization. A strong version is offered by Samuel P. Huntington (1991, p.86) who considers international factors play a decisive role, while Laurence Whitehead (1986) considers internal forces are of primary importance in determining the course and outcome of the democratic transition attempt and international factors play only a secondary role.

12 This article presents a summary of the central arguments made in their book. For detailed discussion, see Rueschemeyer, Stephens, & Stephens, 1992.

13 Arguably, it is based on the assumption that liberation from foreign domination and domestic political repression may produce a special state of mass psychology and corresponding political opportunities for the leading elite to launch radical reform programs.

14 Peter Z. Grossman argues it takes time to install institutions, indicating that it took the United States some 300 years to create its present institutional framework, for more discussion see Grossman, 1999.

15 His explanatory variables are grouped under two titles: (1) Environmental Preconditions: five economic variables (level of economic development, economic growth rate, equality or income distribution, indebtedness, economic system type), one social variable, one external variable, and one cultural variable; and (2) Political Process Variables: the timing of political modernization, models of democratic development, the process of democratization, the origins, or impetus, of democratization, the sequential flow of democratization, the pace & violent potential of democratization, and miscellany.

16 He is executive director of the Center for International Private Enterprise. For more discussion, see Sullivan 1999.

17 Hernando de Soto, author of *The Other Path: the invisible Revolution in the Third World* (New York: Harper & Row, 1989), is president of the Institute for Liberty and Democracy in Lima and director of several Peruvian companies. He was also President Alberto Fujimori's personal representative and principal advisor, and as such initiated Peru's re-insertion into the international economic system and its macro-economic reform programs in June 1990. For more discussion, see Soto, 1999.

18 'Orientations' here and thereafter refers to a broad range of beliefs, values, and assumptions that people hold about social and political life. Such orientations may be cognitive, affective, or evaluative. They are general in the sense that they may structure many more specific attitudes or opinions.

19 Weale points out the impracticality of expecting a non-democratic political system to have a quick transition to a democratic system. For more discussion, see Weale, 1999, p.18. Grossman argues it takes time to install democratic institutions. For example, it took the United States some 300 years to create its present institutional framework. For more discussion, see. Grossman, 1999.

20 It is reported that there is a wide spread of selective policy implementation in the Chinese rural areas. Some of the rural party and state officials try to ignore or distort those state policies that ban local unauthorized appropriation and demand local officials to respect villagers' rights and interests, because these policies run counter to local bureaucratic interests. However, some of illegal local levies and fees are enforced relentlessly because they benefit the vested interests of rural officials. For more discussion, see O'Brien and Li, 1999.

21 Party members account for 71.48 per cent of the total representatives of the Ninth NPC (March 1998).

22 The number of the CPC Politburo Standing Committee members ranges from five to seven since the Politburo Standing Committee was first introduced at the Eighth CPC National Congress in September 1956.

23 In 1954 the first Constitution was approved by the First Session of the First People's National Congress, it was re-written or revised in 1969, 1975, 1978, 1982, 1992, 1995, and 1999.

24 They refer to those law governing criminal offences, civil affairs, the state organs and other matters.

25 It refers to provinces, municipalities directly under the Central Government and autonomous regions.

PART II
TRANSITION FROM MAO ZEDONG TO DENG XIAOPING

Chapter 3

Legacies of Mao Zedong: Constraints and Opportunities

This chapter applies the institutional analytic framework to examining the institutionalizational behavior of the CPC ruling elite in general and the supreme leader, Mao Zedong in particular in 1949-1976, and Mao's institutional legacies: the economic and political consequences, which represented macro environments where the Mao successors maneuvered to pursue their policy preferences in the immediate post-Mao Era.

Types of Institutionalization Processes

There are five major types of policy institutionalization process that have been generalized from the institutionalization outputs of the Chinese ruling elite since 1949. Legally speaking, only an NPC delegation or over 30 deputies, the NPC Presidium, the NPC Standing Committee, each special committee of the NPC, the State Council, the Central Military Commission, the Supreme People's Court, and the Supreme People's Procuratorate may submit bills to the NPC for deliberation and consideration; the NPC Presidium decides both whether or not to put them on the agenda of the session and whether or not to submit them to the session for voting after they are examined, at least, twice. The Council of Chairmen, ten or more members of the NPC Standing Committee, and the above-mentioned entities may submit bills to the NPC Standing Committee. The Council of Chairmen decides whether to refer them to the Standing Committee for examination at its meeting and whether to submit them to the plenary meeting of the Standing Committee for voting. This process has become a dominant form of institutionalization in the later stage of the economic reform, when a series of laws need to be drafted by the NPC since the market economy was endorsed by the CPC in 1992. This institutionalization process is classified as **Type A Process**: parliamentary institutionalization.

However, as the ruling party, the CPC Central Committee, the Politburo and its Standing Committee enjoy the privilege of submitting legal proposals or policy guideline proposals directly to the NPC for consideration. This institutionalization usually considers important policy shifts, a change of the basic laws, or amendments to the Constitution. This institutionalization process is classified as **Type B Process**: oligarchic decisions plus parliamentary institutionalization.

During the early stages of the economic reform and the open-door policy since 1978, the chief actors of the CPC did not bother, perhaps out of the vanguard party's revolutionary tradition,[1] or did not have the time since the National People's Congress convenes once a year, to go through a Type A or Type B institutionalization process to have a law enacted or regulations adopted: they would rather just have resolutions or decisions issued jointly by the CPC Central Committee and the State Council to push forward the economic reform and to further open China to the outside world.   This institutionalization is classified as **Type C Process**: oligarchic decision plus administrative endorsement.

Since 1949 the CPC Central Committee, the Politburo, or its Standing Committee has issued quite a number of resolutions, decisions, and policy circulars to initiate a mass movement, launch a revolutionary campaign, or to start economic reform.   This institutionalization is classified as **Type D Process**:[2] oligarchic institutionalization.

China has a deep-rooted legacy of feudalism of over 2000 years, where the ruler enjoyed an absolute monopoly of power.   The CPC supreme actor, Mao Zedong, did not escape from the influence of the feudal legacy.   In the late 1950s, Mao strongly advocated, on several occasions, to rule by man, which he believed was more effective than to rule by law.[3]   However, by 'rule by man', Mao actually meant to rule China according to the party's decisions and policies that had been made by the CPC actors, which is labeled above as Type D Process.   Mao did not enjoy the rule of man in the sense of making decisions by one man until he initiated the Cultural Revolution in 1967.   During the ten years of the Cultural Revolution 1967-1976, Mao was the supreme actor of the CPC and he discarded the party collective decision-making game and issued instructions directly to the party members and the masses at large.   This autocratic decision-making behavior is classified as **Type E Process**: autocratic institutionalization. Table 3.1 summarizes these types of institutionalization processes in their simplified versions.

Table 3.1 Types of Policy Institutionalization Processes[4]

Type A Process: parliamentary institutionalization			
Stage 1	**Stage 2**	**Stage 3**	**Stage 4**
A bill is submitted to the NPC or its Standing Committee for deliberation and consideration. The NPC Presidium decides whether to submit it to the Congress for examination.	Usually a bill needs three readings (examinations) before it may be put to vote at a session of the NPC or at a plenary meeting of the Standing Committee.	A bill is to be adopted by a simple majority vote. However, amendments to the Constitution are to be adopted by a vote of over two-thirds of all the deputies to the Congress.	It is promulgated by Chairman of the People's Republic of China.

Type B Process: oligarchic decisions plus parliamentary institutionalization

Stage 1	Stage 2	Stage 3	Stage 4	Stage 5
The Supreme Actor initiates new ideology and a new policy proposal usually at a meeting of the Politburo or its Standing Committee.	If it is accepted, it may be submitted either to the CPC Central Committee for approval or directly to the NPC for consideration.	If the CPC Central Committee approves the proposal, it may recommend it to the NPC or its Standing Committee for consideration.	If it is accepted, a law bill will be drafted and examined by the NPC or its Standing Committee.	It will go through all the Type A stages from Stage 1 to Stage 4.

Type C Process: oligarchic decision plus administrative endorsement

Stage 1	Stage 2	Stage 3
The Supreme Actor initiates new ideology and a new policy proposal usually at a meeting of the Politburo or its Standing Committee.	If it is accepted, the Politburo or its Standing Committee may submit it either to the CPC Central Committee for approval or jointly issues, with the State Council, a resolution, decision, or circular to the party members and the whole nation.	If the CPC Central Committee approves the proposal, it jointly issues, with the State Council, a resolution, decision, or circular to the party members and the whole nation.

Type D Process: oligarchic institutionalization

Stage 1	Stage 2	Stage 3
The Supreme Actor initiates new ideology and a new policy proposal usually at a meeting of the Politburo or its Standing Committee.	If it is accepted, the Politburo or its Standing Committee may submit it either to the CPC Central Committee for approval or directly issues a circular, resolution, or decision to the party members and the masses at large for action.	If the CPC Central Committee approves the proposal, it issues a circular, resolution, or decision to the party members and the masses at large for action.

Type E Process: autocratic institutionalization

Stage 1	Stage 2
The Supreme Actor issues instructions directly to the party members and the masses at large for action.	The CPC Central Committee, the Politburo or its Standing Committee issues a circular, resolution, or decision, to provide details of how to carry out Mao's instructions.

Coalition Parliamentary Policy Institutionalization

When the People's Republic of China was established in 1949, a coalition government was set up in Beijing based on the Doctrine of New Democracy advocated by Mao Zedong. Although the CPC secured the leading position in the coalition, in the early years of the People's Republic of China, a collective institutionalization process based on the multi-party coalition principles was basically maintained in drafting and formulating the Constitution, basic laws, and principle policies. In retrospect, that the CPC ruling elite chose the power sharing arrangement in preference to the CPC monopoly of power was conditioned by the domestic and international economic and political situation at that time.

External Conditions

The international powers, including the Soviet Union, wished to see a certain kind of coalition government in China with the dominance of the KMT government, which is clearly indicated in the World War II settlement arrangement.

With the Second World War drawing to its end, Roosevelt, Churchill, and Stalin reached an agreement at Yalta in February 1945 regarding a post-war settlement in East Asia. The United States received Stalin's pledge to attack Japan within two or three months after Germany surrendered, which could minimize casualties of American soldiers in East Asia. Stalin also promised to acknowledge the legitimacy of the KMT Government and not to support the Chinese Communists' attempt to overthrow the KMT Government, insuring the installment of a post-war Chinese government that would be both friendly to the United States and contain the expansion of Soviet Communism. In return, the Russians could annex southern Sakhalin and the Kuriles, secure their influence in Outer-Mongolia, establish a naval base at Port Arthur, recover Russia's pre-1904 rights in Manchuria, including its 'pre-eminent interests' in the Chinese-Eastern Railroad and the South-Manchurian Railroad and the port of Dalian (Leffler, 1992, pp.81-140; Cohen, 1980, pp.175-83). In this context, the post-war settlement produced a loser – the Communist Party of China.

On 2nd April 1945, Patrick Hurley, American Ambassador to China, made it clear that the American government would support only the KMT regime. On 14th August 1945, the Soviet Union and the KMT Government signed the Sino-Soviet Treaty of Friendship. The CPC elite had no other choice but to negotiate with the KMT for a coalition government while preparing for the outbreak of the civil war after the defeat of the Japanese aggressors. Although talks between the CPC and the KMT produced a joint statement on 10 October 1945, civil war seemed imminent with Chiang confident of receiving military aid from the United States and settling the dispute through military means.[5] However, the result of the Chinese civil war in the late 1940s was neither what the United State wanted, the victory of the Nationalist Government, nor what the Russians wished to see, a divided and weak China (Cohen, 1980, p.187). By 1949 the CPC People's

Liberation Army defeated the KMT army on the major battlefields in China and controlled the majority territory of Mainland China. The CPC elite seized the opportunity to set up a coalition government in October 1949 in Beijing before the whole country was liberated.

Coalition Government

The CPC elite kept its promise to install a coalition government both for the purpose of distinguishing itself from the corrupt, autocratic, one-party KMT regime and out of the following economic and political considerations:

- The Russian economic, political, and military support had not been secured yet, which might be a major source of assistance for China's reconstruction;
- A coalition government might be more acceptable to Western countries headed by the United States, which might be another source of assistance for China's economic reconstruction;[6]
- Lacking experience, personnel, and resources to conduct economic reconstruction, the CPC elite had to rely on the material and human resources of the national bourgeoisie and intellectuals for kicking off the economic reconstruction;
- A coalition government would win over co-operation and support of the non-proletarian classes for national economic reconstruction who had supported the CPC's proposal for a coalition government after the defeat of the Japanese aggressors.

The main ideas of a coalition government were initiated by Mao Zedong[7] and summarized as follows:

- To establish a democratic republic under the joint dictatorship of all the anti-feudal and anti-imperial classes, including proletariat, peasants, intellectuals, petty bourgeois, and national bourgeois, with the working class as the leading class (Mao, 1965, pp.635-37, p.957).
- The government at various levels is elected by the corresponding people's congress (Mao, 1965, p.638). First, to set up a coalition government after defeating the Japanese aggressors through consultation among all the democratic parties and representatives of people with no party affiliation, and then at a suitable time in the future, to inaugurate a formal coalition government by the National People's Congress attended by representatives through free election (Mao, 1965, pp.969-70).
- The new democracy is the first stage of the Chinese Revolution before China enters the second stage, socialism (Mao, 1965, p.633, p.644); during the first stage, the new democratic political system is based upon the coalition of several democratic classes that is different from the socialist system based

upon the dictatorship of the proletariat and the monopoly of power by one party as in the Soviet Union (Mao, 1965, pp.962-3).

- To reflect this particular political system, China's economy should be composed of five components: state-owned economy, collective economy, private capitalist economy, private individual economy, and state capitalist economy[8] while the land of the gentry, legacy of the feudal economy, is confiscated and redistributed among peasants who have no or little land of their own (Mao, 1965, p.639, p.959).

Mao's ideas about New Democracy were accepted by the other democratic parties and the majority of the people as his offer looked better than the old KMT rule. The deteriorating economic situation under the KMT rule between the end of the anti-Japanese War and the defeat of the KMT army in Manland China in 1949 illustrates the desperate feeling of the whole country in favor of a regime change, even if under communist rule. Because of the financial mismanagement of the KMT-led National Government, prices increased by 30 per cent per month during 1945-1948 in the KMT-controlled areas. From August 1948 to April 1949, note issues increased by 4,524 times, and the Shanghai price index rose astronomically by 135,742 times. The escalating inflation plus rampant corruption of the Nationalist officials who returned to the Japanese-occupied areas after the war totally discredited the KMT-led National Government. It was small wonder that the majority of the people even looked forward to a change of government (Hsiung, 1970, p.640).

In 1949 the CPC invited the democratic parties and non-party members to participate in the institutionalization of a new republic based upon Mao's blueprint. Between 21 and 30 September 1949, the 1st Plenary Session of the First Chinese People's Political Consultative Conference (CPPCC) convened in Beijing. Attending the Session were 662 deputies, who represented 46 political organizations including the CPC, the 11 democratic parties,[9] non-governmental organizations as well as public figures with no party affiliation. The CPC took about 44 per cent of the total 662 deputy seats, the democratic parties some 30 per cent, and non-party members 26 per cent. In the elected 180-member National Committee of the First CPPCC the democratic parties occupied 60 seats. 31 members of democratic parties and non-party members were elected into the 62-member Central People's Government. Mao Zedong was elected Chairman of the Central People's Government, and three of the six vice chairmen were members of democratic parties or non-party members. In the 21-member Government Administration Council, the executive branch, the democratic parties occupied 11 seats. The Government Administration Council had 34 government agencies or organizations, 15 of which were headed by members of the democratic parties. The CPPCC First Plenary Session enshrined the principles of new democracy in the Common Program of the CPPCC, which was the provisional constitution of the country, the Organic Law of the Central People's Government of the People's Republic of China, and the Organic Law of the CPPCC.

Practice of Coalition Parliamentary Policy Institutionalization

Although the CPC secured its leading position in the coalition and declared its ultimate goal of socialism leading to communism in the Common Program, in the early years of the People's Republic of China, a collective institutionalization process, based on the multi-party coalition principles, was maintained in drafting and formulating the Constitution, basic laws, and principle policies. Democratic parties and non-party members were actively involved in the political decision-making process, creating new institutions and administration of the new republic. The dominant institutionalization process during the early period of the Republic was a Type B Process (see Table 3.1).

This institutionalization process that was practiced at the very beginning of the People's Republic facilitated the active participation of the democratic parties and non-party members in the policy institutionalization process. Although as the largest political party in the coalition, the CPC had a large say in institutionalization, the institutionalization process could still offer opportunities for democratic discussions and deliberations if decision-makers, especially those representatives from democratic parties and non-political affiliations, could act independently and free of political pressure. By 1957 quite a number of important legal documents had been adopted through Type A and Type B Processes,[10] such as the Constitution, adopted by the First Session of the First National People's Congress (NPC) in September 1954.

After 1953 the CPC ruling elite began to push forward socialist transformation of agriculture, handicrafts industry, and capitalist industry and commerce, which was originally expected to be completed within 15 years.[11] The socialist transformation was implemented much faster than most people, even the CPC's chief actors, expected. By the end of 1956, 87.8 per cent of the peasants had joined advanced agricultural producer's co-operatives, 92 per cent of the handicraftsmen had joined handicraftsmen co-operatives, and 99 per cent of the industrial private enterprises and 82.2 per cent of the commercial private enterprises had been transferred either into state-private enterprises or co-operatives (Zhang, Kong and Deng, 1993, p.545). The socialist transformation was carried out in such haste and intensity, producing tensions between the peasants and private businessmen on one side and the CPC on the other. How to ease the tensions was a critical test of both the legitimacy of the newly established institutions, although limited in their numbers, and the willingness of the chief actors of the CPC to observe the institutions and honor the newly established institutionalization process when facing direct policy challenges from the democratic parties and intellectuals. History tells us that the chief actors of the CPC reversed to their traditional institutionalization habit when they perceived such policy challenges a class struggle.

From a Type B Process to a Type D Process: CPC-dominated Institutionalization

With the completion of the socialist transformation, the chief actors of the CPC anticipated a new era of economic construction based on domestic as well as foreign experience of economic development. In April and May 1956, Mao Zedong made a speech at a Politburo Meeting and a Government Administration Council Meeting, respectively, suggesting to his colleagues how they might best mobilize for China's economic development: domestic and foreign factors, party members and non-party members, individuals and work units, the Han nationality and minorities, the central and the periphery, the coastal and the inland areas, and the light industry, agriculture, and the heavy industry. Mao suggested that if during the early years of the Republic, China had to learn from the experiences of the Soviet Union, it was the time now for China to devise its own general guidelines for socialist economic construction. Mao Zedong wanted to avoid the mistake of the Soviet Union's over-emphasis on the heavy industry and to understand the advanced science, technology and management techniques from foreign countries including capitalist countries (Mao, 1977, pp.267-88).

The CPC chief actors and decision-makers reached a consensus on the party economic and political policies at the CPC Eighth National Congress in September 1956, the main points of which are as follows:

- The contradiction between the proletariat and the capitalist had been basically resolved with the completion of the socialist transformation; the main contradiction facing China was the one between the advanced socialist system and the backward social productive forces – as a result, the main task was to turn China from a backward agrarian country into an advanced industrial one.
- The socialist economic system of China[12] included (1) the state economy and the collective economy which formed the main body of the socialist economy, to be supplemented by the individual economy; (2) production was mainly according to the state economic plan, to be supplemented by production according to the market within the limits of the state economic plan; and (3) the state designated markets were the principle markets, to be supplemented by free markets within the state-designated areas.
- To establish and improve the rule of law through gradually formulating comprehensive laws, with a view to both making laws available for the party and the government to abide by and subjecting their activities to existing laws.
- To stress prevention and fight against any individual cult of personality, and to stick to the collective leadership system with personal responsibilities.

Under these CPC policy guidelines, China seemed to enter not only a period of large-scale economic construction but also, more importantly, a period of drafting comprehensive legal institutions to safeguard its economic construction. Without the Anti-Rightists Campaign of 1957, the Type B Process of institutionalization might have been honored by the CPC actors, at least for some time and the development of China's legal institutions might have not been delayed for more than 20 years. The Great Leap Forward might have not been started or at least not in its present form. China's political history of the 1950s might have been re-written.

The Anti-Rightists Campaign of 1957

The CPC policy guidelines were based on an assumption that the CPC had settled class struggle with the bourgeoisie. In the middle of 1957 the CPC perceived class struggle between the proletariat and the bourgeoisie re-emerged and intensified, the CPC discarded their policy guidelines. Gone with the CPC guidelines was the coalition parliamentary institutionalization process. Since 1957 the CPC ruling elite simply shifted to Type C and Type D institutionalization processes for policy guidelines.

Compared to the CPC ruling elite's enthusiasm for socialism and industrialization, the general public were more concerned with their daily necessities. After the collectivization, the peasants were demoralized by the egalitarian distribution of income prevailing in the co-operatives. Many co-operatives were poorly managed owing to lack of management experience among the CPC cadres. In addition to natural disasters, such as flooding in parts of China, agricultural production declined in 1954. Many cities began to feel the shortage of supply in grain, meat, and daily commodities in 1956. As a result, many peasants wanted to quit the co-operatives, and workers went on strike in many cities. It was estimated that more than 10,000 labor strikes erupted across China between October 1956 and March 1957. In Shanghai, more than 200 strikes occurred in the spring of 1957 alone, while in 1925, the most tumultuous year in the history of Shanghai, there were only 175 strikes (Perry 1995, pp.302-26).

The international situation was also turbulent in 1956. In the Soviet Union Khrushchev denounced Stalin's brutality and personality cult during his rule and advocated that the proletariat seize power and realize socialism through parliamentary means rather than armed struggle. In Poland and Hungary, serious strikes, demonstrations, and riots broke out. To make the situation worse for the CPC, the KMT troops launched a counter-offensive campaign against the CPC rule in the southern part of China, while the United States tightened its containment policy of China.

Against these internal and external situations, Mao Zedong initiated, at the Second Plenary Session of the CPC Eighth Central Committee on 15 November 1956, a rectification campaign. The rectification campaign was designed to eliminate elements of 'bureaucratism, factionism and subjectivism' among the party cadres and government officials, which were considered to be the main causes of the complaints of peasants, workers, and bourgeoisie. It was a party internal rectification campaign and did not need to seek approval and endorsement from the National People's Congress (NPC). However, in order to deepen the rectification campaign, Mao tried to mobilize the general public, especially the intellectuals to air their views, to criticize the mistakes of the party and the government by advocating 'Let a hundred flowers bloom and a hundred schools of thought contend'. On 30th April 1957, Mao even invited 44 democrats and other non-party members of the society to discuss the CPC rectification campaign, welcoming non-party members to criticize the CPC and help it with its rectification.[13]

Intellectuals from the democratic parties and those without party affiliation took the lead in criticizing the CPC and the government at seminars, public meetings, and in newspapers. Some criticized the arrogance of the CPC cadres who sought quick success and instant benefit regardless of the actual conditions; some pointed out the CPC's direct interference in the affairs of the government by issuing directives and managing the daily administration of the government; some demanded that the CPC should withdraw from government agencies, schools, and the state-private enterprise; and some even suggested that the CPC and other democratic parties should govern the country in turn.

The intellectuals' sharp criticism was beyond Mao's tolerance. Only two weeks later, Mao Zedong decided to switch from the party Rectification Campaign to launching another mass political campaign – the Anti-Rightists Campaign, to root out the 'poisonous weeds': bourgeois rightists who, in the name of helping CPC with the rectification, attacked socialism and intended to overthrow the leadership of the CPC. On 15th May 1957, Mao Zedong wrote an article entitled 'The Situation is changing' 《事情正在起变化》 to be circulated among the party cadres (Mao, 1977, pp.423-9). In the article Mao identified those actively criticizing the CPC and the government as anti-communist-rightists, who were concentrated in the democratic parties and high learning institutions. Mao warned that a battle against the rightists was imminent but he asked the CPC to allow those bourgeois rightists to show themselves in order to root out these 'poisonous weeds'. On 8th June 1957, the CPC Central Committee issued to the party cadres a directive 'To Organize Forces to Fight against the Reckless Attacks of the Rightists' 《组织力量反击右派分子的猖狂进攻》, which was written by Mao himself (Mao, 1977, pp.431-3). In the document, Mao particularly asked the CPC members to pay close attention to the attacks of the democratic parties and to choose proper time to organize counterattacks against rightists in every organization and school. By the summer of 1958, over 550,000 people were rooted out and labeled as counterrevolutionary rightists, including four non-communist ministers,[14] thirty-eight legislators in the First NPC, four provincial governors, and eighteen provincial deputy-governors, with the majority of the victims being intellectuals (Zheng, 1997, pp.68-71; and Teiwes, 1993, p.275). All the rightists were deprived of any right granted by the 1954 Constitution; they even lost their freedom of occupational choices and were relocated to factories and the countryside to receive re-education from the peasants and workers.

Institutional Consequence of the Anti-Rightists Campaign

The Anti-Rightists Campaign was initiated by Mao and implemented only after the Type D Process of institutionalization. Through the Campaign, Mao consolidated his position in the party and developed his theory of the continual revolution under the proletarian dictatorship. It set a precedent that the CPC supreme leader could use a Type D Process to launch a mass movement or nation-wide revolution whenever he sensed that a class struggle was in the wind. Mao would resort to his notorious theory whenever he found himself constrained by the political institutions and challenged by the other actors and decision makers of the CPC, who demanded the restoration of such rules as the democratic centralism and the collective decision making process stipulated in the party resolutions and constitution. After the 1957 Anti-Rightists Campaign, Mao's challenges came mainly from within the CPC. Again Mao identified any such challenges as the counterrevolutionary rightists, bourgeois revisionists or capitalist representatives within the party. His final decision to settle his battle against these counterrevolutionary elements was to launch the Cultural Revolution, when he successfully destroyed all the political institutions and personally ruled China for 10 years.

The Anti-Rightists Campaign had a great negative impact on the newly established political coalition. Up to 1957, the legal institutions guaranteed, to a great extent, not only free election of the deputies of the people's congress at all the levels and participation in the decision making by democratic parties and non-party members, but also freedom of speech, press, assembly, association, religious beliefs, and demonstrations. In practice, these freedoms were enjoyed by the democratic parties and the public because the CPC tried to distinguish itself from the KMT's dictatorship rule by forming the Central People's Government with democrats taking senior administrative positions and by allowing the democratic parties to participate in the decision making process. Some democratic parties had their own newspapers before 1957, such as Shanghai's *Wenhui Daily* 《文汇报》 controlled by the Chinese Peasants' and Workers' Democratic Party, and Beijing's *Guangming Daily* 《光明日报》 by China Democratic League, which was another sign of real democratic freedom. After 1957 the CPC took direct control of the media with tight censorship imposed on information and articles to be published in newspapers and magazines. Those legislators of the NPC who survived the Campaign did not dare to express opinions different from the party general guidelines, and therefore, there was little to propose except to follow the party lines; as a result, the bills proposed to the assembly by the NPC legislators declined dramatically from 243 in 1957 to 81 in 1958, 80 in 1959, and 46 in 1960 (Zhang, 1997, p.72).

Another significant change in administering national affairs was that in the late 1950s the Central Government stopped issuing directives independently. In 1959, for instance, the CPC issued 23 directives independently and issued another 12 directives jointly with the Central Government (Zhang, 1997, p.90). Since then, the NPC became a rubber-stamp and the Central Government became a policy-implementing agency of the CPC and the dominant institutionalization process was a Type D Process (see Table 3.1). In other words, the CPC completely dominated the institutionalization, which was still a collective decision-making process but was gradually turned into a Type E Process, dominated by Mao Zedong in the late 1960s.

From a Type D Process to a Type E Process: Autocratic Institutionalization

The shift from the Type D institutionalization to the Type E institutionalization was much more difficult than the previous institutionalization shift from Type B Process to Type D Process because the autocrat needed to nullify both the CPC collective leadership and the power of the government, the bureaucracy responsible for administering state affairs. In other words, the autocrat must deprive his colleagues of the decision-making power in the party and the government. Mao Zedong eventually achieved his autocratic institutionalization by launching the Cultural Revolution, which paralyzed both the party and the state bureaucracies. The making of the Cultural Revolution and Mao's control over the process was conditioned by composite factors that influenced each other. This section examines three such major factors below: international isolation of 1960s, ideological dispute with the Soviet Communist Party, and disputes over the failure of the Great Leap Forward.

International Isolation of 1960s

The 1950s witnessed China leaning towards the Soviet Union for economic aid and national security and the early 1960s witnessed the former breaking away from the latter as predicted by the American diplomats in the late 1940s (Sutter, 1978, p.32). China's disenchantment with the Soviet Union could be traced back to the middle of the 1940s when Stalin refused to support the CPC to fight the KMT for power, as he feared the Chinese civil war might develop into a new global conflict. When the CPC won the civil war, Stalin pressed China to be in conformity with the Soviet Union because he was afraid of having another Tito in the socialist camp. The chauvinist attitudes of the Soviet Union ruling elite annoyed CPC chief actors.[15] The relationship between the two largest socialist countries deteriorated from bad to worse in the 1960s. On 16 July 1960 the Soviet Union unilaterally declared an end to all the economic aid contracts it had signed with China and withdrew its experts from China and in 1969 a border military clash occurred in Helongjiang Province.

In the south, the United States was escalating its military involvement in Vietnam in the middle of 1960s by sending over half a million troops into South Vietnam and launching a large scale air war against North Vietnam. It was clearly evident to the CPC chief actors that the imperialists were encircling China by whatever means available, including military intervention. The 1960s was a decade when China was encircled in the north by the Soviet Union, the socialist imperialists, and in the south by the capitalist imperialists headed by the United States. The harsh geopolitical situation offered Mao Zedong a good opportunity to launch a class struggle campaign to eliminate his opponents in China. He made it clear that a domestic class struggle between the proletariat and the capitalist was a reflection of an international class struggle. In other words, the external threat provided the CPC supreme actor the rationale to wage class struggle against his colleagues, other CPC chief actors, who had different views regarding socialist economic construction.

Ideological Dispute with the Soviet Communist Party

When Khrushchev abandoned the principle of Leninism – armed struggle to seize power, Mao Zedong considered such an act as revisionism. Mao warned the party that the revisionism was one type of bourgeois thought that confused both the distinction between socialism and capitalism and the distinction between the proletariat dictatorship and the bourgeois dictatorship (Mao, 1977, p.418). Mao orchestrated nine editorials in newspapers criticizing the Soviet revisionism in the early 1960s and supported anti-imperialist struggle in Asia, Africa, and Latin America. Mao's posture as a defender of the principles of Marxism and Leninism in the international arena made it impossible for other CPC chief actors to challenge Mao's class struggle initiative. The CPC's ideological dispute with the Soviet Communist Party consolidated Mao's position as the supreme actor at home and provided Mao with a certain rationale and a kind of mandate to wage a class struggle against domestic revisionists in China.

Disputes over the Failure of the Great Leap Forward

Although Mao was against the Soviet revisionism, he was much encouraged by the economic development in the Soviet Union. When China finished its First Five-Year Plan in 1957, Mao wanted a faster socialist construction. At a Politburo Meeting in March 1958, Mao formally proposed a general guideline for faster economic development: 'Go all out, aim high and achieve greater, faster, better and more economical results in building socialism'. When the annual agricultural and industrial growth rates reached 20 and 25 per cent or over, respectively, it was considered a great leap forward (Li, 1998b, p.272). Subsequently, the Great Leap Forward became the official economic development target, which contained two main components (Li, 1998b, p.278):

- The 1957 steel production was 5.3 million tons, the targets for 1958 and 1959 production were 10.7 million and 27 million tons, respectively;
- In 1957 China produced 185 billion kilograms of grain, the grain production targets for 1958 and 1959 were set at 300 to 350 billion kilograms and 400 to 500 billion kilograms.

In order to obtain the target, the peasants were organized into people's communes. The agricultural collectivization deprived peasants of the private ownership of land and means of production, a step forward towards socialism and communism. The general guideline for faster economic development, the Great Leap Forward, and the people's commune were officially referred to as the Three Banners of Socialism.

Such an important economic development strategy should have been institutionalized through a Type B Process according to the Constitution, but the CPC implemented it after it had been passed through a Type D Process (see Table 3.1). The reason was perhaps very simple — the CPC supreme leader believed that the socialist camp was in a competition race with the capitalist camp in economic development. To be a great socialist country, Mao (1974, p.296) claimed China should surpass the United States in steel production in 50 or 60 years, otherwise China would have no place in the world. Therefore, economic development was perceived by Mao as a life-and-death political struggle between socialism and capitalism, and the vital decision to launch the Great Leap Forward should be in the hands of the CPC.

After being implemented, serious problems surfaced: unobtainable production targets were set, blind directions were issued, highly exaggerated outputs were praised, while egalitarian income distribution and mobilization of the agricultural labor and materials for steel production without compensation were prevalent. If the Anti-Rightists Campaign of 1957 caused irreparable damage to the intellectual and spiritual property of Chinese society, the Great Leap Forward 1958-1960 inflicted fatal damage to its material property.

By the end of August 1958, only 4.5 million tons of iron and steel were produced, 6.2 million tons short of the set target. The masses were mobilized to realize the target by the end of 1958. To realize the target became the most important political task of the whole party and the people. In November and December 1958, over 90 million people were mobilized to produce iron and steel by indigenous and primitive methods. Millions of small furnaces emerged like mushrooms throughout China, in courtyards, schools, organizations, enterprises, and people's communes. By the end of 1958, some 11 million tons of iron steel were produced, three million of which were utterly useless dross (Li, 1998b, p.280). The state subsidized a dozen billion RMB *yuan* to the mass iron and steel production. This unprecedented high waste of labor, materials, and money was only possible in a period of ignorance. The Anti-Rightists Campaign, which deprived over half a million intellectuals the right to participate in discussing economic and political policies, greatly reduced the nation's ability to question the feasibility of the outrageous targets. To a large extent, therefore, the Anti-Rightists Campaign inaugurated such a period of ignorance in China.

It is not strange that Mao's ideas of Great Leap Forward were implemented to the extreme by boastfulness and exaggeration. If anyone showed doubt about the targets of the Great Leap forward, their pessimism would be severely criticized as Rightist Opportunism. In such an atmosphere, few would question the validity of the exaggerated production. Stories of unrealistic high-yield production were reported and praised in newspapers, including *People's Daily* 《人民日报》, the CPC newspaper, which was nicknamed as 'launching a satellite'. The highest reported rice annual yield per *mu* of land (about 666 square meters) was 65,217 kilograms[16] and the highest reported annual wheat yield was 4,292.5 kilograms.[17] The consequences of the boastfulness were devastating.

For example, in Henan Province, the actual grain output in 1958 was only 14 billion kilograms, but it was claimed to be 35.1 billion, which led to unrealistically high state grain purchase quotas. In order to fulfill the state purchase quotas, county and commune party cadres and leaders forced peasants to sell grain to the state. The arresting and beating of peasants who failed to realize their grain sale quotas was common practice in the countryside. By the end of November 1958, incidences of peasants starving to death were reported in the Mi County of Henan Province. 1958, 1959 and 1960 were officially classified as three years of natural disasters of flooding and drought, when millions of starving peasants fled their homes and tried to find food and shelter in cities. It was estimated that during the three years of Great Leap Forward 1958-1960 over 27 million people died of unnatural causes (Li, 1998b, p.605).

After 1957 the general public received the screened information from the media under the tight control of the CPC. The CPC chief actors and policy-makers themselves could, however, still receive more reliable information through the party internal information system and through personal investigation trips to the countryside and other parts of China. Based on the information they received some CPC chief actors and policy-makers stepped out to question and challenge Mao's general guideline for the Great Leap Forward. Two such incidents are analyzed here in order to understand how Mao gained the upper hand over his colleagues through waging class struggle within the party.

The first such challenge happened at the Enlarge Politburo Meeting in Lushan resort in Jiangxi Province from 2nd July to 2nd August 1959. The strongest criticism came from Peng Dehuai, a Politburo member and Minister of Defense, who criticized the Great Leap Forward both during group discussions and in a personal letter submitted to Mao Zedong on 14th July, one day before the scheduled close of the meeting.[18] His main points were summarized as follows:

- Mobilizing masses to produce iron and steel was a 'Leftist' approach to economic construction;
- It was too early to organize peasants into people's communes because the people's commune had not been properly tested;
- The democratic life within the party was abnormal because the party first secretaries at various levels usually neglected the collective leadership of the party committees at each level and usually made decisions without consulting other committee members;

- The 'Leftist' tendency was prevailing and many people deliberately avoided voicing different opinions because they were afraid of being labeled as 'Rightists';
- Chairman Mao and the party enjoyed the highest prestige among the Chinese people that could not be found in other parts of the world; however, abuse of this prestige should not be tolerated.

Two days later, Mao distributed Peng's letter among the meeting attendants and proposed to comment on the nature of Peng's letter. So the meeting was prolonged without any set date to close. Many attendants thought the opinion contained in the letter conformed to the reality and some even publicly supported Peng's opinion, such as Huang Kecheng, Chief of the General Staff, Zhou Xiaozhou and First Party Secretary of Hunan Province, Zhang Wentian, Deputy Minister of Foreign Affairs Ministry.

Under Mao's proposal the Eighth Plenary Session of the CPC Eighth Central Committee convened from 2nd to 16th August at Lushan. Mao successfully drew his colleagues' attention away from the alleged abuses of collective leadership within the party and the consequences of the Great Leap Forward and persuaded them into believing that the struggle on the Lushan was the life-and-death class struggle between the proletariat and the capitalist. Mao considered the attacks by Peng and his Anti-Party Clique on the party's general guideline and the Great Leap Forward was no coincidence with the international attacks by the Soviet Union Communist Party and the United States.[19] On 16th August, the Eighth Plenary Session adopted several resolutions, including 'Resolution on Safeguarding the Party's General Guideline and Fighting against "Rightist Opportunism"' and 'Resolution on the Anti-Party Clique Headed by Peng Dehuai'. These resolutions declared that 'Rightist Opportunism' became the major danger for the CPC and the party's main task was, thus, to safeguard the general guideline and to defeat the attacks of 'Rightist Opportunism'. Mao concluded that this kind of class struggle would last, at least, for 20 years, or half a century; in a word, class struggle would not stop until classes cease to exist. After the Lushan party meetings, the party institutional rules, such as the democratic life in the party and the collective leadership based on the democratic centralism, were further undermined by Mao.[20] However, other chief actors and decision-makers continued to challenge Mao's ideas of class struggle whenever opportunities came.

Mao Zedong won the political battle at Lushan but the economy of China went from bad to worse. Agriculture suffered most because of massive investment in heavy industry (some 1,000 investment projects in 1959), declining by 23 per cent from 1958 to 1960. The grain output shrank from 200 billion kilograms in 1958 to 170 billion kilograms in 1959 and to 14.35 billion kilograms in 1960 (Li, 1998b, p.284). Industrial output fell by 40 per cent in 1961 (Li, 1998, p.457). Faced with these harsh realities, the CPC Central Committee convened in May and June 1961, when both Mao Zedong and Liu Shaoqi[21] called for an examination of the experience and lessons. However, Mao and Liu had their own understanding of these problems. Mao still held that the party's general guideline and the Great Leap Forward 1958 were basically correct.

Li Shaoqi, nevertheless, raised the question whether the problems since 1958 derived from the natural disasters or the errors and mistakes of the party. After discussing with the party leaders of Shanxi Province, Hebei Province, Shandong Province, Henan Province, and Hunan Province, Liu (1981, pp.337-421) concluded that the major cause was the errors and mistakes of the party, citing the words of the Hunan peasants '30 per cent from natural calamities and 70 per cent from man-made disasters'. On 27th January 1962 in his speech at the Enlarged Working Conference of the CPC Central Committee,[22] Liu Shaoqi even criticized the split of achievements and mistakes into 'a ratio of nine fingers to one finger'[23] and argued that in general, the mistakes and achievements might be split into a ratio of three fingers to seven fingers in the whole country; but in some areas, the ratio might be seven to three fingers. Liu Shaoqi also raised the following points, which were further in contradiction with Mao's ideas:

- If the people's communes were not promoted, we might have been better off;
- Quite a number of the issues raised in Peng Dehuai's letter to Mao Zedong tallied with the actual situation. The writing of a letter by a Politburo member to the party Chairman could not be reckoned as making a mistake even if some of opinions in the letter were not correct;
- If the party relied on suppression to implement policies instead of relying on democratic centralism, there might be a danger that the nature of the party and the state regime would change;
- The General Guiding Line and Great Leap Forward should be maintained since it was too early to reach a conclusion. In five or ten years, we might be in a better position to make a correct judgment.[24]

Mao Zedong was a strategist and he did not counterattack Liu Shaoqi's opinions on the spot owing to the actual economic reality in favor of Liu's opinion. Mao again managed to shift his colleagues' attention away from the issue of the collective leadership and the consequences of his policy initiatives and to focus their attention on the issue of class struggle within the party. Mao slowly but firmly consolidated his position by institutionalizing his ideas of continual revolution under the proletarian dictatorship into the party resolutions. In a series of party meetings in Beidaihe,[25] Mao Zedong maneuvered enough support for his ideas of continual revolution under the dictatorship of the proletariat. He criticized the opinion of some members who assessed the situation as being all black and little bright, which would cause confusion among the party members, and a loss of confidence in the future.

First, Mao successfully gathered enough support in criticizing the proposal of a family production contract responsibility system submitted by Deng Zihui,[26] Director of the Agricultural Department of the CPC Central Committee. The proposal received support from Liu Shaoqi, Chairman of the People's Republic of

China, Chen Yun, Head of the CPC Financial and Economic Leading Group, Deng Xiaoping, Secretary of the CPC Central Committee Secretariat, and Tian Jiaying,[27] Mao's personal secretary. Mao argued that the proposal aimed to discard the agricultural collectivism and socialism; namely, it was capitalist in nature. He criticized Deng Zihui as a capitalist agricultural expert and accused the Agricultural Department of restoring capitalism and it was subsequently disbanded. Liu Shaoqi, Chen Yun, Deng Xiaoping, and Tian Jiaying also received Mao's criticism for their support of the system.

Second, Mao orchestrated a severe criticism of Peng Dehuai, who wrote a second letter to Mao Zedong, requesting a redressing of his case. Mao accused him of making use of the party's temporary difficulty to launch new attacks against the party. Mao even charged that Peng's reopening of his case by letter was in a timely co-operation with the international anti-China wave organized by the United States and Soviet Union.

Third, Mao reiterated that domestically there still existed contradictions between proletariats and capitalists, between socialism and capitalism, between rightists/revisionists and the people/Marxists. Thus, there was a persistent danger of the restoration of capitalism in China. Therefore, class struggle was universal during the whole period of the transition from capitalism to communism. Mao's ideas of continual revolution were institutionalized in the Communiqué of the Tenth Plenary Session of the CPC Eighth Central Committee, one section of which, considered as the theoretical basis of the doctrine of the continual revolution under the dictatorship of the proletariat, is quoted below (Li, 1998b, p.640):

> During the whole historical period of the proletarian revolution and dictatorship (which may need several decades or even much longer time) there is class struggle between the proletariat and the bourgeois, there is a struggle between the two roads: socialism and capitalism. The deposed counterrevolutionary classes will never put up with their elimination and they always try to seek a restoration of their lost status. Besides, there exist the bourgeois influence and the traditional power left by the old society and the natural bourgeois tendency of some small individual producers. Therefore, there are still some people who have not been transformed by the socialism. Although their number only occupies a small fraction of the population, they will attempt to deviate from the socialist road whenever an opportunity comes and embark on the capitalist road. Class struggle seems unavoidable under such a situation, which is a historical principle that have long been elucidated by Marxism and Leninism and which we must never forget. Such class struggle tends to be complex, twisted, coming and going, and even acute sometimes. Such class struggle will certainly be reflecting in (finding its way into) the party. The pressure of the external imperialism and the influence of the domestic bourgeoisie are social origins of brooding revisionist ideology within the party. While fighting against domestic and external class enemies, we much always keep alert and against any kind of ideological tendencies of opportunism within the party.

What Mao wanted to get across to the party members amounted to two warnings: (1) never forget class struggle, and (2) never forget the danger of emerging revisionism in China. The policy disputes of 1959 and early 1960s at the

CPC central power made Mao believe that revisionism might develop in China under certain domestic and external conditions.

Liu Shaoqi was spared and even managed to persuade Mao to restrict the circulation of the meeting documents within certain ranks of party cadres in order to avoid connecting everything with class struggle. In the end the documents of the 1962 Beidaihe CPC summer meetings were only circulated down to 17th rank of cadres and China's economic readjustment could thus be successfully completed as scheduled by the end of 1965.[78] Although Liu Shaoqi escaped political punishment this time, he became the No.1 target in Mao's next campaign – the Cultural Revolution.

The Cultural Revolution: Settling the Policy Disputes for Good?

In retrospect, the Cultural Revolution was originally designed to purge feudal, bourgeois, and revisionist elements from ideological and cultural spheres. As Mao found it difficult to promote the Cultural Revolution, he concluded that the party apparatus and the state bureaucracy were under the control of 'capitalist roaders' who were representatives of the bourgeoisie and against the Cultural Revolution and who should be the target of the Cultural Revolution. Therefore, the Cultural Revolution was transformed from a class struggle for the supremacy of socialist ideology and culture to a class struggle for the control of the political power.

Since the 'capitalist roaders' were not only pervasive but also powerful, in occupation of high positions in the party and the government, Mao needed more solid ideological preparation to launch the Cultural Revolution. Firstly, he took the opportunity of the CPC's ideological dispute in the early sixties with the Soviet Communist Party over such issues as Stalin's mistakes, continuation of class struggle, and peaceful accommodation with the capitalism, to achieve ideological unification on these issues among the CPC members and the general public through publishing nine commentaries of the CPC Central Committee. These commentaries were written under the direction of Mao Zedong and published in the form of open letters. What is ironic about these commentaries is that what they attacked at that time is what the CPC has been advocating since 1978, such as abandonment of class struggle as the focus of socialist construction, peaceful accommodation and economic co-operation with the capitalist countries, restoration of the private sector, and development and protection of private ownership. However, at that time, these open letters laid an ideological foundation for Mao to launch a revolution at his convenience.

Secondly, Mao started the Cultural Revolution in the cultural spheres. Although the CPC Central Committee set up in July 1964, under Mao's proposal, a five-member Cultural Revolutionary Work Team [29] to supervise the party's ideological and cultural work, Mao relied on his wife, Jiang Qing to promote the revolution. With Mao's support, Jiang Qing made initial achievements in organizing an ideological crusade against feudal and capitalist tendencies in cultural and artistic works, such as plays, operas, films, and novels, because Mao believed that they might be used by counterrevolutionaries to publicize feudal, bourgeois, and revisionist ideas and to oppose the party and socialism.[30] Many plays, films, and novels were marked for criticism, such as 'Madam Li Hui 《李慧娘》' (a local opera) and a dozen films, including 'An Everbright City 《不夜城》', 'Red Sun 《红日》', and 'Early Spring Comes in February 《早春二月》'. In November 1965 this ideological and cultural criticism became political when a commentary was published in a Shanghai newspaper *Wenhui Daily*,[31] entitled 'Comment on the New Historic Play "Dismissal of Hai Rui" 《评新编历史剧〈海瑞罢官〉》'.[32] The playwright was accused of using the play to praise Peng Dehuai, the Defense Minister who had been deposed by Mao in 1959. Therefore, the play was allegedly an attack on the dictatorship of the proletariat by the bourgeois. The playwright was none other than Wu Han, vice mayor of Beijing. For 19 days after the article appeared in *Wenhui Daily*, the party official newspaper *People's Daily* and Beijing's other major newspapers did not reprint the article, which deepened Mao's mistrust in and dissatisfaction with his colleagues – other chief actors and decision makers. Mao angrily accused the Municipality of Beijing as an independent 'Kingdom', which was waterproof and needle-proof. This incident convinced Mao that the government bureaucracy was no longer under his control.

At the 11th Plenary Session of the CPC Eighth Central Committee in August 1966, Mao launched an attack against Liu Shaoqi and his associates, through writing a open personal letter entitled 'Gun Down the Headquarters — a Big Poster of Mine 《炮打司令部—我的一张大字报》', accusing some CPC central and local leaders of exercising the bourgeois dictatorship and suppressing the vigorous developments of the Cultural Revolution. It was unprecedented that the CPC supreme actor personally employed such an informal approach to promote a revolutionary campaign. Liu Shaoqi and Deng Xiaoping became the target of criticism for their alleged role in suppressing the developments of the Cultural Revolution. The CPC decision-makers were divided over Liu and Deng's errors. Some viciously poured out their condemnation; some mixed their praise with criticism; some kept silent; and still some even showed their sympathy. Although Mao succeeded in having 'The CPC Central Committee Resolution on the Cultural Revolution' adopted at the Plenary Session on 8th August 1966, Liu Shaoqi was re-elected to the Politburo Standing Committee and no official resolution on Liu's errors was reached at the Plenary Session, which might further convince Mao of the necessity of directing the Cultural Revolution personally rather than relying on the CPC collective institutionalization.

After this, Mao's instructions were transmitted to the party members and the general public through radios and in newspapers directly from Beijing and the Cultural Revolution was falling out of the control of the CPC Central Committee. On 6th January 1967, the Shanghai Rebelling Groups headed by Wang Hongwen took over the authorities of the Shanghai Party Committee and the Municipal Government and set up a Revolutionary Committee of the Cultural Revolution. It was not very long before all the provincial and local party committees and governments were taken over by the Revolutionary Committees. The two networks of the party apparatus and the state bureaucracy were paralyzed and the army was brought in to restore order.   All the mass revolutionary organizations, the Revolutionary Committees at every level and the army looked towards Mao for instructions and orders.   Mao finally realized his personal autocratic institutionalization: Type E Process in the midst of political chaos in China (see Table 3.1).

In January 1975 Mao Zedong institutionalized the Cultural Revolution – his ideas of continual revolution under the proletarian dictatorship, in the Constitution of the state. The institutions established by Mao became powerful constraints on Deng Xiaoping who wanted to pursue his ideas of economic construction after Mao died on 9th September 1976.

Consequences of the Cultural Revolution

On 9th September 1976 Mao Zedong, Chairman of the CPC Central Committee and Chairman of the Central Military Commission, passed away in Beijing.[33] After the People's Republic of China was established in 1949 he launched successive revolutionary campaigns one after another in attempt to achieve his vision of socialism in China. The Cultural Revolution was his last effort to realize his vision of socialism and communism in China. This section reviews the consequences of the Cultural Revolution: weak party and state apparatus and strong army involvement in politics, the struggle for succession to the CPC supreme actor, a broken society, and looking towards the West for technology and investment. These legacies of Mao's era posed challenges and opportunities to the post-Mao leadership.

Weak party state apparatus and strong army involvement in politics

Before the Cultural Revolution broke out in 1966, China had already developed a very strong government bureaucracy alongside the CPC hierarchical system, which had a power center around the head of state, the Chairman of the People's Republic of China. In contrast to the largely honorary and titular position of the Chairman of the Presidium of the Supreme Soviet in the former USSR, the Chairman of the People's Republic of China enjoyed constitutional power in the following key areas:

- Nominating candidates for the premiere-ship of the State Council and the vice-chairmanship and membership of the National Defense Council;[34]
- Acting as ex-officio Chairman of the National Defense Council, with the armed forces of the country under his command;[35]
- Acting as ex-officio Chairman of the Supreme State Conference.[36]

The nomination of candidates for the premiere-ship and other senior positions granted the Chairman of the Republic more authority over his colleagues and thus world help to attract more followers within the party and state apparatus. The second power allowed the Chairman of the Republic to be directly involved in the standardization of the armed forces and their daily management, infringing upon the traditional exclusive power of the Chairman of the CPC Central Committee, ex-officio Chairman of the Central Military Commission of the CPC Central Committee, in commanding the armed forces. The third power allowed the Chairman of the Republic to convene the Supreme State Conference whenever necessary, and he would in turn submit the conference's views regarding important state affairs to the NPC or the NPC Standing Committee, the State Council, or other governmental bodies for their consideration and decision. In fact, it was another policy-making channel created by the 1954 Constitution, with the Chairman of the Republic as the government chief policy initiator although key policy guidelines still came from the CPC Politburo and its Standing Committee. Although the government policy-making process mainly concerned the daily running of state affairs, the policy initiation power offered the Chairman of the Republic tangible state powers compared to the traditional ideology-initiation power of the Chairman of the CPC Central Committee.

These institutional policy-initiating and decision-making powers created, naturally, a power center around the Chairman of the Republic, who might present challenges to the traditional political and military authorities of Chairman of the CPC Central Committee. Between 1954 and 1959 when Mao Zedong held the Chairmanship of both the CPC and the Republic, no such challenge could develop. Starting from 1959 when Liu Shaoqi assumed the Chairmanship of the Republic and Mao Zedong still held the office of the party Chairman, policy splits gradually appeared between the state power center and the party power center. Liu Shaoqi expressed, on some important occasions, opinions and ideas on the relationship between politics and economics, agricultural policies, and class struggle, which deviated from the party lines advocated by Mao Zedong. Particularly, Liu was critical about the Great Leap Forward in his speech at the Enlarged Working Conference of the CPC Central Committee on 27th January 1962.

Firstly, as a spiritual leader of the CPC, Mao could not tolerate this ideological deviation; and secondly Mao might consider the development of Liu's ideology would consolidate Liu's power base as the head of state, which would further undermine Mao's authority as the party Chairman. No wonder that Liu Shaoqi became the No. 1 target of the Cultural Revolution and was accused of taking the capitalist road and attacked as a revisionist and a Chinese Khrushchev. Liu was eventually ousted in October 1968 from all party and government posts and the Chairmanship of the Republic was deleted from the state bureaucratic system.[37] During the Cultural Revolution, the state bureaucracy had no head of state and the premier was nominated by the CPC Central Committee.

Mao finally brought the government hierarchy under his control, but at a price. Although during the Cultural Revolution the CPC still maintained its hierarchical structure: the Politburo and its Standing Committee, the Central Committee, and provincial and local party committees, its political power was decimated because most of the party elite had been prosecuted and it was estimated that about three million cadres had been ousted from their posts (Jiang and Fu, 1994, p.31); as a result, the credibility and authority of the CPC had greatly declined, and in the end, Mao had to call in the army to maintain order. However, Mao's personal authority soared to its summit; his words bypassed any party and government bureaucracy and directly reached party members and masses alike, prevailing over any existing regulations and laws if there was any discrepancy between his words and the existing institutions. Mao's words became the only credible source of the revolutionary ideas, on which the party work, the government administration, the people's life, and every organization and work unit relied for new direction.[38] The Cultural Revolution turned the one-party authoritarian regime into one-man rule. While the credibility and authority of both the party and the government declined, the army's political power increased substantially. It is another feature of the China's political power structure in the Cultural Revolution. When Mao passed away in 1976, the military proved a decisive force in the power struggle for succession.

The first large-scale involvement of the military in the civilian administration was in 1949 when the administration of cities became an acute problem owing to a shortage of cadres capable of municipal administration. Mao assigned the PLA a new temporary role – to take over and manage cities. Many PLA commanders became city majors and provincial governors. In early 1967 when the Cultural Revolution was running out of control and creating large-scale disorder in the whole country and when both governments and party apparatus at national, provincial, and local levels were paralyzed and unable to control the deteriorating situation, Mao again called in the PLA to maintain order[39] and re-organize governments into a 'three-way' alliance between the PLA representatives, 'revolutionary' party cadres, and representatives of the 'revolutionary' masses. Again, military commanders assumed civilian and political offices. As a result, the military maintained an unprecedented high presence in the CPC central and provincial apparatus during the Cultural Revolution.

Table 3.2 Military Representation in the CPC Central Committee and the Politburo during the Cultural Revolution

(in percentage)

Political Organs	11th 1977	10th 1973	9th 1969
Central Committee	34.8	37.5	50.0
Politburo	47.8	33.3	45.5

Notes: 1. Data includes full members only.
2. Military background defined as those who held a military rank in 1955.

Sources: Adapted from Domes, 1979, p.100.

The CPC 9th Central Committee and the Politburo had 50 per cent and 45.5 per cent of their members with military background, respectively.[40] When Mao died in 1976, the military presence in the 10th Central Committee and the Politburo was still over 30 per cent respectively. After the Gang of Four were arrested, the military presence in the Politburo of the 11th Central Committee reached a new high since 1969 (see Table 3.2).

At provincial levels, 70 per cent of the First Secretaries of party committees, 42 per cent of the Chairmen and Vice-Chairmen of the Revolutionary Committees were military commanders in 1972 and two-thirds of the ministers in the State Council were military men. The military presence in the above party and state apparatus in 1975 declined but still remained substantial (see Table 3.3).

Table 3.3 Military Presence in the State Council and the Provincial-level Party and Government Apparatus
(in percentage)

Political Organs	1978	1975	1972
First Secretary of Provincial-level Party Committees	20.0	34.0	70.0
Chairmen and Vice Chairmen of the provincial-level Revolutionary Committees	10.6	25.7 (1976 figure)	42 (1968 figure)
Ministers in the State Council	10.4	20.7	66.6

Sources: Adapted from Domes, 1979, p.45, p.100.

But this time, the military entered the political game in the general context of the inept leadership of the CPC committees at national, provincial, and local levels, thus offering the military greater leverage in the power struggle for succession to Mao Zedong. When Mao was still alive, all the political forces within the power structure turned to Mao for new supreme guidelines. With Mao's death, the military proved absolutely decisive, firstly, in arresting the Gang of Four in October 1976 and then, in backing Deng Xiaoping in 1978.

The Struggle for Succession to Mao

In order to avoid the fate of Stalinism (Hsiung, 1970, p.104), Mao tried, on the one hand, to eliminate ideological deviators through the Cultural Revolution and on the other hand, to seek a faithful successor who might perpetuate his revolutionary theories. Unfortunately, Mao failed to settle his succession issue during his lifetime. His first prospective successor, Liu Shaoqi, was elected collectively as the No. 2 leader of the party by the CPC Eighth Central Committee in September 1956. Liu was discredited during the Cultural Revolution. Thereafter within a short period of six years (1969-1975) Mao Zedong handpicked three successors successively.

As the strong supporter of the Cultural Revolution, Lin Biao, Minister of Defense, was chosen by Mao as his designated successor at the CPC Ninth National Congress in April 1969. In 1971 Lin orchestrated a failed coup against Mao and died in a plan crash. In 1973 Mao selected Wang Hongwen[41] as his successor, who was elected as Vice-Chairman of the CPC 10th Central Committee, and ranked third place after Zhou Enlai in the CPC hierarchy. However, Mao was forced to abandon Wang Hongwen because the old-generation faction of the party, headed by Zhou Enlai and Marshal Yie Jianying, was firmly against the confirmation of Wang Hongwen as Mao's successor, although the radical faction—organizers of the Cultural Revolution backed Wang's nomination.

The power struggle between the two factions turned hot in the late 1974 before the Second Plenary Session of 10th CPC Central Committee and the Fourth NPC that were scheduled to open in February 1975. The radical faction proposed Wang Hongwen to be appointed Vice-Chairman of the NPC Standing Committee and Zhang Chunqiao, First Vice-Premier of the State Council, while the old generation faction proposed Deng Xiaoping be appointed First Vice-Premier, Vice-Chairman of the State Military Commission, and Chief of the General Staff. As an experienced political actor, Mao clearly understood that the radical faction if given the political power, would continue his designated revolutionary course, but Mao also knew very well the old generation faction would certainly block the radical faction from seizing the power, even if supported by Mao himself. He had only two choices:

- To support the radical faction to power but he had to crush the old generation faction's military power base first, that is to purge those generals who were against the radical faction; however, that might create two unacceptable consequences: (1) a bad scenario was instability in the armed forces and (2) the worse scenario was a possible military revolt against his authority; both scenarios might invite the military invasion of the Soviet Union, which Mao tried his best to avoid;
- To nominate the candidates of the old generation and put them in check by the radical faction with the support of the media, and his revolutionary course might be secured.

In the end Mao accepted the proposal of the old generation faction, putting Deng Xiaoping in charge of the daily administration of the party, the state, and the military. With the support of Premier Zhou Enlai, who stayed most of the time in hospital for cancer treatment, and the support of the military, Deng Xiaoping started to rectify, readjust, and reorganize every sector of the society, including agriculture, industry, transportation, education, arts, science, the armed forces, the government, and the party. He criticized the prevailing piece-meal and one-sided style of studying Mao Zedong Thought and advocated studying, propagating, and implementing Mao Zedong Thought in its entirety. What Deng Xiaoping tried to do was to rectify the leftist ideological errors of the Cultural Revolution, which was beyond Mao's tolerance, because Mao considered his ideological line was beyond dispute. In November 1975 Mao initiated a political campaign to criticize Deng Xiaoping and labeled Deng's rectification program as Rightist Deviation that attempted to reverse his verdicts of the Cultural Revolution.[42]

On 8th January 1976, Zhou Enlai, Deng's protector, died in Beijing. Who was to succeed Zhou as Premier? Deng Xiaoping had been discredited by Mao for his attempted over-all ratification of the Cultural Revolution. Jiang Qing, Mao's wife, proposed Zhang Chunqiao, second Vice-Premier, for the premiership. As one of the chief actors of the radical faction, Zhang Chunqiao was certainly unacceptable to the old generation faction, whose favorable candidate was Deng Xiaoping. In the end, Mao made a decision on 7th February 1976, which startled everyone, that Hua Guofeng, sixth Vice-Premier and Minister of Public Security, was appointed as acting premier. Hua's appointment indicated Mao tried very hard to maintain the power balance, that is, to find someone who would be acceptable to both factions and could act as a political stabilizer between the two opposing factions (Yang, 1998, p.102). Hua Guofeng was Mao's fellow townsman, a faithful follower who would, in Mao's eyes, safeguard his ideological legacy after his death.

However, Hua's appointment did not please the two factions and even did not impress the general public, particularly the Beijing people who doubted his abilities to govern the country. Public disappointment broke out between 29th March and 5th April 1976 when people in Beijing took the opportunity of Qing Ming Festival, a time when the Chinese traditionally would visit the ancestral tombs and mourn the dead, to mourn the death of Premier Zhou Enlai at Beijing Tiananman Square and displayed their disappointment of Hua's appointment and support of Deng Xiaoping. On 5th April 1976 over 100,000 people gathered at the Tiananman Square in a protest demonstration, which soon went out control and was suppressed by the security guards and militiamen.

The CPC Politburo, on Mao's recommendation, passed two resolutions on 7th April 1976. One resolution dismissed Deng Xiaoping from all party and government posts and the other resolution appointed Hua Guofeng as Premier of the State Council and first Vice-Chairman of the CPC Central Committee. Thus, Hua Guofeng emerged as the designated heir of Mao Zedong. However, Hua had no solid power base in the CPC Central Committee, the Politburo, the government, and the army. If Mao had lived longer, Hua might have built and consolidated his power base in the center. Caught in the crossfire of the two opposing factions, Hua was left with few options, either to join one faction against the other or to skillfully co-ordinate the two factions to achieve a kind of power balance – co-existence for all parties involved. But the second option required not only political experience but also political charisma that Hua lacked. In fact, Hua had only the first option at his disposal.

On 30th April 1976 Mao offered Hua three policy tips in a hand written instruction: (1) 'Carry out the work slowly, not in haste'; (2) 'Act according to past principles'; and (3) 'With you in charge, I am at ease'.[43] Mao's 30th April instruction indicated that Mao had trust in Hua and certain confidence, as the spiritual leader of the CPC, that his party and the general public would help Hua to consolidate his leadership. Five months later, Mao passed away and left Hua's succession to be confirmed and open to challenge again.

A Society in Disarray

In the 1950s China's socialist transformation eliminated all the exploiting classes without destroying the mortal flesh of these feudal and capitalist classes. However the transformation did little to change their 'Four Olds': old ideologies, old traditions, old customs, and old habits. The Cultural Revolution, as its name indicated, was originally designed to do the second part of the job of the socialist transformation, that is, to replace the 'Four Olds' with the new ones of the proletariat.

The 'Four Olds' received the first wave of the attack of the Red Guards in the summer of 1966. Signboards of shops, factories, streets that contained Chinese characters with the names of former celebrities, traditional values, and historical significance were smashed because they carried bourgeois, feudal, and colonial connotations. Any form of religious practice was forbidden except for the worship of Mao Zedong. People who kept stylist hairstyle and garment fashion were physically attacked on streets. Any pleasure entertainment and artistic endeavor was condemned and criticized publicly as petty bourgeois tastes. Traditional literature, plays, films, and art works, including those produced after 1949, were under general attack and criticism and proletariat model works were selected, made, and recommended to the general public. For instance, *Bright Sky* 《艳阳天》, a novel about the agricultural collectivization, was recommended as the best novel depicting a 'true' picture of the collectivization.

Perhaps, the greatest effort of the radical faction to convince the general public what a revolutionary and proletarian form of art works should look like was the production and recommendation of the Eight Model Plays in 1966,[44] produced under the direction of Jiang Qing, Mao's wife. To follow suit, provincial and local opera and ballet troupes reproduced these eight model plays in theatres; the film industry made them into films to be shown in every part of China; and the national, provincial, and local radio stations broadcast them on a daily basis, to such a propaganda effect that most people over forties can still hum one or two tunes of the Eight Model Plays.

In such a politicized atmosphere, innovative artistic creativity was suffocated and blind submissiveness was rewarded. That is why during the Cultural Revolution no original and creative art works, novels, plays, and films could emerge. In this sense, the Cultural Revolution was a decade of cultural barrenness. However, the greatest irreparable loss the Cultural Revolution inflicted upon China is the breaking down of China's educational system, ruining normal educational opportunity of, at least, one generation

The educational system was denounced for its bourgeois educational line, bourgeois teaching materials, bourgeois academic authorities, and bourgeois products – 'intellectual aristocrats', who were divorced from the workers, peasants, and masses, from the proletarian politics, from socialist production, and from scientific research. Professors were criticized and humiliated for their academic views and pedagogical practices. Universities stopped admitting students. When they resumed recruiting students in the middle of 1970s, they had to accept workers, peasants, and soldiers recommended by their work units. At first, universities accepted these worker-peasant-soldier students based on academic assessment tests administered by universities. However, even this nominal screening process was severely criticized and was abolished the following year. As a result, after a decade of social and political turbulence, large numbers of professors, specialists, and researchers still remained largely idle, because there were no academic standards to be supervised.

Generally speaking, in the later years of the Cultural Revolution there was a growing feeling of disillusionment among the general public about the Cultural Revolution. In the early years of the Cultural Revolution, people were enthusiastic about the prospects of the Cultural Revolution – to revolutionize people's ideology and as a result to achieve greater, faster, better, and more economic results in all fields of work. Therefore, people followed the supreme commands of Mao strictly and stopped any kind of leisure and entertainment activities, such as raising pets, growing flowers, fishing, and hunting because they were bourgeois tastes. Students longed for army uniforms and shoes as they represented revolutionary character and style. However, in the later years of the Cultural Revolution people gradually grew disillusioned and cynical as the Cultural Revolution failed to deliver the economic benefits it had promised and only gave people a puritan style of life.

People began to treat political meetings and study sessions as routines and with little enthusiasm and started to indulge themselves in secret leisure activities.[45] The general mood during the latter years of the Cultural Revolution was a sober, graduate withdrawal into a private self from the bustling political revolution that was running out of steam.

Table 3.4 Grain Production and Consumption, 1957-1976

Year	Grain output (million tons)	Population (millions at year end)	Per capita grain output (kg)	Per capita grain consumption Urban (kg)	Per capita grain consumption Rural (kg)
1957	195	647	301	196	205
1966	214	745	287	206	186
1976	286	934	306	212	186

Source: Adapted from Selden, 1988, pp.16-8.

Statistically speaking, China's economy as a whole kept growing during the Cultural Revolution except in 1967, 1968, and 1976 when political turmoil drove the economy to utter chaos and to the brink of bankruptcy. Its GDP maintained an average growth rate of 5.9 per cent between 1966 and 1976.[46] In the same period, the grain output increased by 33.6 per cent, but the per capita grain consumption remained stagnant and did not regain the 1957 level (Selden, 1988, p.16). Compared to that of urban dwellers, rural per capita annual food consumption was much worse (see Table 3.4). Shortage of food and commodities ushered in a commodities distribution system in cities based on ration coupons. It was estimated that up to 1993 when the last grain and oil ration coupons were abandoned, over 2,000 kinds of ration coupons had been issued in different parts of China.[47]

There were several main reasons behind this scenario of steady growth with low consumption and declining living standards:

- High growth of population, an increase by a quarter between 1966 and 1976, consumed a lion's share of the benefits of the economic growth, leaving little to be distributed anyway;
- The party and the government adopted a policy of high rates of state accumulation for industrialization and a policy of egalitarian low income and low consumption;[48]
- To keep the masses happy with the austere living standards based on shortage of commodities and egalitarian distribution of the limited resources, the party indoctrinated the masses with austere and thrifty living styles[49] based on Mao Zedong Thought. This ideological transformation worked quite well until Mao's death in keeping people's attention from their materialistic orientations to socialist spiritual perfection through class struggle;
- A large share of the accumulated wealth went to industrialization, particularly heavy industry, and the agriculture was an under-invested sector (Selden, 1979, pp.50-1);
- The unfair income distribution policy was in favor of the industrial sector and at the cost of the agricultural sector, in the form of high prices for industrial products and lower prices for agricultural products.[50] This unfair distribution not only greatly hindered peasants' enthusiasm from producing more agricultural products the country most needed to feed its ballooning population, but also crippled their ability to purchase more industrial products, which might stimulate the industrialization the country was keenly seeking; and
- The egalitarian income distribution within both industrial and agricultural sectors further dampened people's enthusiasm to produce or to invent to produce more.

The 1960s were a decade of isolation and self-reliance for China that was contained both by the Soviet Union and the West. The isolation completely blocked China from taking part in or even sharing information on the fourth wave of technology development in petrochemicals, electronics, and aviation. The situation was made worse by the CPC ruling elite's ideological objection to any form of modern management techniques developed in capitalist countries. It stuck, instead, to its ideological mobilization of masses to produce, although inefficiently and sometimes quite wastefully. This emphasized, on the one hand, output more than return on investment, and on the other hand, sacrificed material comfort for spiritual satisfaction.

China's backwardness in technology and rejection of modern management techniques drove its economy to a dead end – a negative return on investment. It was estimated that in 1970-1977 to produce each additional dollar of industrial output required an investment of 3.26 US dollars (Selden 1988, p.23). The official view blamed this bleak economic performance on the Cultural Revolution, or more specifically, on the four culprits: the Gang of Four.[51] The reality is that seeds of all these causes had been planted by Mao and his party from the very beginning of the socialist transformation of the economy, and had only fermented and been intensified with each political campaign or revolution, most notably, the Anti-Rightists Campaign, the Great Leap Forward, and the Cultural Revolution. Like other political campaigns, the Cultural Revolution is only part of the Grand Scheme of Mao – a series of successive specific programs leading to the fundamental program of communism, which drove China to the brink of bankruptcy in the middle of the 1970s.

After Lin Biao's failed coup in 1971, Mao began to rehabilitate quite a number of old cadres,[52] including Deng Xiaoping,[53] No. 2 target of the Cultural Revolution, in an attempt to raise production. Mao even agreed to the modernization program,[54] which was announced by Zhou Enlai at the Fourth NPC in January 1975. Deng Xiaoping sponsored drafting programs to implement the four modernizations. Deng's programs contained three key dimensions that were in contradiction with the principles of the Cultural Revolution:

- The modernization programs stressed controlling and combating the anarchy caused by 'ultra-left' forces in the management of factories and businesses where production was being sacrificed for revolution, which undermined Mao's mass line of class struggle;
- The modernization programs emphasized both import of foreign advanced technology and equipment and export of goods, which deviated from the self-reliance principle;
- The modernization programs advocated the positive roles of intellectuals and specialists in the four-modernization drive and called for an end to the incessant criticism of 'bourgeois academic authorities', which deviated from Mao's mass-line principle of production that relied solely on the creative contribution of workers and peasants.

Deng Xiaoping's programs were abortive because he attempted, in fact, to rectify the chaotic situation in all sectors, based on the assumption that the Cultural Revolution had created big chaos rather than great order, which was beyond Mao's tolerance no matter how capable Deng was in handling economic affairs. Deng was again deposed from all his party and government posts in the early 1977 power struggle.

In a word, when Mao died he left behind him a broken society with chaos and confusion prevailing in every aspect of the society, including culture, economy, and people's daily life.

Looking Towards the West for Technology and Investment

China's external relations have different themes at different times and exert a strong influence on China's domestic political as well as economic policies. In the 1950s China maintained a close tie with the Eastern Camp headed by the Soviet Union and was the target of the containment policy of the Western Camp headed by the United States; and China's economic development was logically based on the Soviet model: rapid collectivization and industrialization at the expense of agriculture. The 1960s were perhaps the most difficult decade for China because it was in direct confrontation with the Soviet Union and the West, fighting on two fronts simultaneously; and economically, China looked inward and readjusted its economic development on self-reliance, and politically, Mao Zedong launched the Cultural Revolution to safeguard China against both the revisionism and the restoration of capitalism in China, which made China further lag behind the industrialized countries.

China's dispute with the Soviet Union started from the ideological sphere and spilled over to bilateral relationship, which eventually escalated into a military conflict in 1969 in the Ussuri River. The Sino-Russian border conflict revealed vividly the backwardness of the hardware of the Chinese armed forces, indicating China's low-level technology and weak industry in general. This harsh reality made Mao look towards the West, stronger than the Soviet Union in the above mentioned areas, for assistance. At that time, the United States was plagued by the Vietnam War and planned to pull its troops out of Vietnam and China might provide some assistance in that respect. In early 1970s the United States changed its policy towards China from containment and confrontation to negotiation. Threatened by possibilities of the Soviet Union's military attack, Mao Zedong welcomed US new policy and agreed that direct negotiation could obviate the Sino-American difficulties (Snow 1971, p.47). Since then, Sino-American rapprochement developed swiftly.

Soon after Zhou Enlai warmly received the American table-tennis players in Beijing and started the 'Ping-Pong Diplomacy' to further warm up Sino-American relationship, Henry Kissinger, President Richard Nixon's security advisor, paid a secret visit from 9th to 11th July 1971 to Beijing to arrange for Nixon's state visit to China. On 18th February 1972, Nixon visited China and discussed normalization of relations with his Chinese counterparts. On 28th February 1972, China and the United States signed the Shanghai Communiqué to lay down the foundation for the normalization of Sino-American relations. Since then China broke its isolation and started the process of its integration into the world community.

On 15th October 1971 China resumed its seat in the United Nations. On 25th September 1972 Premier Tanaka of Japan arrived in Beijing for a five-day visit. After Japan recognized the People's Republic of China, other western countries followed suit: West Germany in October 1972, New Zealand in December 1972, Australia in January 1973, and Spain in March 1973. In March 1972 China and Britain upgraded the diplomatic relations from Office of the Charge d'Affairs to Ambassadorship. By the end of 1972, China established formal diplomatic relations with 28 countries. During the same time, China was also engaged in serious talks with the Soviet Union to normalize bilateral relations.

By the middle of the 1970s, China was no longer isolated. China's international recognition, restoration of diplomatic relations with the West, and normalization of the relationship with the Soviet Union created very favorable conditions for the political actors to propose new domestic policy initiatives. Even before Mao's death, many deposed cadres who had experience of economic development were rehabilitated, and four-modernization program was announced at the Fourth NPC. Although these developments were in their initial stages, they laid a useful platform from which to launch new policies by ambitious successors of Mao.

Conclusion

The previous sections have examined the shift of the institutionalization of the CPC from a Type B Process to a Type D Process and to a Type E Process between 1949 and 1976. The examination has revealed some features of the institutionalization behavior of the CPC ruling actors and the consequences of their behavior. This section provides a summary of the features and the consequences of Mao's institutionalization legacies, which represented challenges and opportunities to Mao's successors. They are summarized under the following subheadings: Mao's manipulation of class struggle, the rationality of Mao's institutionalization behavior, and the consequences of Mao's legacies: challenges or opportunities.

Mao's Manipulation of Class Struggle

Since 1949 Mao Zedong initiated a series of class struggle campaigns in an attempt to realize his vision of socialism. In terms of the change of Mao's targets of class struggle, revolutionary campaigns in Mao's Era after 1949 may be divided into two broad categories: General Campaign – class struggle within the whole society, and Specific Campaign – class struggle within the CPC and state apparatus. The new democratic revolution up to 1953, the socialist transformation in 1953-1956, the agricultural collectivization in the late 1950s, and the Anti-Rightists Campaign in 1957 may be grouped under the category of general campaigns. The anti-rightists campaign at Lushan in 1959, the anti-opportunists and anti-revisionists campaign in the early 1960s, and the Cultural Revolution in 1966-1976 may be grouped under the category of specific campaigns.

The new democratic revolution in 1949-1953 targeted bureaucratic capitalists, comprador bourgeoisie, the landed gentry, and the imperialist in the entry-ports. The socialist transformation in 1953-1956 economically and politically eliminated the national and petty bourgeoisie. Agricultural collectivization in the late 1950s turned peasants from private owners of land and means of production into agricultural proletariats. The Anti-Rightists Campaign in 1957 targeted liberal intellectuals in the society, particularly those in democratic parties, education, and media, and effectively deprived them of the right to voice different views and opinions about the CPC policies. In sum, these revolutions were initiated by Mao to realize his vision of socialism in China, transforming a private-dominated economy into a public-dominated economy and a multi-party coalition governance into a one-party regime. The institutionalization was shifting from a Type B Process to a Type D Process to promote and facilitate these revolutions.

If Mao nullified any possible opposition and challenge from the society and cleared the way for his vision of socialism through launching these general campaigns, Mao initiated specific campaigns to remove any possible opposition and challenge from within the CPC. The anti-rightists campaign at Lushan in 1959 and the anti-opportunists and anti-revisionists campaign in the early 1960s suppressed the opposition and challenge among the CPC decision-makers and chief actors. The Cultural Revolution in 1966-1976 eliminated all the overt opposition and challenges from within the CPC decision-makers and chief actors. These inner party class struggle campaigns effectively turned the institutionalization from a Type D Process to a Type E Process, signifying a shift from the party oligarchic to the personal autocratic institutionalization.

Rationality of Mao's Institutionalization Behavior

The examination of the institutionalization behavior of Mao has shown clear signs of a rational and self-interested calculator, who cherished two basic interrelated goals: to maintain the status of the CPC supreme actor and to maintain the monopoly of power by the CPC. Mao was rational because he understood that these two basic goals were the prerequisites for implementing his vision of socialism and communism; that is why Mao repeatedly resorted to class struggle in order to have them realized. Whether the perceived challenge came from the society, such as the intellectuals' criticism, or from within the party, such as the policy disputes among the CPC chief actors and decision-makers, class struggle was always his reliable tool in securing these two basic goals. He was rational also because his policy preferences were subject to the constraint of the domestic and international economic and political conditions.

Some scholars would consider China's foreign policy preference, such as leaning towards the Soviet Union and anti-American stance in the late 1940s, as predetermined by the ideology of the CPC or Mao (Goldstein, 1980, pp.235-78; 1989, pp.119-42). I would like to see the selection of an international enemy as manipulated by Mao in order to optimize the chance of realizing the two basic goals. In retrospect, only after the CPC lost any hope of having accommodation with the United States did the CPC develop a strong anti-American stance (He, 1995, pp.337-48; Stueck, 1995, pp.348-56), which could be explained as the only feasible option left to the CPC chief actors that could guarantee them Russian economic aid and national security protection.   To a certain degree, therefore, China's leaning over towards the Soviet Union in the late 1940s and the 1950s for the sake of its economic development and national security was due to the disappointing failure of the CPC to seek recognition of its rule in China by the United States in the late 1940s (Sutter, 1978; Esherick, 1974; and Hunt, 1980).

In a similar vein, China's breakaway from the Soviet Camp in the 1960s could be explained both as the CPC's efforts to maintain its independence against the big bullying brother and as Mao's efforts to enhance his position as the spiritual leader[55] by denouncing the Soviet revisionism and the Soviet imperialism.   China's self-reliance or autarkic development strategy in the 1960s could be attributed largely to its international isolation in the 1960s, when it was fighting on two fronts: against the Soviet revisionist imperialism and against the capitalist imperialism headed by the United States, because there was no way to seek economic and technological assistance from either of the two superpowers.   The Cultural Revolution might be seen as the desperate attempt made by Mao to secure the two basic goals in such a harsh international situation.

At the early 1970s China's domestic economic problems and the military threat from its strong neighbor in the north – the Soviet revisionist imperialism compelled China to look towards the West, particularly the United States, for its economic development and national security, which could help to secure the two basic goals of the CPC chief actor.   This time Mao's strategic flexibility received positive response from the United States that was trying to scale down its military involvement in Vietnam and in East Asia while it could still contain the Soviet expansion.

Mao was rational also because he was self-interested.   When the two basic goals, namely, to maintain the status of the CPC supreme actor and to maintain the monopoly of power by the CPC, in contradiction with each other, Mao chose to sacrifice the latter.   The Cultural Revolution is a case in point.   If Mao had not waged the Cultural Revolution, the party state apparatus could not possibly have been collapsed in the early years of the Cultural Revolution, its capacity could not have been decimated in the subsequent years, and the army need not have been called in to maintain order and could not have enjoyed prominent presence at the political power center.   However, Mao might have lost his status as the sole initiator of policy institutionalization with the consolidation and expansion of Liu Shaoqi's power base as the head of the state, which was cutting away a large share of policy institutional initiation from Mao's sphere of power in managing state affairs.   Mao's status as the supreme actor might even gradually have been declining owing to Liu's success in promoting economic development based on the advanced technology and expertise of experts, which was different from Mao's mass line approach exemplified in the Great Leap Forward.   Mao chose to secure the goal of maintaining his status as the supreme actor by launching the Cultural

Revolution, which was claimed by him to eradicate revisionists and 'capitalist roaders' from the party and the government. Practically, the Cultural Revolution helped Mao reach his power zenith and changed the party oligarchic institutionalization into his personal autocratic institutionalization at the expense of other CPC chief actors and at the cost of the power of the party state apparatus.

In sum, the analysis of the institutionalization behavior of Mao has revealed that his ideology exerted strong influence on his strategic policy preference but did not predetermine it. The underlying factors that determined his choice of policy preference were the two basic goals, whose realization were subject to both his self-interests and the domestic and international conditions, rather than subject to his ideology only.

Mao's Legacies: Challenges or Opportunities

It was a fact the Mao left behind him rich legacies of his rule between 1949 and 1976. Whether Mao's legacies would become challenges or opportunities to his successors, however, depends on the skills of his successors to manipulate the legacies. This chapter has touched such main legacies of Mao as follows:

(a) Mao's ideology still occupied a significant place in China's politics, even beyond challenge;
(b) His designated successor, Hua Guofeng, as the CPC supreme actor needed to be confirmed by the CPC Central Committee;
(c) Mao's death put an end to the personal autocratic institutionalization because his designated successor, Hua Guofeng, not only lacked Mao's charisma but also had no power basis at the center; he was sandwiched between two political forces: the Gang of Four, the leftist faction, and the old generation faction;
(d) The party state apparatus did not recover from its structural deconstruction inflicted by the Cultural Revolution, with nearly three million cadres deposed, while the military overshadowed the political establishment, with a large proportion of military personnel involved in the institutionalization process;
(e) By the end of the Cultural Revolution, the People's living standard was even worse than in 1957 and public disillusionment grew;
(f) The economy was in a shabby state and the CPC supreme actor, chief actors and decision-makers reached a consensus that China needed a modernization program;
(g) China ended its isolation by building constructive relations with the West headed by the United States, opening an opportunity of tapping western technology and investment for China's economic development.

It stems from our examination that Mao was paradoxical in the later years of the Cultural Revolution when he realized something must be done to correct problems of the Cultural Revolution but he would never tolerate any correction in political and ideological spheres. However, Mao did not have the time and possibly the courage to make any meaningful correction himself. Therefore, at his death three political forces at the power center, as indicated above, were struggling not only for political power but also, perhaps more importantly, for dominance and supremacy in policy institutionalization. The next chapter will explore the manipulation of Mao's legacies by the political actors in the immediate post-Mao period.

Notes

1   Zhang believes that the CPC's revolutionary ideology, organizational principle, and methods of mass mobilization, which had spelled the party's success before 1949, became increasingly obstacles to the political institutionalization after 1949. For more discussion, see Zhang, 1997, p.255.

2   It was the predominant institutionalization process before 1949, when the CPC was the decision making center for issuing revolutionary orders, directives, and resolutions.

3   For more discussion of Mao's tendency towards the rule of man, see Xiang 1991, pp.2-12; Chen 1999, pp.8-9.

4   Adapted from Table 3 Institutionalization Process of the NPC and its Standing Committee. See Pu, 1999, p.144.

5   The Russians basically kept their promise not to support the CPC, except facilitating the movements of the CPC military personnel in late 1945 and leaving behind them stocks of Japanese weapons to the CPC when they withdrew from Manchuria in early 1946. The KMT National Government received comprehensive military aids from the Truman administration in 1946: over US$800 million for military supply, transportation, training; over US$500 million worth of non-military supplies; and a military advisory group of over 900 US military officers. For more discussion, see Cohen, 1980, p.84-7; Leffler, 1992, pp.86-7.

6   In early 1949 Huang Hua, head of the CPC Alien Affairs Bureau, and Zhou Enlai, the CPC Politburo member, approached American Ambassador Stuart in Nanjing and the American Consular General in Beijing, respectively, exploring the possibility of US diplomatic recognition and economic assistance for China's reconstruction. There were final attempts made by the CPC to set up working relations with the United States before China leaned totally towards the Soviet Union for economic assistance and national security. For more discussion, see Stueck, 1995, pp.348-56; He, 1995, pp.337-48.

7   On 24th April 1945, Mao Zedong laid out a blueprint of a coalition government based upon a united front for China in his political report at the CPC Seventh National Congress, which was later entitled as 'On Coalition Government'.

8   According to the Article 31 of the Common Program, the state capitalist economy means those economic co-operation that involved both the state and the private sector, namely, (1) private enterprises manufactured according to orders from the state; (2) private businessmen managed state enterprises on a lease agreement; and (3) joint ventures involving state and private capital.

9   Before 1949, China used to have 11 democratic parties. After the First CPPCC some democratic parties dissolved or merged with other parties and now there are 8 democratic parties with little autonomy even in their own political preferences.

10 By the end of 1957, some 731 laws, decrees and administrative regulations were promulgated and issued by the National People's Congress, including the Organization Law of the Chinese People's Political Consultative Conference (September 1949), the Organization Law of the Central People's Government (September 1949), the Marriage

Law (April 1950), the Land Reform Law (June 1950), the Trade Union Law (June 1950), the Election Law of the National People's Congress (March 1953), the Organic Law of the National People's Congress (September 1954), the Organic Law of the State Council (September 1954), the Organic Law of the People's Court (September 1954), the Organic Law of the People's Procuratorates (September 1954), and the Organic Law of the Local People's Congresses and Local People's Committees (September 1954). For more discussion, see Xin, 1999, pp.329-31; Zhang, 1997, pp.54-62.

11 Mao made this prediction in June 1953 and Zhou Enlai made this prediction in his speech at the 49th Enlarged Meeting of the Standing Committee of the First CPPCC National Committee on 8 September 1953.

12 They were proposed by Chen Yun, newly elected member of the Standing Committee of the Politburo, which were later usually referred to as the Theory of a Bird in a Cage.

13 We cannot say that at the very beginning the intention of the chief actors of the CPC to welcoming criticism from intellectuals was menace in design, but they could not face strong criticism bravely when criticism was targeted at the CPC general guidelines, the CPC monopoly of power, and the legitimacy of the CPC leading position; they did not take action within the limits of the existing legal institutions; rather, they simply resorted to their traditional class struggle to crush the 'Rightists' ruthlessly.

14 Zhang Naiqi (Minister of Food), Zhang Bojun (Minister of Communications), Luo Longji (Minister of Timber Industry), and Zhang Xiruo (Minister of Education).

15 In 1956 and 1957 Mao Zedong complained, on several occasions, about the wrong policies of Stalin towards the CPC and China's revolution and economic reconstruction, see Mao, 1977, p.286, p.344.

16 *People's Daily*, 18th September 1958.

17 *People's Daily*, 22nd September 1958.

18 Peng's criticism was based on his personal investigation trip to several places; he was deeply impressed by difficult conditions of the peasants in his hometown, Wu Shi, Jiangxi Province, which he visited in December 1958. For more discussion, see Li, 1998b, pp.286-306. For excerpts from Peng Dehuai's talks, see *The Case of Peng The-Huai*《彭德怀案件专辑》*1959-1968*, Union Research Institute (1968), Hong Kong.

19 Khrushchev, Secretary of the Soviet Union Communist Party, criticized the Chinese people's commune movement as beyond present China's socialist conditions, while John Foster Dulles, Secretary of State, United States, commented on the imbalance of the Chinese economy.

20 For more discussion, see Li, 1998b, pp.286-406.

21 Liu Shaoqi was Chairman of the People's Republic of China since 1959 and a member of the CPC Politburo Standing Committee.

22 This meeting was attended by more than 7000 party cadres and state officials, including members of the CPC Central Committee, ministerial level officials, provincial level cadres and officials and was later referred to as 'Meeting of 7000 Attendants'.

23 This comparison was made by Mao Zedong at the Lu Shan Enlarged Politburo Meeting when Mao assessed the achievements and mistakes of the Great Leap Forward.

24 For more discussion, see Li, 1998b, pp.456-67, pp.510-6.

25 The Working Conference of the CPC Central Committee 25th July-24th August 1962, the Preparatory Meeting of the Tenth Plenary Session of the CPC Eighth Congress 26th August-23rd September 1962, and the Tenth Plenary Session of the CPC Eighth Congress 24th-27th September 1962.

26 During the agricultural collectivization, peasants in some provinces invented the family production contract system to solve the egalitarian problem, which worked like this: a

household of peasants was given a piece of land to take care of and was held responsible for an agreed production target and paid according the actual output. Deng Zihui dispatched a working team to investigate it in Anhui Province and proposed to let some areas practice the family production contract system in a report submitted to the CPC and Mao Zedong. For more discussion, see Li, 1998b, p.623-32.

27   In March and April 1962, Mao sent Tian Jiaying to conduct a fact-finding investigation in Mao's hometown Shao San, Hunan Province. Tian Jiaying was against the family production contract system before the investigation but he supported the system after returning from the investigation. For more discussion, see Li, 1998b, pp.476-9.

28   For more discussion, see Li, 1998b, p.642.

29   The Team leader was Peng Zhen, the first Secretary of the Beijing CPC Committee, with other members including Lu Dinyi, Secretary of the CPC Secretariat and Director of the propaganda Department of the CPC Central Committee, Zhou Yang, Executive Deputy Director of the Propaganda Department of the CPC Central Committee, and Wu Linxi, Chief-of-staff of the people's Daily Agency and the Xinhua News Agency.

30   As early as 1962, the novel entitled 'Liu Zhidan' was criticized at the CPC Beidaihe Meeting for its alleged praising Gao Gang, who used to be a member of the CPC Politburo Standing Committee and was purged in 1955.

31   It was mainly academic newspaper, mainly publishing news on academic developments, research articles, and academic comments.

32   The play was about a county magistrate called Hai Rui (海瑞) who was praised by the masses as the 'Clear Sky' for upholding justice and speaking for the poor and weak in the Qing Dynasty; Hai Rui was deposed by the Emperor and was later rehabilitated.

33   Mao Zedong was elected Chairman of the CPC Central Military Commission in January 1935 and was elected Chairman of the CPC Central Committee in April 1945. However, Mao became the party boss in March 1943 when he was selected Chairman of the CPC Politburo and Chairman of the CPC Secretariat.

34   Article 27 of the 1954 Constitution.

35   Article 42 of the 1954 Constitution.

36   Article 43 of the 1954 Constitution.

37   Although the Chairmanship of the Republic was resumed in early 1980s, its power was degraded to such a degree that it could no longer give a political actor enough power to challenge the party power center.

38   During the Cultural Revolution the 'revolutionary' party members, cadres, and masses were organized to listen to Mao's new Supreme Order from the radio broadcasting, usually in the evening, to be followed by a celebration march to the local Revolutionary Committee—local government with comprehensive power, including the law enforcing and the judiciary power.

39   After Mao remarked that 'the army must support the Leftists' on 20 January 1967, the CPC Central Committee, the State Council, the Central Military Commission, and the Cultural Revolution Group under the Central Committee jointly issued a directive, stating that 'the PLA should actively support the revolutionary Leftists'.   Later the PLA's mission was defined as Three-Support and Two-Military: to support the Leftists, to assist in industry and in Agriculture, to exercise military control of local communities, work units, or cities whenever necessary, and to give military training to the revolutionary masses.

40   The CPC Eighth Central Committee (1956) had 25.3 per cent of members from the military, in other words, the military commanders were directly elected into the Central

Committee; while in the Cultural Revolution, a great number of military commanders first assumed civilian offices and then were elected as civilian officials with military background into the Central Committee.

41 Wang Hongwen used to be a worker in Shanghai No. 17 Cotton Mill Factory. He became the chief commander of the Rebelling Workers Groups of Shanghai in late 1966. In January 1967 Wang Hongwen led the Rebelling Workers Groups to take over the authority form the Shanghai CPC Committee and the Shanghai Government, inaugurating a wave of seizing the power from the local party apparatus and governments throughout China. Later it was referred to as 'January Storm'.

42 For more discussion, see Yang, 1998, pp.54-63, pp.63-73.

43 *Peking Review*, 24th December 1976, p.8; and also see Thornton, 1978.

44 Two ballets: *The White-Haired Girl* 《白毛女》 and *The Red Detachment of Women* 《红色娘子军》; five Peking Operas: *Taking Tiger Mountain by Strategy* 《智取威虎山》, *Raid on White Tiger Regiment* 《奇袭白虎团》, *The Red Lantern* 《红灯记》, *On the Docks* 《海港》, and *The Shajia Lake* 《沙家浜》; and a symphonic music *The Shajia Lake* 《沙家浜》. By 1976 eighteen model theatrical works were put on stage, including Peking operas: *Ode to the Dragon River* 《龙江颂》 and *Azalea Mountain* 《杜鹃山》.

45 In the factory where I worked in 1971-1978, workers began to entertain themselves on Sundays in various ways. Some workers made hunting guns themselves and went hunting in the farmland on Sundays, some went fishing, and still others played cards and other games.

46 *Data source: China Statistical Yearbook 1999*, p.57.

47 Take Shanghai, the largest industrial base of China, for example. Between 1961 and 1963 ration coupons issue reached its climax when over 30 types of ration coupons were in use in Shanghai, such as grain, oil, cloth, soap, match, meat, fish, egg, cake, cigarette, and bicycle ration coupons. See *Jie Fang Daily*, Weekend Issue, 1st August 1998.

48 It was estimated that investment grew from approximately one-fourth of national output in the mid-1950s to one-third or higher in the 1970s. For more discussion, see Selden, 1988, p.23.

49 There was a much-publicized saying that 'A dress will last three years new, three years old, and another three years mended'.

50 A survey revealed that although in 1965-1977 grain yields rose by 30 per cent, peasants' average daily income dropped by 20 per cent because of the 54 per cent increase in agricultural costs. See Selden, 1988, p.19.

51 Hua Kuofeng accused the Gang of Four of their sabotage and interference in 1974-1976 that resulted in a loss of 100 billion RMB *yuan*'s worth (US$60 billion) of industrial output, 28 million tons of steel, and 40 billion RMB *yuan* in state revenues. (Report on the Work of the Government, delivered by Hua Guofeng at the First Session of the Fifth NPC, on 26th February 1978, in *Peking Review*, 10th March 1978, p.12.)

52 By September 1976, 19 per cent of the Central Committee members, 21.3 per cent of chairmen and vice-chairmen of provincial-level Revolutionary Committees, and 19.5 per cent of ministers and vice-ministers were formerly purged cadres.

53 Deng Xiaoping was appointed Vice-Chairman of the party, first Vice-Premier, and Chief of Staff of the Army. In fact, he was serving as acting premier in charge of the

daily work of the party and the State Council owing to the illness of Premier Zhou Enlai, who stayed in hospital for treatment.

54　Modernization of agriculture, industry, national defense, and science and technology.

55　Although the CPC Eighth National Congress adopted an anti-cult of personality article into the party constitution following revelations that a lot of Stalin's mistakes were due to his cult of personality, Mao personally held reservation on the party newly-established institution against the personality cult.　At the Chengdu Politburo Conference in March 1958 Mao even challenged the party newly established institution against the personality cult, by commenting that there were two kinds of personality cult, to worship the correct theories of Marx, Engles, Lenin, and Stalin was a good practice of personality cult, while to worship indiscriminately was a bad practice of personality cult.

Chapter 4

Transformation of the Ideological Environment and Deng Xiaoping's Rise

This chapter examines how Mao's successors settled the succession issue and how Deng Xiaoping managed to make a significant change in the ideological environment to his favor, winning the succession struggle and paving the way for a takeoff of economic reforms and opening to the outside world.

Ups and Downs of Deng Xiaoping

Deng Xiaoping was a complex figure among the CPC ruling elite. He was both a devout follower of Mao's political guidelines and a stubborn dissenter against some specific policies of Mao. He firmly supported Mao's controversial political campaigns as the 1957 Anti-Rightists Campaign and the Great Leap Forward at its early stage, while he held different views about Mao's agricultural collectivism[1] and the Cultural Revolution.[2]

Deng Xiaoping was elected into the CPC decision-making elite – the CPC Politburo in April 1955 and elected into the core of the ruling elite – the CPC Politburo Standing Committee in September 1956. As the Secretary General of the CPC Central Committee since September 1956, Deng actually controlled the daily activities of the CPC Central Committee. In his political career, Deng experienced ups and downs three times. He had his first dismissal in 1931 when he supported Mao Zedong's military defensive strategy in the CPC military base area in Jiangxi Province.[3] Ironically, he was ousted by Mao Zedong as the No. 2 'Capitalist Roader' in the early days of the Cultural Revolution when he and Liu Shaoqi, the Chairman of the People's Republic of China, tried to put the Cultural Revolution under control so as to save the party state bureaucracy that Mao wanted to smash. He was under house arrest in Beijing from September 1969 to October 1969 and was then sent to do manual labor work at the Xin Jian County Tractor Repair and Manufacture Factory, Jiangxi Province until his second rehabilitation in 1973. This time, Deng returned to the power center as, perhaps, a very difficult domestic situation China faced since 1949.

In the early 1970s, in the face of a possible military invasion from the former Soviet Union and a dislocated domestic economy, Mao Zedong gave his consent to Premier Zhou Enlai's effort to rectify the economic order and to normalize relations with the United States. The rapprochement with the United States started the process of China integrating into the world community dominated by the industrialized West, which has provided China until today with most favorable external conditions for modernization. China's modernization needed no such class-struggle-minded fighters around Mao during the height of the Cultural Revolution but pragmatic and economic-construction-minded political elite. Mao Zedong must have thought Deng was one of the political elite, otherwise Mao Zedong would not have written favorable comments on a letter presented to him by Deng Xiaoping in 1972, indicating Deng Xiaoping had made a contribution to the Chinese revolution and his deviation had belonged to contradictions among the people. Premier Zhou Enlai and Marshal Ye Jianying quickly seized the opportunity to engineer Deng's rehabilitation. In March 1973 Deng Xiaoping resumed the job of Vice-Premier of the State Council. In January 1975 Deng was elected as Vice-Chairman of the CPC Central Committee and a member of the CPC Politburo Standing Committee and was appointed as the First Vice-Premier of the State Council, responsible for managing daily affairs of the party and state apparatus. As Deng tried to systemically readdress the economic problems generated by the Cultural Revolution, Mao was afraid that the rectification of the economic mistakes of the Cultural Revolution would eventually lead to an overall rectification of the Cultural Revolution. Deng Xiaoping was therefore dismissed from all his positions for the third time.

1976 was very bad for the People's Republic of China because it lost its three charismatic founders successively within nine months.[4] The death of Mao Zedong practically ended the era of the CPC leadership based on personal charisma and made China's political future uncertain with three political forces struggling for dominance at the power center. In the end the old generation faction defeated the other two political forces and began the CPC ruling elite (party veterans) collective leadership with Deng Xiaoping as their chief representative. It took them less than a month after the death of Mao Zedong to ally with Hua Guofeng, Mao's designated successor, to wipe out the radical faction from the power center through the arrest of the 'Gang of Four',[5] although subsequent cleansing of the radical faction's influences took a much longer time. It took the old generation faction two years and two months to take over all the decision making power from Hua Guofeng, Chairman of both the CPC Central Committee and the CPC Central Military Affairs Commission after the Gang of Four were arrested in October 1976. It took them another two years and six months to force Hua Guofeng to resign his two chairmanship positions. It took them five years to rehabilitate three million party and state cadres who had been dismissed or convicted during the Cultural Revolution and other political campaigns. Finally, it took them more than ten years to purge the followers of the Gang of Four from the party and state apparatus. All these paved the way for Deng Xiaoping, chief representative of the party veterans, to launch and implement his reform measures.

Arrest of the Gang of Four

The death of Mao Zedong stimulated struggles among the three political forces for succession. As Mao's designated successor, Hua Guofeng would certainly continue to realize Mao's socialist and communist visions through class struggle and endless revolutions. However he had little power base at the central party and state apparatus. He used to be the First Secretary General of the CPC Hunan Provincial Committee before he was transferred to the State Council in 1971. Since then Hua Guofeng rose quickly, perhaps too rapidly, at the central party and state apparatus for him to build his power base. He was promoted into the CPC Politburo in August 1973, elected as Vice Premier in January 1975 and appointed as the First Vice Chairman of the CPC Central Committee and Premier of the State Council in April 1976. Since Hua Guofeng had few followers at the central party and state apparatus, he had to rely on either the radical faction or the old generation faction to consolidate his leadership. The radical faction was committed to continuing the Cultural Revolution and throwing the remaining old veterans of the party out of the CPC Central Committee. With the media under its control, the radical faction began to prepare the party and the people for its political objective. On 4 October 1976, an editorial appeared in *Guang Ming Daily* 《光明日报》 with the title 'Forever Follow Chairman Mao's Designated Guiding Principles' 《永远按毛主席的即定方针办》. The old generation faction, headed by Marshal Yie Jianying, did not give the radical faction time to fulfill their task and persuaded Hua Guofeng, Mao's designated successor, to take a decisive action against the radical faction. In the evening of 6th October 1976 four key members of the radical faction were arrested, who were later called the Gang of Four.

With the radical faction eliminated, the disagreement between Hua Guofeng and the old generation faction became prominent over many issues, including the rehabilitation of the dismissed party veterans, particularly Deng Xiaoping, and the re-evaluation of the Cultural Revolution. The old generation faction settled its dispute with Hua Guofeng through an orchestrated theoretical discussion on the 'Criteria of Truth'.

Theoretical Discussion on the 'Criteria of Truth'

After Hua Guofeng was confirmed as Chairman of the CPC Central Committee and Chairman of the Central Military Commission,[6] Marshall Yie Jianying and many other party veterans repeated the suggestion several times to Hua Guofeng that Deng Xiaoping should be rehabilitated as soon as possible. Hua Guofeng, however, insisted on condemning both the Gang of Four and Deng Xiaoping. Hua employed the ideological legacy of Mao Zedong to defend his position, calling for the safeguarding of whatever decisions Mao Zedong had made and the upholding of whatever instructions Mao Zedong had given, which were later referred to as 'Two Whatevers'. Since Deng Xiaoping's dismissal and criticism was approved by Mao Zedong, it was necessary to continue that way.

Eventually, Hua succumbed to the pressure from the old generation faction, reinstating Deng in his former positions. For the third time, Deng resumed all his lost positions, including CPC Vice Chairman, Vice Chairman of the CPC Central Military Affairs Commission, Deputy Premier, and Chief of the General Staff, at the Third Plenary Session of the CPC Tenth Central Committee in July 1977. However, Hua Guofeng managed to uphold class struggle and the 'Two Whatevers' as the guiding principle of the party, perhaps, the only basis of his legitimacy to the top leadership.

Two of Hua Guofeng's policies were extremely unpopular among the party veterans. Since Hua Guofeng stressed that the Cultural Revolution was absolutely necessary, millions of party and government officials who had been dismissed during the Cultural Revolution had little chance of rehabilitation under his party chairmanship. The prevailing feeling among the party veterans was that the Cultural Revolution only brought chaos and destruction to China and the dismissed cadres should be rehabilitated immediately.

Secondly, Hua followed Mao's mass line of agricultural collectivism, continuing to promote it after the model of the Da Zhai Production Brigade, which was based on mass line mobilization of peasants to work the land collectively. This collective agricultural policy had been repeatedly challenged by the peasants and the party veterans because the agricultural productivity under collectivism was much lower than when peasants had been not organized into agricultural co-operatives in 1953.[7]

At that time, nobody dared to directly challenge Hua's 'Two Whatevers' because the Chinese people had been indoctrinated into believing that Mao Zedong and his Thoughts were infallible. Deng Xiaoping clearly saw the 'Two Whatevers' becoming the key obstacle to the redressing of the Cultural Revolution, which was the precondition for charting a different route to economic development. To counter Hua's 'Two Whatevers', Deng Xiaoping wrote a letter in April 1977 to the CPC Central Committee before he was rehabilitated and proposed to employ the correct and whole Mao Zedong Thought to guide the party, the army and the people in China's socialist construction (Deng, 1983, pp.35-6). It must be clear to Deng that Mao's ideological legacy was so powerful that he had to work within the ideological environment, accepting the correct part of Mao's ideology.

When the Third Plenary Session of the CPC Tenth Central Committee formally reinstated all his positions in July 1977, Deng Xiaoping made a speech, advocating guiding the party's future work with the correct and undistorted Mao Zedong Thought and outlining three major components of what he considered the correct and undistorted Mao Zedong Thought (Deng, 1983, pp.39-44):

- Full trust in the general public;
- Seeking truth from facts; and
- Promoting democracy.

Deng was trying to sort out those elements of Mao Zedong Thought that could be used as the working ideology or guiding principles for the party state apparatus. In other words, he tried to present a 'correct and undistorted' Mao Zedong Thought to replace Hua's 'Whatever' version of Mao Zedong Thought. However, to invalidate Hua's 'Whatever' version, Deng and other reform-minded political elite waited for an opportunity to launch a theoretical crusade, which came to them in April 1978.

At the beginning of April 1978, the full-page proof of the 77th Issue of Philosophy Column of *Guang Ming Daily* laid open on the desk of the new Chief Editor, Yang Xiguang, for his routine examination and approval for publication. In this issue to be published on 11 April, there was an article entitled 'Practice is the Criteria of Every Truth' 《实践是检验一切真理的标准》, whose first draft was submitted in October 1977 by Mr. Hu Fuming, a philosophy teacher of Nanjing University.

Before the Cultural Revolution Yang Xiguang was an alternate party secretary of the Shanghai CPC Municipal Committee, responsible for Shanghai's cultural and educational work. He was labeled No. 3 Capitalist Roader of Shanghai when the Cultural Revolution storm hit Shanghai. In the fall of 1977 he entered the Party School of the CPC Central Committee in Beijing for further training when Hu Yaobang, Vice-Principal of the Party School, was responsible for running the Party School. Hu Yaobang echoed Deng's position on Mao Zedong Thought, stressing two principles: (1) the correct and undistorted application of Mao Zedong Thought, and (2) practice is the criterion for testing truth (Tao, 1999, p.243). Heated discussions followed among the teaching staff and trainees – medium- and high-ranking party officials, which were encouraged by Hu Yaobang who advocated to emancipate the mind and to assess the party history according to facts. Yang Xiguang also took part in the discussions.

As soon as Yang Xiguang completed reading 'Practice is the Criterion for Testing Every Truth', he instructed a revision of the article before publishing it on the front page. The revision of the article involved not only the original author and editors of *Guang Ming Daily* but also two personnel from the Theoretical Research Unit of the Party School of the CPC Central Committee. In essence, the revised article criticized the views of those who were upholding the 'Two Whatevers' and echoing Deng Xiaoping's call for a correct and undistorted understanding of Marxism, Leninism, and Mao Zedong Thought. If the revised article had been sent to Wang Dongxin for examination and approval, a member of the Politburo, who was responsible for the party propaganda work, including the media, it would have been rejected for publication. To go around the obstacle, the article was arranged to be published first in *Theoretical Trend* 《理论动态》 an internal magazine of the Party School of the CPC Central Committee, and then be reviewed by Hu Yaobang, Vice Principal of the Party School, for examination and approval. *Guang Ming Daily* reprinted the article in the second day. To make a greater impact, Yang Xiguang reached an agreement with the *Xinhua News Agency* 《新华社》, *People's Daily* 《人民日报》, and *Liberation Army Daily* 《解放军报》 on their reprinting of the article on the following day.

As planned, the revised article entitled 'Practice is the only Criterion for Testing Truth' 《实践是检验真理的唯一标准》 was published in *Theoretical Trend* on 10th May 1978 and in *Guang Ming Daily* on 11th May. It was reprinted on 12th May by *People's Daily*, *Liberation Army Daily* and other six provincial newspapers. On 13th May another 15 provincial newspapers reprinted the article and within a month nearly all the major provincial newspapers reprinted the article, initiating a nation-wide discussion on the 'criteria of truth'.

Inter party disputes over policy guiding principles are not uncommon among the CPC chief political actors but it was unprecedented that the dispute surfaced and brought in front of the whole nation. One of the main reasons why Hu Yaobang and Deng Xiaoping openly challenged Hua's 'Two Whatevers' was that they enjoyed the backing of the army.[8] Hua immediately understood that he was the target of the article and asked the other newspapers not to reprint it and instructed the CPC Propaganda Department and provincial leaders not to comment or participate in the discussion of the 'criteria of truth'. Wang Dongxin, one of the organizers of arresting the Gang of Four, was Hua's supporter. Wang criticized on many occasions the article as anti-Mao Zedong Thought and accused the chief editors of having no party discipline who published it in their newspapers. Deng Xiaoping publicly supported the article on several important occasions. On 2nd June 1978, Deng Xiaoping made an important speech at the Ideological Working Conference of the All Army Forces, calling for the emancipation of the mind, seeking truth from practice and getting rid of the distortion of Mao Zedong Thought made by the Gang of Four and Lin Biao.[9]

Hu Yaobang organized another two articles to be published in newspapers. Academics and researchers joined in the discussion and wrote articles to support 'Practice is the Only Criteria of Testing Truth'. It was estimated that by the end of 1978, more than 650 articles were devoted to the discussion and appeared in national and provincial newspapers and magazines. From August to November 1978, provincial and municipal leaders and army field commanders, one after another, wrote and spoke publicly to support the article 'Practice is the Only Criteria of Testing Truth'. Through the public discussion of the criterion of truth, provincial and municipal leaders, ministers, and army officers reached a consensus that practice was the sole criterion of truth (Jiang and Fu, 1994, p.20; Ma and Ling, 1998, pp.63-7; and Yang, 1998, pp.126-30).

Significant Changes in the Ideological Environment

By the end of 1978, public discussions on the 'criteria of truth' reached an ideological consensus among the general public, the academics and the ruling elite, and Deng and his associates succeeded in winning the legitimate right to interpret Mao Zedong Thought. The discussions on the 'criteria of truth' were conducted in the name of defending Mao Zedong Thought, that is, the ruling party needed to have a correct and undistorted understanding and application of Mao's ideological legacies. As this new strategy presupposed an individualistic interpretation of Mao's ideological legacy, it certainly offered Deng and his associates a free hand in pursuing whatever policies they would consider observing the correct and undistorted application of Mao Zedong Thought.

On 13th December 1978, Deng Xiaoping made a speech to the Working Conference of the CPC Central Committee, entitled 'Emancipate the Mind, Seek

Truth from Facts, Unite, and Look Ahead' 《解放思想，实事求实，团结一致向前看》, outlining his vision of building four modernizations in China. The main points are summarized as follows (Deng, 1983, pp.130-40):

- To shift the focus of the party work from class struggle to economic construction: the realization of the four modernizations;
- To emancipate the mind and seek truth from facts, which are the principles to be observed in solving historic and new problems, renovating new methods and formulating new policies to realize the four modernizations;
- To reach a correct democratic centralism, full democracy must be practiced first, insuring workers and peasants democratic freedom, including democratic election;
- To strengthen the legal system, great attention should be focused on drafting various laws to regulate relations between and among people, enterprises and the state;
- The criteria for evaluating the political work of the party committees at each level would be advanced management, technology renovation, productivity growth, profits increase, workers income increase, and collective welfare improvement;
- To enlarge autonomy to industrial enterprises and agricultural production teams;
- To learn advanced management and new technology from foreign countries;
- Economic policies should allow some areas and some people to become rich first, setting a good example for others to follow, in this way all the people could reach prosperity more quickly;
- To call on the party cadres to unite and to study economics, scientific technology and management.

Deng's speech became the key tone of the Third Plenary Session of CPC Eleventh Central Committee between 18th and 22nd December 1978, which confirmed Deng's leadership in the CPC Central Committee although Hua Guofeng still held the positions of the Chairman of the party and the Chairman of the CPC Central Military Affairs Commission. Hua Guofeng resigned his two chairmanship positions at the Sixth Plenary Session of the CPC Eleventh Central Committee in June 1981. Hu Yaobang replaced Hua Guofeng as the party Chairman and Deng Xiaoping took the Chairmanship of the CPC Central Military Affairs Commission.

Deng's pragmatic ideas of how to conduct modernization and economic development in China were accepted by the CPC Thirteenth National Congress as the party general guidelines during the preliminary socialism.[10] It consists of one core idea and two basic points. The core idea is the principle of setting economic construction as the first priority of the party, abandoning Mao's doctrine of continual class struggle. The development targets for China's modernization were set for GDP to be redoubled by the end of 20th century and be doubled in the middle of the 21st century, with per capita GDP reaching the level of middle-income countries.[11]

The two basic points are (1) the perseverance in reform and the open-door policy, and (2) the adherence to the four cardinal principles: socialism, the dictatorship of the proletariat, the leadership of the CPC, and Marxism, Leninism and Mao Zedong Thought.

The four cardinal principles are taken from Mao's ideological legacy without any modification. The essence of these principles is to maintain the rule of the CPC although contents of these principles may be in a state of constant change owing to the impact from economic development, reforms and opening up. The perseverance in reform and the open-door policy represents new parameters of the party operational ideology created by Deng Xiaoping. They are dynamic in the sense that the outcomes of the reform and open-door policy, however it is well planed and well executed, may be quite different from what the policy designer expects.

The party's priority of economic construction represents a significant modification of Mao's operational ideology that was based more on endless class struggles than on economic construction. Economic construction may not necessarily produce economic development; it may deliver economic destruction as in the later years of Mao's era. Whether it produces negative or positive economic development, social and economic transformations generated by economic development become dynamic constraints on the policy choices of the ruling elite to continue, abandon, or revise the reform and open-door measures, or to devise new reform and opening up agendas.

By reform, Deng meant both economic reform and political reform. Deng initiated political reform in 1980, intending to solve the problem of over-concentration of power, especially the personal monopoly of power within the party. The over-concentration of power, Deng (1983, pp.288-9) observed, directly derived from the party's unified leadership[12] and its wide spreading had a lot to do with both China's long tradition of feudalism and the tradition of the party leader monopoly of power in each country during the period of the Communist International (1919-1943). He called for the elimination of such feudal legacies from the party leadership as the cult of the individual, patriarchy, and life tenure of leading posts. For Deng the political reform was to establish a clear division of labor between the party and the government with the latter under the political leadership of the former, a collective leadership combined with individual responsibility based on a division of responsibilities among party leaders, socialist democracy and a socialist legal system. The political reform initiated by Deng Xiaoping was not intended to redress the root cause of the political system problem – the monopoly of political power by the party within the country, but to correct the over-centralization of power by individuals within the party, especially by the first secretary at various levels of the CPC. Even this limited political reform received setbacks after the crackdown of the Tiananmen Square student demonstrations on 4th June 1989 and the end of the communist rule in former Eastern European countries and the Soviet Union.

There were two additional factors that were favorable to Deng Xiaoping in his attempt to make a change in the party operational ideology. One was the domestic economic situation, which was totally broken down during the Cultural Revolution. This legacy of Mao's era offered Deng and his reform-minded associates a good excuse for trying new economic policies. In 1978 the annual per capita net incomes of rural and urban residents were 78.6 US dollars and 185.9 US dollars, respectively. The per capita floor space of residential buildings was 8.1 square meters in rural areas and 3.6 square meters in urban areas. There were no TV sets in the households of the Chinese ordinary people (see Table 1.2). Every type of consumer goods and capital goods was in shortage. The socialist economy at that time was closely related with the shortage of goods. Ration coupons were invented to distribute the limited goods.

By the time when the last grain and oil ration coupons were abandoned in 1993, over 2,000 kinds of ration coupons had been issued in China. Take Shanghai, the largest industrial base of China for example. Between 1961 and 1963 ration coupons issue reached its climax when over 30 types of ration coupons were in use in Shanghai, such as grain, oil, cloth, soap, match, meat, fish, egg, cake, cigarette, and bicycle ration coupons.[13] Therefore, the bleak economic situation and poor living standards were the major reason why the ruling elite, party members, and the Chinese public favored a change in the ideological environment.

The second factor influencing people's political preference is the continual improvement in the relationship with the two superpowers in the 1970s. In the 1950s China was isolated by the containment policy of the West led by the United States. The 1960s witnessed a worse international situation for China. After an ideological quarrel and then a border dispute with the Soviet Union, China was under the siege of both the East and the West. The 1970s saw both a gradual warming of diplomatic ties with the West and signs of normalizing relations with the Soviet Union. On 25th October 1971 China resumed its membership in the United Nations. On 13th March 1972 China and United Kingdom upgraded their diplomatic relations from Office of the Charge d'Affairs to Ambassadorship. On 11th October 1972 China set up formal diplomatic relations with West Germany. When Deng was in control of the party state apparatus in 1978, he moved further along this policy line endorsed by Mao Zedong. On 1st January 1979 China and the United States established formal diplomatic ties.

It is obvious that this favorable international environment made Deng Xiaoping's market-oriented economic reform and open policy realistic and attainable. The changes in the ideological and international environments (see Figure 2.2), therefore, made it possible for Deng to chart a new route to economic development. However, to fully implement his reform policy Deng needed, on the one hand, to purge the followers of the Gang of Four from the party and state apparatus, and on the other hand, to create a contingent of reform-minded cadres.

Purge Elements of the Gang of Four from the Party and State Apparatus

The Gang of Four were arrested in October 1976 but their official titles were not removed until July 1977. It took a much longer time to eliminate their influences from the party and state apparatus at every level. Immediately following the arrest of the Gang of Four, a first wave of cleansing was ordered by the CPC Central Committee to purge those officials who had been directly involved in the Gang of Four's scheme to usurp power. Most of the culprits were provincial level officials. In December 1977, the cleansing campaign was extended into every level of the party and state apparatus and the purging target included those officials who had been directly connected to the faction of the Gang of Four. This could practically include all those cadres who had owned their titles in the Cultural Revolution. By the end of 1978 the cleansing task had been basically achieved, purging all those officials from the party and state apparatus who had certain connection, in one way or another, with the faction of the Gang of Four.

In October 1983 a rectification campaign was started within the party, initiating a second round of cleansing elements of the Gang of Four. Its main target was to purge Three Types of Persons from any organizations, including non-governmental organizations, schools, hospitals, research institutes, universities and state-owned enterprises: (1) those who had risen to power because they had actively followed the call of Lin Biao and the Gang of Four to revolt against the party and state apparatus during the Cultural Revolution; (2) those who had shown strong factional tendency; and (3) those who had taken part in beating cadres, smashing public and private property, and plundering everything valuable during the Cultural Revolution.

The second round cleansing campaign ended in May 1987. It was reported that 33,896 persons had been expelled from the party, 90,069 persons barred from the party membership registration, 145,456 persons suspended from the party membership registration until further notice, and 184,071 persons received disciplinary sanctions within the party (Jiang and Fu, 1994, p.33).

Deng's Contingent of Cadres

To run a large country like China and to implement economic reform measures, a loyal army was not enough. Deng Xiaoping needed a large contingent of loyal cadres as well, which would consolidate his leadership. Deng adopted three key measures to build his contingent of loyal cadres: (1) promoting his protégés to crucial jobs; (2) rehabilitating old cadres who had been dismissed in the Cultural Revolution; and (3) promoting young people to replace the old generation of cadres.

In December 1977, Hu Yaobang was appointed as Director of the Organization Department the CPC Central Committee to push forward the rehabilitation of the old cadres. He was elected as a member of the CPC Politburo in December 1978 and was raised to the rank of the CPC Politburo Standing Committee and Party Secretary General in February 1980, responsible for running the party day-to-day activities. Hu Yaobang replaced Hua Guofeng as the Chairman of the CPC Central

Committee in June 1981. Deng Xiaoping also managed to promote his other protégé, Zhao Ziyang, to the CPC Politburo in September 1979 and the CPC Politburo Standing Committee in February 1982. Zhao Ziyang replaced Hua Guofeng as Premier of the State Council in September 1980. In late 1980 Deng Xiaoping actually took control of the daily activities both of the party and the state through his two protégés, Hu Yaobang and Zhao Ziyang,

As soon as Hu Yaobang took over the CPC Central Organization Department in December 1977, a large-scale rehabilitation of the dismissed cadres took off seriously. The rehabilitation eventually reached those who had been dismissed not only during the Cultural Revolution but also in the political campaigns since 1949. The former Chairman of the People's Republic of China, Liu Shaoqi, who had been dismissed as the 'No. 1 Capitalist Roader' in October 1968, was fully rehabilitated. So was the former Defense Minister, Marshal Peng Dehuai, who had been labeled as anti-CPC and Right-opportunist in August 1959. By the end of 1982 more than 3 million party and state officials had been rehabilitated and reinstated in their previous positions or assigned new jobs (Jiang and Fu, 1994, p.31).

The rehabilitation of all those dismissed cadres boosted Deng Xiaoping's power base when he was competing against Hua Guofeng for the leadership within the party. However, since the majority of the rehabilitated cadres were old and tended to be more conservative, they might become obstacles to Deng's reform policy implementation. Deng Xiaoping initiated the retirement system of old cadres and the recruitment of younger people into the contingent of cadres in January 1982. The CPC Central Committee adopted the decision on the retirement of old cadres in February 1982, ending the life tenure in office within the party and state apparatus. To facilitate the old-to-young-leadership transition, advisory committees that consisted of retired party veterans were established in the CPC Central Committee and provincial level committees in September 1982, which were abolished in October 1992. The leadership transition had been completed by the end of 1984. At the central party and state apparatus the ruling elite's average age was cut down from 64 to 60; at the provincial level, the average age was reduced from 62 to 55; and at the county level, the average age was slashed under 45 except in Beijing and Shanghai.

Conclusion

The above sections have discussed how Deng rose to the leadership of the party state apparatus. With the support of the army, Deng skillfully manipulated the legacies of Mao, continuing Mao's modernization drive with the economic construction as the first priority, making a change in the ideological environment while keeping some of Mao's ideological legacy, purging the elements of the radical faction, and building his contingent of cadres. Deng achieved these because the favorable international conditions, the poor performance of Mao's socialist construction and the political support of the majority of the ruling elite, including the army veterans, were three important initial institutional environments (see Figure 2.2) that offered Deng an opportunity to launch his version of economic development.

Among them the support of the army veterans was his crucial political capital when he took a risk to chart a new economic development route. However, it is through the discussion of the 'criteria of truth' that Deng Xiaoping made a necessary change in the ideological environment, which not only established his leadership among the central and provincial ruling elites, and decision makers within the party state apparatus, but also gave him a free hand or a political mandate to pursue whatever policies he would perceive worthwhile trying.

Although the leadership transition from Hua Guofeng to Deng Xiaoping was started when the former unwillingly agreed to reinstate the latter all his positions, it is at the Third Plenary of the 11th CPC National Central Committee in December 1978 that Deng had his leadership confirmed in principle. It is the beginning of the era of Deng's leadership, although Hua Guofeng resigned his two chairmanship positions two years later. It was unprecedented and the first time in the history of the CPC Central Committee that the collective leadership was observed with the policy preference of the majority of the ruling elite prevailing over that of the Chairman of the CPC Central Committee and the Chairman of the CPC Military Affairs Committee.

Through the purging of the elements of the radical faction and the building of his contingent of cadres, Deng Xiaoping laid down a firm power base at both the central and the local levels for the implementation of his economic reform measures. However, with the common opponents eliminated, disputes over policy guidelines erupted again among Deng and his reform-minded associates and the party conservatives. The next chapter will examine how Deng managed to push forward economic reform and the open-door policy, with an emphasis on institutional and historical limitations on his reform efforts.

Notes

1   In order to solve the output deteriorating problem of 'Eating from the Big Pot' encouraged by the agricultural collectivism – the People's Commune, various forms of production-related contract schemes such as the fixing of agricultural output quotas on the household basis and the fixing of agricultural output quotas on the farmland basis were innovated in the aftermath of the Great Leap Forward. It was estimated that more than 20 per cent of the People's Communes adopted such production-related responsibility schemes. Deng's attitudes towards such new innovation were pragmatic and deviated from Mao's preference. Deng (1989, p.305) believed that an optimal form of agricultural production should be (1) that could more easily and more quickly recover and boost agricultural production; (2) that the peasants would prefer to adopt; and (3) such an optimal production form should be legalized if it was an illegal practice. This was later referred to as Deng's 'Cat Theory' that a cat is a good cat that can catch a mouse.

2   During the very early stage of the Cultural Revolution from May to July 1966, Liu Shaoqi and Deng Xiaoping proposed to send Work Teams to universities and high schools to organize the Cultural Revolution in an orderly manner and to avoid any possible social chaos, which was in opposition to Mao's intended preference to destroy

the party and state apparatus that had been, in Mao's view, under the control of Socialist Revisionists and Capitalist Roaders.

3   Deng Xiaoping received a serious warning sanction and was dismissed from the positions of Director of the Propaganda Department of the CPC Jiangxi Provincial Committee and Secretary of the CPC Huichang Zhongxing County Committee.

4   Premier Zhou Enlai, head of the government, died in January. Marshal Zhu De, commander in chief of the People's Liberation Army, died in July. Mao Zedong, Chairman of the CPC Central Committee and Chairman of the CPC Central Military Affairs Commission, died in September.

5   The Gang of Four referred to the three Politburo Standing Committee members: Jiang Qing, Mao's wife, Zhang Chunqiao, and Wang Hongwen, vice party Chairman, and Yao Wenyuan, member of the Politburo. For more discussion, see Zhang, Long and Deng, 1993, pp.570-5; Yang, 1998, pp.92-8.

6   Hua's two titles were confirmed at a special Politburo meeting immediately after the Gang of Four were arrested.

7   It is estimated that the agricultural productivity of 1978 was only 77.6 percent of that of 1952. For more discussion, see Ma and Ling, 1998, p.43.

8   Although Hua Guofeng was Chairman of the CPC Central Military Affairs Commission, Marshal Ye Jianying was Vice Chairman responsible for the Commission's daily routine work and all other vice chairmen and standing committee members were party veterans.

9   For more discussion, see Ma and Ling, 1998, pp.57-63.

10   The Congress convened from 25th October to 1st November 1987.

11   Deng Xiaoping's economic development targets were more specific than the party document, with per capita GDP reaching 800 to 1,000 US dollars by the end of 20th century and 4,000 US dollars in the middle of the 21st century. See Deng, 1993, pp.224-5.

12   Under the party's unified leadership, all the power is centralized in the party committees at various levels, further centralized in the hands of several party secretaries, and still further concentrated in the hands of the First Secretary, which easily leads to a personal monopoly of power.

13   Special Weekend Issue, *Jie Fang Daily*, 1st August 1998.

PART III
POLICY INSTITUTIONALIZATION IN THE POST-MAO ERA

Chapter 5

Institutionalization of Agricultural Reform and Open-door Policy

This chapter examines the institutionalization of the agricultural reform and the open-door policy, which have jointly played a decisive role in transforming China from a command economy into a market economy. The agricultural reform provided the reform-minded elite with necessary stimulus and pressure to initiate market-oriented measures, phasing out the old economic system, while the success of the open-door policy in continuously opening China to the outside world strongly demonstrated that not only foreign capital and technology but also market mechanisms could be introduced into China. However, the results were not what had been expected when the reform was started in 1978. The analysis will show how the agricultural reform and the open-door policy, which were intended to be complementary to the planned economy, created a market-oriented economic environment that eventually led to the replacement of the planned economy by a market economy.

Early Consensus on the Economic Reform: a Planned Economy with Supplementary Market

When Deng Xiaoping was fully reinstated in July 1977 following the efforts of the old ruling elite headed by Marshal Ye Jianying, he was in a position to put his vision of China's economic construction into practice. However, Deng would face some innate and historical constraints over his policy choices and preferences. Firstly, he did not have the spiritual charisma that Mao Zedong had acquired, the statesmanship that the late Premier Zhou Enlai had enjoyed, or the military glamour that Marshal Zhu De, Commander-in-Chief of the People's Liberation Army, had developed. Secondly, his rise to the leadership of the party and state apparatus was owed, to a large extent, to the political consensus of the old generation faction of the CPC who had suffered under the personal dictatorship of Mao Zedong. They would not tolerate, therefore, Deng's leadership if his policy preference turned out to be not in their interests. Thirdly, since Deng had been busily engaged in managing routine activities of the party and state central apparatus since 1956, he had not developed any theory of his own on party ideology, state building or economic construction. Lastly, when Deng won enough support for his economic construction and reform guidelines and became the de facto leader within the party by the end of 1978, Hua Guofeng still held the three most important titles of the party and state apparatus: Premier of the State Council, Chairman of the CPC Central Committee and Chairman of the CPC Central Military Affairs Commission. Hua's consent was still routinely required for implementing, if not for initiating, reform measures before he resigned all his positions.[1] These constraints affected his ability to have his reform policies institutionalized into the party documents, the state regulations, and the state laws and constitution.

Although Deng Xiaoping had persuaded his colleagues to accept his general guidelines for economic reform and the open-door policy at the Third Plenum of the 11th CPC Central Committee in December 1978, there were different views among the ruling elite on how to reform the economy and what to reform. One view believed that the system of the planned economy should be reformed since it had been centralized to such an extent that all capital goods and many vital consumer goods such as grain and oil were under unified state allocation or distribution. The highly centralized planned economy suppressed and rejected any form of organizing production of commodities according to the law of value.[2] In other words, it predominantly relied on the central administrative means and mandatory plans to allocate resources, to organize production and to distribute goods. Deng Xiaoping was among those ruling elite who held this view, considering that the socialist economy was still a type of commodity economy and therefore, the centralized economy system should be reformed in accordance with the operational principle of commodity economy.[3] He made it quite clear in early 1980 (Deng, 1983, pp.211-3) that in the last 30 years or so China's socialist economic construction had only achieved a slow, unstable and uncoordinated development of productivity and had failed to improve Chinese people's living standards; therefore, the economic system needed to be reformed, although he compromised with the majority of the CPC ruling elite who held the following conservative view.

The conservatives considered the centralized economic system was still a rational form of economic system under socialism. Chen Yun[4] was among those ruling elite who believed the centralized economic system should be retained and the economic reform was only to add some market functions to the centralized economic system. They would prefer to let the plan play the principal role while allowing the market to play a supplementary role, which was in essence a copy of the 'Three Principals and Three Subordinates' economic model[5] proposed by Chen Yun in 1956 to remedy the deficits of the highly-centralized planned economic system based on the Soviet model.

Li Xiannian,[6] another member of the Politburo Standing Committee and responsible for the fiscal and economic policies in the late 1970s and the early 1980s, agreed with Chen Yun's view on the relationship between the state principal planning and the market supplementary regulation. At the Fifth Session of the Fifth National People's Congress on 2nd December 1982, Chen Yun explained the relationship between plan and market by analogy with the relationship between a cage and a bird in the cage. The bird could move freely within the confinements of the cage that could be adjusted according to how much movement you wanted the bird to have. Without the cage the bird would fly out of sight, signifying a loss of control. Chen Yun's Bird in the Cage Analogy was a big advancement in comparison with Mao's economic view and the previous rigid economic system. Under his model, the central planning was divided into two types: mandatory plans and guidance plans, with the former taking the driving seat while the latter the back seat.[7] It was accepted by the majority of the ruling elite and became the general guideline of economic reforms until October 1984 when a policy compromise more favorable to market regulation could be reached among the ruling elite.

In the political report of the Third Plenum of the 11th CPC Central Committee in December 1978, the keynote speech on how to realize modernization through reform, Deng (1983, pp.132-3) scorned those leaders who never did their work according to the actual conditions but followed the party directives and their superior's instructions to the letter. He called on the party committees at each level to encourage and support party members and the general public to innovate in new ways of conducting China's economic construction and to shake off its poverty and backwardness. Deng's pragmatic strategy to let people innovate and sort things out was vividly reflected in his advocated 'Cat Theory' that it is a good cat so long as it can catch rats no matter what color it is.[8]

The agricultural reform and the open-door policy are good examples of Deng's policy institutionalization. The institutionalization of the agricultural reform had several stages, including: unofficial innovative practice of hungry peasants, tacit consent of the local and provincial leaders, openly support of the national ruling elite, official recognition by the party and state apparatus, and formal legal institutionalization. The institutionalization of the open-door policy was a different process since it involved a major change in the country's external economic policy although it was targeted at specific areas, involving a substantial delegation of power from the center to the periphery. Its institutionalization process started with initiation of the provincial leaders, support from the ruling elite, endorsement of the party and state apparatus, and formal legal institutionalization.

The Agricultural Reform – Restoring Peasants' Independent Producers

Before the CPC came to power in 1949, Chinese peasants were classified by Mao Zedong (1969, pp.1-11, pp.113-5) into five categories: landlords, rich peasants, middle peasants, poor peasants and workers (farm laborers). The land reform turned millions of landless peasants into landowners or expanded their land holdings, making every peasant an independent farmer.[9] Through the socialist transformation in 1953-1956 and the people's commune movement in 1958, peasants were organized first into co-operatives and then into people's communes, handing over their property such as land, farm animals and equipment, and forest to people's communes and losing every right as independent farmers. As one of the CPC ruling elite admitted in 1998 (Wan, 1998a), peasants were treated as 'slaves' in people's communes, who had lost their individual right to produce and to distribute agricultural products.

The agricultural household contract responsibility system refers to various forms of contracting output or grain quota to households that were assigned a plot of land and farm animals according to labor. The peasant who signs the output contract should hand over the contracted output to the production team and receives the payment from the production team according to the agreed production cost and workpoints; while the peasant who signs the grain quota contract should deliver to the state the grain quota, submit the agreed amount of produce or income to the production team, and retain the remaining produce and income. It had been repeatedly practiced by peasants in certain parts of China whenever agricultural production was badly hit by natural disasters or by the agricultural collective system itself before it resurfaced in 1978. By 1978, China had experienced three major waves of the simultaneous adoption of the household contract responsibility system by Chinese peasants. It first appeared in Zhejiang and Sichuan provinces during the Socialist Transformation in 1953-1956. It appeared again in Hu Bei, Henan, Gansu and Shanxi provinces after peasants had been organized into the people's commune in 1958. It reappeared in the aftermath of the Great Leap Forward in Henan, Sichuan, Anhui and Gansu provinces in the early 1960s.[10] One simple reason behind the repeated unofficial adoption of the household contract responsibility system was that it could stimulate peasants' enthusiasm to work diligently and efficiently and produce more.[11]

Although the household contract responsibility system could help to raise grain production, it was suppressed by Mao Zedong each time before it spread across the nation. On this issue, Mao Zedong refused to sacrifice his socialist principle to economic benefits. He criticized his colleagues in 1962 who supported the agricultural household contract responsibility system,[12] for he believed it would lead up to dismantling the agricultural collectivism – the people's commune. But the resurfacing of the household contract responsibility system in the late 1970s went much further than Mao had contemplated. It not only led to the dismantling of the agricultural collectivism but also contributed to the replacement of the command economy with a market economy. Like the previous three attempts, it was initiated by peasants and grass-root agricultural officials. Its success was due to a number of factors. The liberal political atmosphere, which had been created through the discussion on the 'criteria of truth' in the second half of 1978, encouraged peasants and grass-root leaders to unofficially adopt it again. The collective leadership of the ruling elite, whose decision-making was based on consensus rather than on ideology and personal dictatorship, helped to win valuable time for it to prove itself as a viable form of agricultural production. The lack of legal tradition, a weak legal system and the strong CPC organization and leading position, offered the ruling elite at various levels discretionary powers to try and implement it before it was formally enshrined in the Constitution in 1993.

In 1978 hungry peasants and grass-root leaders in some parts of China adopted the household contract responsibility system again. Anhui Province took the lead in the resurrection of the household contract responsibility system owing to a severe drought in the summer and autumn of 1978 that prompted peasants and production team leaders to adopt it secretly again.   At that time, most of the production teams contracted output or grain quota to groups of households,[13] which was openly supported by the provincial leaders, particularly by the First Secretary of the Anhui CPC Committee, Wan Li.[14] When the peasants' spontaneous adoption of the household contract responsibility system in the Shan Nan People's Commune, Shan Nan District, Fei Xi County, was reported to Wan Li, he sent the Agricultural Commission of the Anhui CPC Committee to investigate. After a discussion of the Commission's report, the Standing Committee of the Anhui CPC Committee reached a decision in February 1979 to let the Shan Nan People's Commune continue the household contract responsibility system as an experiment, on the agreement that it should not be publicized among the agricultural community nor be released to the public media. With the tacit or verbal consent of the provincial leaders, 40 per cent of the production teams in Fei Xi County implemented the household contract responsibility system in 1979.

The household contract responsibility system was also adopted secretly by the peasants and team leaders of the Xiao Gang Production Team, the Li Yuan People's Commune, Feng Yang County.   Their unofficial practice received a negative response from the leaders of the Li Yuan People's Commune but received support from the Secretary of the Feng Yang County CPC Committee. Therefore, the peasants of the Xiao Gang Production Team were able to carry out their practice, which was kept secret until January 1980 when Chen Yuanting, the county party secretary, submitted a special report to Wan Li, the First Secretary of the Anhui CPC Committee, during the Provincial Agricultural Conference on 1st – 11th January 1980. Wan Li visited the Xiao Gang Production Team on 24 January 1980 and praised their achievements after personally talking to the peasants.

This time, the peasants who initiated the household contract responsibility system would make history.   In December 1978 a contract was signed by 21 peasants and the team leaders of the Xiao Gang Production Team, the Li Yuan People's Commune, Feng Yang County. The contract assigned all the land to the 20 households that promised to deliver their quota of grain to the state and also promised to look after the children of the team leaders if they were prosecuted.[15] The promise taken by the peasants to look after the offspring of the team leaders reflected their deep concern over the political risk the team leaders were taking. It was estimated that the suppression of the third wave of the household contract responsibility system in the early 1960s led to the prosecution of over 100,000 agricultural officials in Anhui, with many of their families ruined (Li, 1998b, p.179).

What the peasants were doing was against the Constitution of 1975 and the agricultural policies of the CPC Central Committee. The Seventh Article of the Constitution stipulated that the people's commune was a three-level collective ownership system that comprised the commune, the production brigade, and the production team, with the production team as the basic accounting unit. Their practice was also against the 'Decision of the CPC Central Committee on Some Questions Concerning the Acceleration of Agricultural Development (Draft for Trial)' and the 'Regulations on the Work in Rural People's Communes (Draft for Trial)' that had been issued by the CPC Central Committee in November and

December 1978. Both of the CPC documents strictly prohibited any form of assigning land to households and contracting output quota to households.

At that time both the group and household contract responsibility systems were simultaneously adopted only in some provinces, such as Henan, Sichuan, Anhui and Gansu that had experienced the Great Leap Forward Famine in the late 1950s.[16] Most rural officials in other provinces were not ready for or even held negative views about the household contract responsibility system. On 15th March 1979 the *People's Daily* published a reader's letter with the editor's comments, initiating a public crusade against the household contract responsibility system. The peasants and rural officials, who were involved in the practice of the household contract responsibility system in Anhui, were placed under great pressure. Fortunately, the initial results of the household contract responsibility system gave them encouragement. Those people's communes that had practiced the household contract responsibility system increased their summer wheat production. For example, the Shan Nan People's Commune had a record high wheat production of 1,005 tons (Yang, 1998, p.186).

With the initial success, the Anhui provincial leaders did their best to lobby the central ruling elite in support of the household contract responsibility system. At a meeting on rural work in March 1979, Zhou Yueli, the Anhui representative, managed to persuade Hua Guofeng to let Anhui continue with its experiment although Hua was strongly promoting the agricultural collectivism on the model of the Dazhai Production Brigade.[17] In July 1979 Deng Xiaoping paid a visit to Anhui and encouraged Wan Li to employ whatever ways and methods to help peasants to get rich, the sooner the better. In September 1979, Wan Li tried very hard to persuade Hu Yaobang,[18] who was supervising the drafting of the 'Decision of the CPC Central Committee on Some Questions Concerning the Acceleration of Agricultural Development', to cancel the two prohibitions, 'no contracting output to households' and 'no contracting grain quota to households' from the 'Decision'. Eventually, a compromise was reached among the ruling elite that the final 'Decision' would allow the contracting of output to isolated and inaccessible households in mountainous areas and some places with special problems. It was a small crack in the collective system although the 'Decision' still categorically prohibited production teams from dividing the collective land to households and contracting output or grain quota to households.

The practice of the household contract responsibility system in the Xiao Gang Production Team, Feng Yang County, produced even more encouraging results. It had a bumper harvest in 1979 and delivered to the state 15,000 kilograms of grain, the first time in last 23 years.[19] Its per capita disposable income was over 400 RMB *yuan*.[20] On 31st May 1980, Deng Xiaoping publicly supported the household contract responsibility system and praised the results of its experiment in Fei Xi County and Feng Yang County, Anhui Province. However, Deng's personal opinions had to be institutionalized into party or state documents before they could gain official status because a rule had been laid down by the ruling elite at the Third Plenum of the CPC Central Committee that personal opinions should not be taken as 'official instructions' of the party or the state.

The official endorsement of the household contract responsibility system did not happen easily. At the beginning of 1980, Wan Li was promoted to Vice-Premier, responsible for agricultural work, which must be Deng Xiaoping's arrangement for promoting the agricultural reform. At a rural work meeting, attended by the party first secretaries of each province, Wan Li tabled his proposal to endorse the household contract responsibility system. After a heated discussion, only three provincial party first secretaries openly supported Wan Li's proposal. A compromise was reached in the end among the provincial and central leaders that allowed poor and backward areas to contract output or grain quota to households. On 27 September 1980, the CPC Central Committee issued a document that officially granted, for the first time since 1956, a green light to the restoration of private agricultural cultivation of the assigned collective land on the basis of household contract.[21]

Since 1980, the household contract responsibility system had rapidly spread to other parts of China. Those peasants who wanted to adopt the production responsibility system could easily claim they belonged to the category. The reform minded ruling elite took the opportunity to continually push forward the agricultural reform after taking into consideration the peasants' demand and the actual progress of the agricultural reform. A series of documents were issued by the CPC alone or jointly with the State Council in the first half of the 1980s, to offer policy guidelines to peasants and rural officials regarding the agricultural reform. The gradual upgrading and broadening of the agricultural reform can be reflected in the following series of the party and state documents issued in the first half of the 1980s, predominantly a Type D institutionalization process (see Table 3.1).

On 27 September 1980, the CPC Central Committee issued 'The Circular on Several Issues Concerning the Strengthening and Improving of the Rural Contracted Production Responsibility'. Major new policy guidelines include:

- to allow poor and backward areas to adopt the household contract responsibility system;
- to allow those areas that have already adopted the household contract responsibility system to continue their practice;
- to forbid peasants to sell land and hire laborers.

On 1st January 1982, the CPC Central Committee endorsed and issued 'The Summary of the National Rural Work Conference (December 1981)', with the following major new policy guidelines:

- to encourage the production team to develop specialized production households and transfer surplus labor to sideline production;
- to allow individuals to transport farm and sideline products for sale.[22]

On 2nd January 1983, 'Current Issues of the Rural Economic Policy', was approved and issued by the Politburo of the CPC Central Committee, stipulating the following major new policy guidelines:

- to encourage specialized production households to form economic associations, a kind of loosely united cooperatives to improve economic efficiency and begin to allow peasants to hire laborers;
- to encourage co-operatives and individuals to engage in commerce and to broaden commodity distribution channels.

On 1st January 1984, 'The CPC Central Committee's Circular on the 1984 Rural Work' was issued, including the following major new policy guidelines:

- to allow peasants to transfer their responsibility contract to other peasants;
- to encourage peasants to specialize in production of commodities;
- to encourage peasants to form specialized economic co-operatives—village and township enterprises.

On 1st January 1985, 'Ten Policies of the CPC Central Committee and the State Council on Further Revitalizing the Rural Economy' was issued, including the following major new policy guidelines:

- to began to replace the state monopolized purchase of agricultural products with contract purchase and free market purchase;
- to provide village and township enterprises with preferential treatments in credit and taxation;
- to expand rural-urban economic exchanges and encourage the construction of small towns and to allow peasants to enter towns and cities to engage in commercial, manufacturing and service activities.

From 1982 to 1985, at the beginning of each year the first document of the party state apparatus concerned the agricultural reform, indicating a close monitoring of the reform development and a series of policy adjustments based on the experience and lessons of the previous year. By the end of 1983 about 98 per cent of the production teams had adopted the household contract responsibility system and over 99 per cent had done so by the end of 1984.[23] This institutional innovation was the beginning of the end of the people's commune. By the spring of 1985 when township governments and village committees had been established throughout China, the people's commune ceased to exist. The new agricultural production institution is a hybrid of Chinese traditional farming and socialism. It restored the traditional practice of farming on the basis of households but kept the collective ownership of the land, while assigning or leasing the land to peasants for farming on a per capita basis. As it was not well adapted to modern farming that is based on technology, machinery, and the economies of scales of production, it represented a drawback from China's drive for its agricultural modernization. However, when put into serious implementation in a country with 82 per cent of its population, or 790 million people, living in the rural areas,[24] this hybrid system turned 'collective slaves' into individual producers. The peasants' enthusiasm to produce and seek wealth was thus thoroughly stimulated. The first outcome was an unprecedented large amount of agricultural products made suddenly available for consumption and the second outcome was a growing pool of surplus agricultural labor force. They became potent forces that were pressing for reform of the planned economic system: the state monopoly of purchase and marketing of agricultural and sideline products, the state monopoly of distribution of commodities, and the state monopoly of pricing of goods.

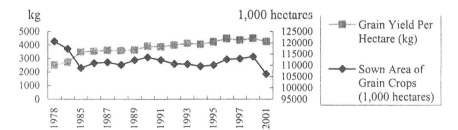

Figure 5.1 Grain Yield Growth, 1978-2001

Source: China Statistical Yearbook 1999, 2002.

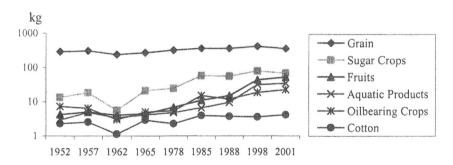

Figure 5.2 Growth of Per Capita Major Agricultural Products, 1952-2001

Source: China Statistical Yearbook 1999, 2002.

Although the new institution did not restore the private ownership of land, it indeed gave peasants control of production on the assigned piece of land and liberated the productive force of peasants by restoring their independent producer's status, which led to substantial growth in agricultural production and peasants' income.[25] The yield of grain has been on the increase since 1978 although the total sown areas of grain crops remained smaller than 1978 until 1996 (see Figure 5.1). The peasants' liberalized production energy can also be illustrated in the steady growth in China per capita major agricultural products since 1978 (see Figure 5.2).

As independent producers, peasants also found that they had large amount of surplus labor available for other purposes. It was estimated that the total rural labor force was over 400 million people in the 1980s and about 160 to 200 million became surplus labor (He, 1998, p.251; Deng, Xu and Sheng, 1997, p.276). The surplus labor either moved into the various economic development zones or was diverted to production of industrial and consumer goods, transportation of agricultural products, and provision of other commercial services.[26]

These rural commercial activities generated by the agricultural reform resulted in, among others, a rapid development of both township and village enterprises (see Figure 5.3) and a private sector, including self-employed and private enterprises (to be discussed in the next chapter). Under the planned economy, the means of production were not regarded as commodities and were put under the state-unified purchase and distribution. In order to develop their own industry, peasants had to buy industrial raw materials such as steel, coal, and timber on the free market at a higher price or to exchange agricultural products for industrial raw materials, which were called 'materials through extra-plan co-operation', making a breach in the planned distribution of capital goods.[27]

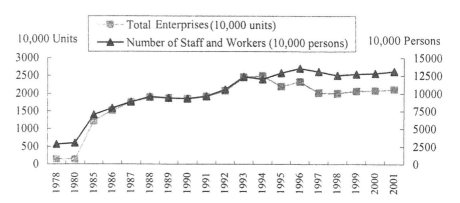

Figure 5.3 Development of Township and Village Enterprises, 1978-2001

Source: China Statistical Yearbook 1997, 1999, 2000, 2002.

To accommodate such drastic changes, the party and state apparatus did react very quickly, rapidly reducing the number of agricultural and sideline products under its monopoly purchase scheme from 46 categories in 1983 to 12 categories in 1984. Since 1985 the state stopped issuing mandatory purchase plans and instead began to purchase grain and other farm products through purchase contracts. At the same time, the state began to reduce the number of manufactured goods under the state planned purchase and marketing scheme. The manufactured goods under the state planned purchase and marketing scheme declined from 120 categories in 1980 to 12 categories in 1997. It also gradually reduced the number of capital goods under the state distribution and allocation, and since 1995, all capital goods, except items such as steel, timber, cement, crude oil, coal, grain, cotton and tobacco, were put under market regulation. Of those capital goods that remained under the state distribution and allocation, most of them, such as grain, cotton, timber and steel may also be purchased on the wholesale and future markets.[28]

The state also began to gradually abolish the planned wholesale system of fixed wholesale dealers, fixed supply of goods, and fixed prices. In 1979 rural and urban free markets were restored and peasants went to cities to sell their products. In 1983 and 1984 the party and state apparatus issued two regulations to allow co-operatives and individuals to purchase, transport and sell agricultural and sideline products in rural and urban free markets.[29] By 1985 there were 61,337 rural and urban free markets.[30]

The rapid development of these rural and urban free markets and the emergence of a large army of self-employed businessmen and individual producers[31] not only broke the state monopoly of the distribution of commodities, another major component of the planned economy, but also provided favorable commercial institutions and active business agents that led to the resurgence of Chinese private enterprises in the late 1980s.

At the same time, the state began to reduce the areas of the state-set pricing while enlarging the areas of the state guidance pricing and the market regulated pricing. The market regulated pricing of the retailing commodities, industrial goods and agricultural products rose from only 3 per cent, almost zero, and 5.6 per cent of their respective total sales in 1978 to 53 per cent, 36.4 per cent, and 53 per cent in 1990, and to 92.5 per cent, 81.1 per cent, and 79 per cent in 1996, respectively (Zhang, Huang and Li, 1998, pp.118-9).

Encouraged by the success of the agricultural reform, the reform-minded ruling elite wanted to keep up the momentum of economic reform. Deng Xiaoping (1993, p.70) argued on 1st October 1984 that the first priority of the party should be to carry out a systemic reform of the present economic system that was hindering Chinese economic development. His close associates, Hu Yaobang, the CPC Secretary General, and Zhao Zhiyang, Premier of the State Council, joined together and worked out a CPC document 'The CPC Central Committee Decision on the Reform of the Economic System' that advocated, among other things, building a planned commodity economy that was based on the public ownership, and starting the urban reform. In order to obtain consent from other members of the Politburo Standing Committee,[32] they redefined the content of the planned economy and accepted the complementary role of market regulation in the planned economy. The planned economy was redefined as consisting of state guidance planning and state mandatory planning with the former expanding and the latter shrinking in their regulating areas; production and exchange of miscellaneous goods were regulated by free markets, playing a complementary role in the economy; and the realization of the state guidance planning should be through economic means while the realization of the state mandatory planning should take the law of value into consideration.

The document received consent from all the members of the Politburo Standing Committee and was adopted at the Third Plenum of the 12th CPC Central Committee on 20 October 1984. Although state mandatory planning was confirmed in the CPC document, it represented a step away from the planned economic system by emphasizing both state guidance planning and the production and exchange of commodities.

The document also laid down guidelines for reforming the urban economic system, including the pricing system, the taxation system, the fiscal system, and the financial system, which would become the major economic means that the state might employ to regulate economic activities through its guidance planning. Besides, the document stressed the revitalization of the state-owned enterprises as the core of the urban economic reform and offered them more autonomous rights in personnel management and in production, marketing, and pricing of their products. The reform of the state-owned enterprises only went as far as the adoption of a collective responsibility system in the 1980s and the early 1990s, which might be defined, respectively, as a production or management contract responsibility system involving a collective entity: a factory, a workshop, or a work team, which was fundamentally different from the agricultural contract responsibility system involving individual households.

However, in the middle of the 1990s, the fast development of the private sector provided the impetus for a new strategy in the reform of the state-owned enterprises, which will be discussed in the next chapter. Nevertheless, all these sectional reforms were preparing China for a transition to a market economy.

The Open-door Policy

In the late 1970s China began to open up to the rest of the world. China had been a self-sufficient, self-centered, self-conceited, and self-closed society until the early 1840s. The opening up forced upon China by the world powers did not go any further than creating five entry ports and some limited fragmentary industry. After the CPC won the civil war in 1949 by driving the KMT (the Nationalist Party) government to Taiwan, China was only open to the Soviet block in the 1950s, receiving loans, technology and equipment for modernization mainly from the Soviet Union.[33] However, the deepening ideological dispute between the CPC and the Soviet Communist Party eventually led to China's break from the Soviet Block and China was plunged into total isolation from the scientific, technological and economic developments of the outside world. When China was poised to open up again in the late 1970s, China's self-imposed isolation had already cost China a chance to catch up with the industrialized countries in the fourth industrial revolution, represented by petrochemicals, electronics and aviation industries.[34] China lagged several decades behind the industrialized countries in science, technology and economic development.[35] The urge to achieve modernization was so strong that an ambitious development program, 'Ten-Year Planning Outlines', was adopted by the First Session of the Fifth National People's Congress in February 1978, which planned to build 120 large industrial projects. In the same year, China signed contracts with foreign partners on building 22 of them, involving about 60 billion RMB *yuan* of foreign loans. Hua Guofeng was an advocate of the ambitious development program, while Chen Yun was against the program and rejected it as 'Buying modernization on foreign loans'. The ambitious program was criticized as a 'Westernized Great Leap Forward' and was abandoned (Li, 1998b, pp.874-7).

Nevertheless, the gap between China and the industrialized countries was quite obvious to the ruling elite, if not so clear to the ordinary people at that time. Deng Xiaoping must have understood China's backwardness after he visited Japan in October 1978 and the United States in January 1979. He warned his colleagues in December 1978 that China's modernization and socialism would be doomed to failure if the CPC could not carry out the reform immediately (Deng, 1983, p.140). The open-door policy, as an alternative way to introduce into China the advanced technology and foreign investment, was endorsed by the ruling elite because it would not interfere with the state central planning and would not rely on the funding of the Central Government.

China opened first its southern coastal region to foreign investment for a mixture of geographical and economic reasons. First, there were millions of overseas Chinese whose hometowns are located in Guangdong and Fujian provinces. Second, Guangdong is closely linked by land with Hong Kong and by sea with Macao. In the late 1970s and the early 1980s Hong Kong had a large pool of cheap capital looking for investment while Guangdong had a large pool of cheap labor looking for work. In January 1979 Guangdong Province and the Ministry of Communications submitted a report to the State Council, proposing to set up an export processing zone in Bao An County, adjacent to Hong Kong and Macao (Yang, 1998, p.247).

Deng Xiaoping's call to emancipate the mind and to seek truth from practice greatly encouraged the ruling elite of Guangdong Province, whose growth rate of agricultural and industrial production had been below the national average, to make good use of both its geographical location close to Hong Kong and Macao and its large pool of Cantonese overseas Chinese[36] in developing its external economic and trade links. In April 1979, the CPC Guangdong Provincial Committee, headed by Xi Zhongxun, First Party Secretary, and Yang Shangkun, Second Party Secretary, submitted a proposal to set up export processing zones, hoping the Central Government would grant Guangdong Province more economic autonomy in its external economic activities. Deng Xiaoping supported the new idea and suggested calling these zones special export zones, which were renamed as special economic zones in 1980. The CPC Central Committee and the State Council instructed Guangdong Province and Fujian Province to submit a detailed plan for implementation. The idea of special export or economic zones received little objection from Deng's colleagues at that time probably because these new zones were considered by the conventional wisdom to be confined within specified geographical locations and their economic activities would be still under the guidance of the central planning and complementary to the planned economy. That is why Chen Yun, a conservative veteran, also agreed to the idea.

On 15th July 1979 the CPC Central Committee and the State Council jointly approved the reports submitted by Guangdong and Fujian provinces to set up four special export zones. They were renamed special economic zones[37] after the Standing Committee of the Fifth National People's Congress adopted on 26th August 1980 'Regulations on the Special Economic Zones (SEZ) in Guangdong Province' submitted by the State Council. The Standing Committee of the Fifth National People's Congress delegated legislative power, on 26 November 1981, to the Guangdong and Fujian Provincial People's Congresses and their Standing Committees to draft economic regulations according to the SEZs' conditions and needs and in accordance with the national laws, regulations and rules. From the beginning of China's opening up to the outside world, the institutionalization of the open-door policy is a combination of Type B, Type C and Type D processes (see Table 3.1).

The legislative institutionalization of the National People's Congress and its Standing Committee was also on a fast track to facilitate its opening development. The ruling elite had little difficulty in having a series of laws on foreign investment adopted and promulgated in the first half of the 1980s.[38] And in order to facilitate the economic reform and the opening, the Third Session of the Sixth National People's Congress delegated legislative power in April 1985 to the State Council to draft and implement temporary regulations and rules in relation to the economic system reform and the opening in accordance with the Constitution, laws and relevant regulations of the NPC.

These special zones initiated China's open-door policy but their impact surpassed their boundaries, affecting Chinese society in general and the command economy in particular, because they not only adopted the most favorable external policies to attract foreign investment but also restructured their internal economic system to facilitate the operation of incoming foreign-funded enterprises.

The main features of the SEZ policies included (1) foreign citizens, overseas Chinese, compatriots from Hong Kong, Macao and Taiwan, and their companies are encouraged to invest and open wholly-owned enterprises or to set up joint-ventures with Chinese partners; their assets, profits and legal rights are protected by the Chinese law; (2) the power to approve foreign investment projects below 30 million US dollars; (3) the exemption of import duty on the imported equipment, spare parts, raw materials, vehicles and other capital goods that are needed for manufacturing in the SEZs; (4) the corporate income tax is 15 per cent, providing tax breaks as a further incentive to long-term investment or hi-tech projects; and (5) the exemption of income tax on the remittance of profits by foreign investors. These foreign investment policies had an indirect impact on China's economic system since their application was targeted at various forms of foreign investment in the SEZs. The internal restructuring of the traditional economic system in accordance with the objective of the SEZs to attract more foreign investment would have far-reaching implications for economic reform in other parts of China. The internal system restructuring[39] in the SEZs covered the following major areas:

- Abolishing state mandatory economic plans and letting market forces regulate production under the guidance of state plans;
- Liberalizing prices of capital and consumption goods, with 97.5 per cent of commodities being priced according to market demand and supply;
- Liberalizing distribution of commodities and resources and allowing commercial and service enterprises to be engaged in their main as well as sideline businesses, and in domestic as well as foreign trade;

- Granting state-owned enterprises every power in managing human resource, finance, production and marketing; assigning management responsibility to the manager in most state-owned enterprises, while contracting or leasing out some small state-owned and collective enterprises, on an experiment basis;
- Organizing public bidding for construction projects;
- The fiscal responsibility system was extended to the district level, while the SEZ Administration shared after-tax profits with state-owned enterprises, allowing them to retain reasonable funds;
- Allowing foreign banks to open branch offices in SEZs; allowing domestic and foreign banks to engage in inter-bank loans and commercial note discount, to accept bills and drafts, and to adjust interest rates; creating non-bank financial institutions to broaden capital raising channels; gradually liberalizing the foreign currency market; establishing a stock exchange and opening stock secondary transactions.

The internal economic system restructuring set SEZs in a, more or less, market economic environment, which instantly became an oasis among the rigid command economy, attracting not only foreign investment but also domestic investment from other parts of the country.[40] With both domestic and foreign investment pouring in, and cheap labor, mainly peasants, flocking into the SEZs, they experienced a marvelous economic development that other parts of China would wish to copy. For example, Guangdong Province has got three of the first four SEZs, Shenzhen, Zhuhai and Shantou and its fast economic development has become the envy of the whole nation. By the end of 1991, its three SEZs had registered about 4,000 foreign direct investment projects[41] and over 7,000 foreign indirect investment projects,[42] with a paid-in foreign capital of 5.2 billion US dollars. They had also established more than 5,200 enterprises jointly with inland provinces and cities, with the latter investing over 4 billion RMB *yuan* in the three SEZs. With three SEZs as windows of opportunity, Guangdong Province had attracted an additional paid-in foreign investment of 9.74 billion US dollars by 1992. The results were extraordinary. In 1978, Guangdong's total export value was only 121 million US dollars and rose to 18.44 billion US dollars in 1992. Its GDP maintained an average growth rate of 12.6 per cent from 1979 to 1991. The annual disposable income of urban families per capita and the annual net income of rural families per capita rose from 412.13 and 193.25 RMB *yuan* in 1978 to 2,535 and 1,158 RMB *yuan* in 1991, respectively, well above the national average of 1,701 and 709 RMB *yuan*.[43]

The contribution of the SEZs' policies to the economic prosperity and technological advancement of the southern coastal regions was acknowledged and appraised by Deng Xiaoping who made a tour of Shenzhen SEZ, Zhuhai SEZ and Xiameng SEZ in February 1984. He advocated opening up other coastal cities to foreign investment. Besides, provincial and regional officials of other parts of China were enthusiastic about investing in SEZs and they were even keener to open SEZs in their own territories. Encouraged by the success of the four SEZs and lobbied by the provincial officials of other regions, the ruling elite began to expand the opening to other regions. On 4th May, the CPC Central Committee and the State Council decided to open 14 coastal cities, including Tianjing, Shanghai and Dalian, allowing 12 of them to establish economic and technology development zones and granting them similar preferential policies as those enjoyed by SEZs. On 18th February 1985, the CPC Central Committee and the State Council agreed to open the Yangtze Delta, the Zhujiang Delta, and the Southern Fujian Triangle, granting 61 cities and counties as coastal economic development zones. In March 1988 the State Council decided to extend the open-door policy to the Liaodong Peninsula, Shandong Peninsula, and the coastal areas that circles the Bohai Sea. On 13th April 1988, the NPC approved the plan of the State Council to establish Hainan Province and to designate it as the fifth SEZ. On 18th April 1990, the CPC Central Committee and the State Council decided to develop and open Shanghai Pudong New Area, granting it similar policies as those enjoyed by SEZs and economic and technology development zones.

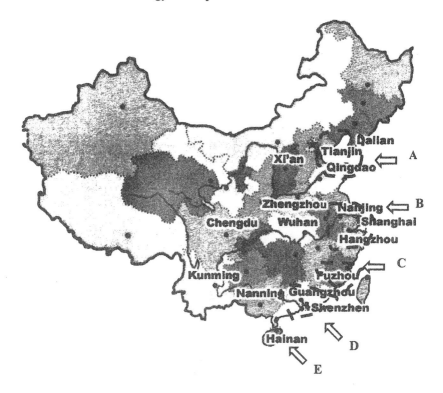

Figure 5.4 Locations of China's Key Coastal Opened-up Areas

A: The Liaodong Peninsula, Shangdon Peninsula, and the coastal areas that circle the Bohai Sea, including Beijing and Tianjin.
B: The Yangtze Delta, including Shanghai, Jiangsu and Zhejiang provinces.
C: The Southern Fujian Triangle, including the Xiamen SEZ.

D: The Zhujiang Delta, including the Shenzhen SEZ, the Zhuhai SEZ and the Shantou SEZ.

E: The Hainan SEZ.

By the end of 1988, 293 cities and counties in coastal areas had been opened up, covering 427,000 square kilometers and a population of 220 million and by the end of 1998, the opened up cities and counties had reached 359, with a area of half a million square kilometers and a population of 320 million[44] (see Figure 5.4).

Deng's Second Southern Tour – Calling for the Market

With the deepening of the agricultural reform and the continual expansion of the opened-up areas, China began to establish markets and liberalize pricing on agricultural and industrial products, including a two-track pricing on industrial capital goods. As the transition from the command distribution of resources to a market distribution was a gradual one, there were distortions of prices during the transitional process, which led to inflation and widespread official corruption. The problem was that people's economic well-being deteriorated between 1987 and 1989 when the inflation rate kept rising higher than their income growth rate (see Figure 5.5). The city dwellers were hit harder than the peasants who usually supplied their own daily necessities. As non-wage earners, the students were most sensitive to the effects of rising prices. Their dissatisfaction multiplied with the official profiteering that usually involved children and relatives of party and state officials.[45]

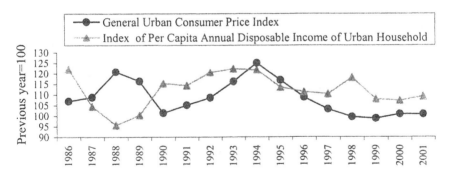

Figure 5.5 General Urban Price and Income Indices, 1986-2001

Source: China Statistical Yearbook 1999, 2002.

To a large extent, rising inflation ignited two waves of student demonstrations, one in December 1986 – January 1987 and the other in the first half of 1989. Their resentment towards their college management against the rising tuition and the poor quality of food in the late 1986 soon turned to blaming the party and state apparatus for the mismanagement of the economy. Therefore, students shifted their original economic demands for lower cost of tuition and better quality of food, to broad political ones for a multiparty system, a free press, competitive elections and the abolition of the official ideology.[46] In fact, the students' political demands were reflections of the intellectuals' quest for freedom of expression and a democratic solution to China's political reform.

The ruling elite were divided over how to deal with the political demands of intellectuals and students. The conservative force within the ruling elite refused to contemplate any concession to their demands. The architect of the discussions on the criteria of truth, Hu Yaobang, Secretary General of the CPC Central Committee, was open to new ideas and the suggestions of progressive intellectuals regarding the political reform, such as expanding the role of the NPC and dividing it into two chambers, subjecting the CPC to outside supervision and challenges, and greater independence to non-party organizations such as the Women's Federation, trade unions, and professional associations. He also declined to take tough measures to deal with liberal intellectuals and student demonstrators. Against these economic and political backgrounds, students began to organize spontaneous demonstrations in 28 large cities. That was beyond the tolerance of the conservative force within the ruling elite with the effect that Deng sided with the conservative force. Hu Yaobang was removed from his position and three progressive intellectuals, Fang Lizhi, Liu Binyan, Wang Ruowang[47] were expelled from the party in January 1987, to be followed by a nation-wide campaign against the 'bourgeois liberalization'. Student demonstrators were persuaded to return to their colleges and campus life seemed to become normal again, at least on the surface.[48]

The death of Hu Yaobang in April 1989 ignited and motivated student political aspirations again and led to a second wave of nation-wide anti-government demonstrations. This time, students received active responses from the mass public, especially, those educated people who worked in the education sector, the media, government offices, and those who worked in the non-government sector: self-employed individuals and private businessmen. The first wave of student demonstrations reached only large cities, and the second wave affected nearly all those cities that had universities and colleges.[49] For one example, Bengbu City, Anhui Province, was a medium city with three colleges and a student population of about 6,000. The local students not only sent representatives to join the demonstration on the Tiananmen Square but also staged daily demonstrations in Bengbu in support to the Tiananmen demonstrators.

Nobody in China had ever witnessed such a large scale demonstration since 1949 that was brought to the attention of over one billion people through daily live television and broadcast coverage up to the military crackdown on the student demonstration on the Tiananmen Square on 4th June 1989. The conservatives within the ruling elite considered that one step backward meant the end of their rule and decided to suppress the demonstration by force. Deng's second protégé, Zhao Zhiyang, Secretary General of the CPC Central Committee, was removed from all his positions and his close associate, Hu Qili, a member of the CPC Politburo Standing Committee, was forced to resign. The suppression of the two waves of student demonstrations indicated that Deng was a conservative on political issues while a reformist on economic issues. The cracking down on the two waves of student demonstrations and the purging of the reform-minded elite from the party and state apparatus set China's economic reform and opening up at its lowest ebb around the 1990.

Subsequently, Deng Xiaoping resigned his last position: Chairmanship of the Military Affairs Commission of the CPC Central Committee in November 1989 and selected Jiang Zemin as his successor. Jiang Zemin came from Shanghai where he served as Mayor in 1985-1987 and Secretary of the CPC Shanghai Committee in 1987-1989. Although he was elected into the Politburo of the CPC Central Committee in November 1987, his power base was regional and had no personal connection with the ruling elite in the center and in the periphery-- provinces. Such a de facto power vacancy created ample space for the 'leftist' conservative force to challenge the market-oriented reform and open-door measures.

Although Deng Xiaoping (1993, p.296) stressed, on 31st May 1989, the continuation of the reform and open-door guidelines, policies and measures that had been implemented since December 1978, some 'leftist' conservative politicians and scholars criticized the market-oriented reform and open-door policy after the Tiananmen incident of 1989. They considered the new bourgeois – owners of private enterprises and self-employed individuals – were the economic sources of support for the 'bourgeois liberalisation'. They argued that more foreign investment led to more capitalist elements in China. They accused the market orientation of the economic reform as the bourgeois orientation towards capitalism, which would turn public ownership into private ownership and the planned economy into a market economy.[50] Most of the crusading articles were published in Beijing newspapers and magazines while people in Shanghai and southern coastal areas were more concerned about further opening up to the outside world. However, the international conditions were developing in the 'leftist' conservatives' favor. The West staged sanctions against China over the Tiananmen incident of 1989, and the Berlin Wall fell with socialism abandoned in the Eastern European countries one after another. The general political atmosphere was so depressed in China that few people, even those reform-minded intellectuals and ruling elite, were unwilling to advocate economic reform and the open-door policy.

After retirement, Deng Xiaoping kept on employing his remaining influence to push forward the reform and open-door policy, whose success or failure would carry his name. To make a show case of China's further opening up, the State Council declared on 18 April 1990 a decision to develop and open up Pudong, an eastern suburb of Shanghai. The limited gesture of further opening up was too weak to silence the conservatives. In December 1990, Deng warned the party ruling elite that China needed both plan and market, dismissing the accusation that the implementation of market regulations was leading towards capitalism (Deng, 1993, p.364). Deng's personal remarks and talks could not silence the 'leftist' conservative crusade against the market-oriented economic reform and the further opening. He came to Shanghai at the early 1991 and stayed in Shanghai from 28 January to 18 February, encouraging Shanghai people and the local ruling elite to be more open-minded, bolder, and faster in economic development and opening up. He reiterated that the market could also be used to serve socialism. Deng's remarks and talks were taken seriously by the ruling elite of the Shanghai party and state apparatus. The *Jie Fang Daily*, the mouthpiece of the Shanghai CPC Committee, published four editorials on 15th February, 2nd March, 22nd March, and 22nd April 1991. They boldly championed economic reform and the open-door policy, advocating further ideological liberalization for further reform and opening up, calling for new measures of opening up, and ridiculing the obsession of the 'leftist' conservative in the 'Socialist or Capitalist' crusade.

These editorials drew strong criticism from the 'leftist' conservatives although many of the 'leftist' conservatives knew the editorials were conveying Deng's ideas. Their crusading articles appeared mainly in Beijing major newspapers and magazines, suggesting a clear ideological division over economic reform and the open-door policy between a conservative Beijing, the political center, and a liberal Shanghai, the commercial center. The on-going crusade against the reform and opening up in Beijing newspapers and magazines indicated that the new party boss, Jiang Zemin, could not possibly control the political situation at the political center, even with the personal support of Deng Xiaoping, which would develop, if unchecked, into a total negation of economic reform and the open-door policy initiated by Deng. What the 'leftist' conservatives wanted was, in essence, to negate all the pragmatic ideas of Deng regarding the reform and opening since 1978, which was beyond Deng's tolerance.

There were two main reasons why Deng's Shanghai remarks and talks of the early 1991 did not reverse the 'leftist' conservative tide. One is that Deng's remarks and talks were not transmitted through the CPC official channel but were leaked to the public, without mentioning the source, in a regional party newspaper's editorials. Their true significance, therefore, did not reach the general public and the majority of the party and state officials. Another reason is that when Deng made these comments, Shanghai's economic development and opening up had no spectacular achievements to show the merits of economic reform and the open-door policy since Shanghai had only begun, a year before, to adopt comprehensive opening measures after the CPC Central Committee and the State Council's decision to develop and open Shanghai Pudong. In early 1992, Deng Xiaoping made a tour of the southern coastal areas, counterattacking the 'leftist' tendency among the ruling elite while inspecting one economic development zone after another. This time, Jiang Zemin acted quickly to make his patron's remarks and talks and comments officially transmitted to the party members and the public, because Jiang's political position at the center needed to be consolidated and to promote the economic reform and opening up could rally political support around him at the CPC 14th National Congress, to be held in October 1992.

The year 1991 witnessed the dramatic death of the Soviet Communist Party and the end of the socialism in the Soviet Union, which was a shock to the CPC ruling elite who were feeling an intense sense of crisis. Lessons were drawn about the failure of socialism in the former Soviet Union and a dominant opinion within the CPC considered that the CPC should strengthen its fight against the 'bourgeois liberalization' in order to avoid the fate of the Soviet Communist Party. Many even associated the market-oriented economic reform and opening measures with the wide spread of the 'bourgeois liberalization' that led ˙ to the student demonstration in the first half of 1989. Before Deng Xiaoping started his tour of the southern coastal areas, he fully understood the political risks, because he intended to criticize the 'leftist' conservative force within the party. From 18th January to 21st February 1992, Deng Xiaoping, at the age of 88, toured Wuchang, Shenzhen SEZ, Zhuhai SEZ and Shanghai, and was warmly received by the provincial and local party and government officials and the mass public. Viewing the achievements of the Shenzhen SEZ made in the past eight years since his last visit in 1984, Deng counter-attacked the 'leftist' conservative view that more foreign investment meant more capitalism. Deng argued that it was not the basic distinction between socialism and capitalism to have more plan elements or more market elements in the economy. He recommended three criteria for judging a reform measure 'socialist' or 'capitalist', namely, to see whether it facilitates (1) the development of the socialist society's productivity, (2) the strengthening of the comprehensive national capabilities, and (3) the raising of the people's living standards. However, unlike his predecessor, Mao Zedong, who ruthlessly dismissed and prosecuted his colleagues holding different views over policies, Deng was liberal enough towards the 'leftist' conservatives within the party, offering them a grace period to ponder and see for themselves and to follow up along his policy later. Deng's conciliatory gesture (Deng, 1993, p.370-83), that is, 'no forced conversion', 'no political campaign', and 'welcoming slow followers', won the support of the majority of the ruling elite and the party members for his market-oriented reform and open-door measures.

Deng's southern tour received a wide coverage in the Hong Kong press while in Mainland China the press was rather quiet about Deng's tour because without the party's permission, it was not allowed to report the ruling elite's speech and talks, especially since Deng had no official title at the time of his southern tour. Some newspapers did leak some ideas of Deng's talks to the public. On 4th February, the *Jie Fang Daily* of Shanghai published an editorial, introducing some ideas of the Deng's southern talks. On 20th February, the *Shenzhen SEZ Daily* 《深圳特区报》 began a series of editorials, reporting the main ideas of Deng's talks during his stay in Shenzhen. On 24 February, the *People's Daily* published an editorial in Beijing, echoing Deng's call for bolder reform measures.

Jiang Zemin acted swiftly to spread Deng's southern talks through the official channel. On 28th February, a week after Deng returned to Beijing from his southern tour, the CPC Central Committee issued to its members 'The Circular of the CPC Central Committee on the Conveying and Studying of Comrade Deng Xiaoping's Important Talks'. The CPC Politburo convened on 9th and 10th March, reaching a decision to accept Deng's remarks and talks as the guidelines for China's next round of economic reforms and opening-up.

After the southern tour, Deng Xiaoping left behind him a 'Deng's Hurricane' (Yang, 1998, p.515), stimulating market-oriented reforms and opening-up. On 21st May, the Shanghai Stock Exchange lifted the cap on the transaction price and the stock price index rose by 570 per cent within three days. In June 1992, 13 border cities in the Northeast, the Southwest, and the Northwest, including Hei He, Shuifeng He, and Huichun, were declared open to the world. In August, 12 provincial capitals and three cities, including Haerbin, Changchun, Shijiazhuang, Taiyuan, Hefei, Chengdu, Xian, and Yingchuan, were declared open. By 1994, China's open areas and regions had spread from the coastal areas into the inner regions along the Yangtze River and the Zhujiang River, along the border lines, covering 354 cities and counties, with a total area of 550,000 square kilometers and a population of over 330 million (see Figure 5.4).[51]

On 9th June 1992, Jiang Zemin gave a speech to an audience of provincial leaders who were on a training program in the Party School of the CPC Central Committee and proposed 'a socialist market economy' as the objective of the economic reform. In the ownership structure, he stressed the public sector, including those owned both by the whole people and collectively, should be the principal component, while other sectors, including private enterprises, self-employed individuals, and foreign-funded enterprises, forming a supplementary part.

His speech was meant to set the tone of the incoming CPC 14th National Congress but also tried to communicate with the provincial leaders, rallying their support for his proposal at the Congress. As expected, the CPC 14th National Congress adopted Jiang's speech, acclaiming the 14-year reform and opening-up achievements, confirming Deng's ideas as Chinese Style Socialism Theory, agreeing to speed up the market-oriented reform and opening measures, and setting a market economy as the reform target. The CPC 14th National Congress also decided to abolish the Advisors Committee of the CPC Central Committee, giving party veterans a complete retirement from future active political involvement. The Congress confirmed Jiang Zemin's leadership within the party and accepted his economic reform target – a socialist market economy, which initiated a hasty drafting and adopting of laws and regulations to uphold the construction of a market economy in China.

Increasing Integration with the World Community

China's strategy of looking towards the West has been a success. The open-door policy has not only led to more economic integration but also cultural and political integration with the world community. Its exports and imports' share of the GDP has increased from 4.6 per cent and 5.2 per cent in 1978 to 22.9 per cent and 21.0 per cent in 2001, respectively.[52] Among the developing countries, China has been the most attractive destination for foreign direct investment (FDI). By the end of 2002, China had approved 424,196 foreign-invested enterprises with a contractual foreign investment of US$828.060 billion and a total paid-in foreign investment of US$447.966 billion.[53] Since 1993, China has absorbed the largest amount of FDI among developing countries, and in terms of FDI value, China ranks the second best destination behind the United States. For example, in 1998 China attracted 45.46 billion USD dollars of FDI, accounting for 27.4 per cent of the total FDI flow into the developing countries.[54] China's WTO membership has boosted its external economic integration dramatically.[55]

Besides the economic integration, China is seeking social and political integration with the world community as well. China signed the International Covenant on Economic, Social and Cultural Rights in June 1998 and the International Covenant on Civil and Political Rights in October 1998. Although the ratification by the National People's Congress of the UN rights treaties will take many years,[56] it creates great expectations among the Chinese people that a freer society is coming nearer and nearer to them.

The increasing economic integration with the world community has also promoted mutual understanding between the Chinese people and peoples of other countries and facilitate cultural exchanges. For example, in 1994 there were over 43 million foreign tourists coming into China and more than 6.1 million Chinese visiting other countries and the number of incoming foreign tourists and outgoing Chinese climbed to over 63 million and 8.4 million in 1998.[57]

Since 1978 China has abandoned its former practice of only conducting cultural exchanges with a few countries and regions and begun to promote cultural exchanges with every part of the world. China's foreign cultural exchanges have taken various forms, including the Central government sponsored, local government-sponsored, non-governmental, and commercial performances and exhibitions. By 1999 China has signed cultural co-operation agreements with 138 countries and sent over 230 cultural delegations abroad and received more than 400 foreign delegations. China has maintained various kinds of relations with several thousand foreign and international cultural organizations in the fields of literature, art, cultural relics, books museums, press, publishing, radio broadcasting, film, television, sports, education, science and technology, public health, youths, women, tourism and religion. Each year, the number of international cultural exchange programs approved by the Ministry of Culture exceeds 1,000, with the number of participants surpassing 10,000. For example, in 1997, the Ministry approved 1,600 exchange programs with the participation of more than 22,000 people. The respective number was 16 and 40 times greater than the annual average number during Mao's era.[58]

With the deepening of reform and opening, the situation of 'walling the culture off from international exchanges' has been broken. Cultural exchanges expanding on such a large scale and covering such a wide range of interests, have been unprecedented and have far exceeded people's expectations before reform and opening. Through actively introducing the excellent cultural achievements of other countries, China has greatly enriched its cultural undertakings and promoted the development of its cultural market. On today's Chinese stages, people can enjoy both classical and modern ballet, folk songs and dances, operas performed by artists from all over the world, performances of famous international symphony orchestras, and films and TV programs made in Europe and the United States. The broadening of Chinese cultural exchanges with other countries has certainly played an important role in remolding people's living habits and attitudes towards personal and public issues, which may facilitate social transformations towards the patterns characteristic of liberal democratic societies. Younger generations seem to be more receptive to such influence than older generations. For example, more

Chinese youngsters like to watch Hollywood films, drink Cocoa Cola, and eat hamburgers and Kentucky fried chicken.

From Economic Reform to Legal Reform

In order to accommodate the market-oriented economic reform, China has begun a gradual but profound shift from the rule of the party towards the rule of law, which is represented by a shift of policy institutionalization towards Type B and Type A processes (see Table 3.1). It may be one important characteristic of China's political reform, leading gradually towards political liberalization and democratization.

From the Rule of Man to the Rule of the Party

In the aftermath of the Cultural Revolution the Chinese pondered the cause of the Cultural Revolution that had devastated the economy, the society, and the party. One famous intellectual, Liang Shuming, concluded that the main cause was the rule of man. The Constitution existed only on paper and had not been treated as the highest authority. China had been governed by man rather than according to law (Wang, 1998a, pp.159-61; Cheng, 1999, p.3). The rule of man had been executed to its zenith by Mao Zedong in the Cultural Revolution. Liang Shuming thought that with the end of the Cultural Revolution China had just embarked on the transition from the rule of man to the rule of law. Although many Chinese scholars stressed that the rule of law should be the principle of governance, it was not until 1982 when the supremacy of the rule of law was written into Article 5 of the 1982 Constitution:

> All state organs, the armed forces, all political parties and public organizations and all enterprises and institutions must abide by the Constitution and the law. All acts in violation of the Constitution and the law must be investigated. No organization or individual is privileged to be beyond the Constitution or the law.

The Constitution, however, did not usher in an era of the rule of law in China. Instead, since China started its economic reform in 1978, it has entered a phase of the rule of the party. The CPC resolutions and policy circulars are looked upon as the rules of game, especially when there is no existing law or regulation available, or when the reform practice is in contradiction with the existing law and the Constitution. For example, the agricultural family responsibility contract system and the dismantling of the agricultural collective system were started as early as 1979 but relevant amendments were not added to the Constitution until 1993. The instrumental view of the rule of law was supported by the CPC ruling elite who would like to build a legal system that could promote economic development without weakening its monopoly of power. Governing under the rule of law was therefore replaced with the building of a socialist legal system under the rule of the party. Since a market economy was accepted as the target of the economic reform in 1992, efforts have been strengthened to draft sets of laws and rules that would safeguard the normal function of the market economy under construction instead of relying on the party's resolutions and policy circulars.

From the Rule of the Party to the Rule of Law

The momentum of the legal reform eventually led to the rule of law being accepted by the CPC[59] and an amendment was added to Article 5 of the Constitution: 'The People's Republic of China is governed according to the law and aims to build a socialist country under the rule of law'. The endorsement of the principle of the rule of law has profound implications for China's political reform. It has speeded up the drafting of laws and regulations. By February 1998, the National People's Congress and its Standing Committee have passed 327 laws and resolutions on legal affairs, the State Council formulated more than 750 administrative regulations, and the local people's congresses and governments have worked out over 5,300 local regulations and rules. By the end of 1999, the Constitution had been revised six times to reflect the fundamental economic and social changes (Jiang, Feng and Ji, 1999, pp.321-7).

Firstly, there are more national administrative regulations than laws, indicating a strong administrative dominance in the institutionalization process.[60] These features reflect the historical, economic and political conditions of China. When China embarked on her legal reform required by the economic reform and opening-up programs, it had more of Mao's personal ideological instructions than administrative regulations and laws. China had to build its framework of regulations and laws from scratch. On the policy initiation front, the CPC Central Committee and its Politburo always takes a lead in initiating reform and opening-up guidelines that may be, sometimes, contradictory to the socialist principles and ideology it upholds. In terms of institutionalizing detailed laws and regulations, since the National People's Congress convenes yearly for a dozen days and its Standing Committee hold meetings periodically, it has to delegate its legislative power to the State Council to draft regulations. Since 1982 the provincial level people's congresses and their standing committees have acquired legislative powers to draft and pass local regulations and rules but, owing to the same institutional handicap, has to delegate legislative power to local governments. Besides, the State Council and provincial governments can draft new rules to regulate activities within their administrative scope, without seeking legislative delegation from the relevant people's congress whenever there are no available pertinent laws and national administrative regulations.

As a result, China witnessed a proliferation of local regulations and rules and a faster growth of national administrative regulations than laws. However, as China's market economy is drawing to its maturity, the legislative institutionalization is in a transition from the administrative dominance, represented by the legislative discretionary powers of the government, to the dominance of the state legislative body. For example, the percentage of the new rules that do not require legislative delegation from the Shanghai People's Congress is declining (see Table 5.1).

Table 5.1 Legislative Discretionary Powers of the Shanghai Government

Year	Total Rules	Administrative New Rules	Percentage
1979 - 1985	186	115	61.83
1986 - 1990	250	150	60
1991 - 1995	234	111	47.44
1996	35	19	54.29
1997	36	16	44.44

Source: Adapted from Gu and Wang, 1999, p.259.

Secondly, most of the national laws and regulations have been drafted after 1978 and concern the establishment of a market economy and the regulation of economic activities, and some of them deal with legislation and the relationship between the state and the society.[61] All these laws will prepare the nation for the rule of law but those regulating legislation and the relationship between the state and the society will have greater implications for building the rule of law in China. For example, on 15th March 2000, the Legislation Law was adopted at the Third Session of the Ninth NPC. The significance of the Legislation Law is its stipulation of the exclusive legislative power to the NPC in enacting national laws, excluding the CPC from any direct involvement in the legislative process, although the leadership of the CPC is confirmed in principle in the preamble. This development represents a shift of institutionalization towards Type B and Type A processes (see Table 3.1.).

On the relationship between the state and the society, three laws have been enacted and put into implementation.[62] They provide legal protection to individuals and economic entities against illegal acts and predatory behavior of the state personnel and agencies and will, through their implementation, promote a legal sense and behavior between the ruling and the ruled. The rapid development of legal right awareness in the society is indicated by a study of administrative litigation lawsuits conducted by Minxin Pei. The study shows that the number of cases accepted and processed by the court has kept rising, from less than 1,000 in 1986 to 79,527 in 1996 (Pei, 1997, pp.832-62). Of those cases tried, the court rulings favorable to plaintiffs are rising from 11 per cent in 1988 to 15 per cent in 1995, while the court rulings favorable to defendants declining from 49 per cent in 1988 to 17 per cent in 1995.

Therefore, with the gradual completion of the laws and regulations for the market economy under construction, a second phase of China's legislation has already been ushered in, focusing on how to regulate the relationship between the state and the society and social and political activities, although the legislation regulating political activities seems more difficult to appear at present. However, economic freedom offered by a market economy in China is leading to a demand for political reform.[63] A case in point is the abortive attempt to add an amendment, proposed by liberal deputies to the Ninth National People's Congress, to Article 12 of the Constitution, which outlaws any infringement of socialist public assets, by including the 'private assets of citizens'.[64] With the growing accumulation of private assets,[65] the Chinese people are likely to become more and more assertive in protecting their private assets. And the ruling elite and experts are again talking publicly about further improving legal protection of the private assets.[66] The issue of a constitutional amendment for further protecting private assets will be raised on future National People's Congresses until private assets have received the same legal protection as public assets.

What Deng Xiaoping wanted from the political reform twenty years ago was to separate the party from the government (the executive branch of the state) and he later even dropped the reform idea owing to the domestic and international political situation in the late 1980s.[67] To turn China into a country under the rule of law needs more than that. Most important, it requires a new relationship between the party and the People's Congress (the legislature), between the party and other minor parties, and between the party and the society. For example, the party should be in the legislature but not above it, turning the party's proposals into laws through legislative procedures. It requires independence of the Judiciary, which is critical in implementing the rule of law. It also needs to set up the mechanism of Judicial Review and an independent Constitutional Court, which are essential in guaranteeing the authority of the Constitution and the citizen's legal rights from being encroached upon by the ruling elite and the government agencies.[68]

Obviously, to transform China from the rule of party to the rule of law is much more difficult than to change its command economy into a market economy, because the CPC has to redefine its role and purpose[69] under the rule of law, such as how to separate itself from the government, how to conduct activities in the legislature (the People's Congress), how to co-operate with other minor parties on equal terms, how to put the party under the supervision and check of the whole society, and most important, how to maintain its leading position in the government through fair and free elections rather than through coercive forces. All these require not only the drafting of laws on political organization, civil society and public media but also the effective enforcement of the laws.[70] Considering the CPC ruling elite control the institutionalization of reform guidelines, it may take a long time for such laws to come through the drafting and approving process because their adoption will further provide freedom to society while, at the same time, further narrowing arbitrary actions of the CPC. For example, the Media Law was proposed as early as 1980 and its drafting started in 1984 but now is still in its drafting stage. Many scholars call for the drafting of Law on Political Organizations but it is not even in the legislative agenda. The reason why they are so difficult to draft is that the principles they uphold, such as free association and free speech, are in direct contradiction with the CPC ideology. Any breakthrough in the second phase of legislation depends, to a large extent, on revising the CPC's increasingly obsolete fundamental ideology.

Conclusion

It took China nearly 14 years to officially abandon its command economic system and to adopt a market-oriented economic system. Considering that the plan is usually considered as one of the principal features of socialism and that the market is normally associated with capitalism, the plan-market transition has created a new economic institutional environment within which the ruling elite make policy choices (see Figure 2.2). This has great implications for China's future economic and political developments. The second important change is in the international environment. After more than twenty years of opening up to the rest of the world, China's increasing integration with the world community in economic, cultural and political spheres has become an important factor in influencing future policy institutionalization. In the context of the changing institutional environments, the institutional behavior of the ruling elite has also been in constant change. Summarized below are patterns of this transitional policy institutionalization, the ruling elite's institutionalization behavior, and their consequences.

Firstly, the institutionalization behavior of Deng Xiaoping was quite different from that of Mao Zedong, perhaps because Deng had no such charismatic leadership qualities as Mao Zedong, Zhou Enlai and Zhu De, or because he was strictly observing the principle of the collective leadership in decision making. The striking difference between Mao Zedong and Deng Xiaoping lies in their manner of initiating, institutionalizing and implementing economic and opening policies. Mao Zedong preferred to devise and formulate policies based on his vision of socialism and communism for China, particularly on his doctrine of continual class struggle that was endless until communism. Mao was also determined to have his policy guidelines accepted by his colleagues and the general public through waging class struggle within the party as well as in the whole society. Mao would like to see that his policies were followed strictly, sometimes to the extreme of refusing to listen to different opinions. Deng Xiaoping preferred to give more general direction for reform and encourage party members and the general public to experiment with various innovations, and then based on the experience and lessons of the reform experiment drew reform policies. Deng would like his reform policies to be followed according to the actual situation of the area where the policies were implemented.

Mao's manner is basically one-way traffic from the center to the periphery, while Deng's manner is a two-way channel, offering an exchange of views between the center and the periphery. This two-way institutionalization behavior of the CPC chief actor was not only conducive to political pluralism among the ruling elite but also provided favorable conditions for policy innovations, making it possible for the agricultural reform and the opening up to survive and prosper. However, on institutionalizing political reform policies, Deng was only a rational political calculator who was concerned more about his political survival than about the political future of the CPC. Perhaps Deng did not get the time to consider how to shift the basis of the legitimacy of the CPC's rule from its self-claimed vanguard leading position in the society in accordance with the social and economic transformations generated by economic reforms and opening up, and according to the rule of law endorsed by the CPC. Or, perhaps, he did not think that it was time to make such a strategic political transition.

Deng's successor Jiang Zemin has much less natural or crafted leadership endowments as his predecessor's and therefore, his institutionalization behavior cannot afford to deviate from the Deng's two-way traffic pattern. Therefore, before he submits policy proposals to the CPC Central Committee for consideration, he usually reveals his policy institutionalization intentions, such as the adoption of a socialist market economy in 1992 and the acknowledgement of the private sector as an important component of the Chinese economy in 1997, to provincial leaders who are usually in Beijing attending conferences or on a training program in the CPC Central Party School.

Secondly, the rationale of the ruling elite's institutionalization has shifted from aiming at the ideological purity of socialism and communism in Mao's era to focusing on pragmatic economic benefits for the general public and the society in the post-Mao's era. Although the ruling elite are still upholding the four cardinal principles,[71] this fundamental shift may generate enough economic, social and political pressure for a revision, redefinition, or even discarding of the contents of the four cardinal principles. The preliminary stage of socialism proposed in 1987 to justify the restoration of private ownership and to tolerate bourgeois exploitation is an example of the revision in the party's ideology on socialism to justify the ruling elite's reform measures, which will be discussed in the next chapter.

Thirdly, policy institutionalization, which used to originate from the center – the supreme actor in Mao's era, may start from the periphery – local leaders and people in the post-Mao era. A classic example was the peasants' innovation of the household contract responsibility system. Since 1982 the people's congresses and municipalities directly under the Central Government and their standing committees may adopt local regulations.[72] Some of the local regulations are later adapted by the Central Government for national implementation. For example, the Shanghai People's Congress adopted 'Regulations of Shanghai Municipality on Liquidation of Enterprises with Foreign Investment' in 1991. Based on the Shanghai regulation, the State Council issued a national regulation in 1996.[73] This backward process of policy institutionalization from the periphery to the center has not only reduced the possibility of irrational national policies but also substantially increased the weight of the periphery in the national policy institutionalization. The central ruling elite would like to tap the peripheral institutionalization resources whenever they consider it necessary. The two southern tours of Deng Xiaoping were two such cases of rallying the peripheral support by the central ruling elite for his national policy initiatives.

Fourthly, when the agricultural household contract responsibility system was introduced and the peasants were given back their independent producer status, the impact on the old system, in the form of large available quantities of agricultural produce and extra labor, was beyond its capacity to deal with the new situation, forcing the ruling elite to adopt market-oriented measures.[74] This indicates that the market-oriented reform has a development path of its own internal logic. The ruling elite could neither dictate the process nor the outcome. For example, the agricultural reform and opening measures had been intended to improve, not to dismantle the old command economic system. When the reform and opening processes were started, however, the ruling elite could not control the impact of the deepening reform and the broadening opening, which eventually led to the end of the old economic system, facilitating the transition from the rule of the party to the rule of law. To a large extent, market-oriented reforms are stripping authoritarian elements out of the economic system, restoring freedom and rights to pursue wealth to the mass public, which may eventually develop into a public demand for a polity where the government accountability is guaranteed.

Fifthly, the formulation of a complete set of laws and regulations to sustain proper functions of a market economy, although dominated by the CPC ruling elite, suggests a shift of institutionalization towards Type B and Type A processes (see Table 3.1), enlarging freedom and rights to the society and the general public while narrowing the discretionary power of the party and state apparatus. It is a meaningful change in the domestic political and constitutional environments (see Figure 2.2) that may have significant implications for democratic institutional developments in China. It may be an evolutionary legal development that is stripping authoritarian elements out of the political system while its economy is growing out of the plan.

As the general public are getting more and more economic freedom and independence of the party and state apparatus, they will become more and more critical of the regime and more and more willing to influence the policy and legislative institutionalization because they are associating their economic well-being with sound and proper policy institutionalization and administration. It represents a change in the domestic civil-social environment that may cultivate and lead to demands for more accountability of the government and the ruling elite, conducive to democratization. The student and mass demonstrations of 1989, although suppressed by the conservative ruling elite, represented a strong indication of the potential force of the mass public. Whenever their economic welfare is seriously affected, the public outrage may erupt again, which is a time bomb that the ruling elite have to disable in a timely and proper manner.

In conclusion, the analysis of the ruling elite's policy institutionalization for the agricultural reform and opening measures indicates some meaningful institutional transformations have occurred in China, namely, (1) an emerging new economic environment represented by people's freedom and right to pursue wealth in a market economy, which facilitates and generates changes in other domestic environments (see Figure 2.2), conducive to further economic and political liberalization; (2) a developing legal environment with the rule of law phasing out the rule of the party; (3) a changing pattern of institutionalization with the periphery increasing their weight in the national institutionalization process; and (4) an awakening general public who would exert their influence over the policy institutionalization when the time came. Under these changing domestic environments, the ruling elite seem to have little choice but to have authoritarian elements to be dismantled, although little by little, out of the economic system, and they may also have little choice but to have authoritarian elements to be gradually stripped off the political system, willingly or unwillingly.

Notes

1   Hua Guofeng resigned his premiership in September 1980, party chairmanship and military commission Chairmanship in June 1981.

2   Under the unified state allocation or distribution were 227 categories of goods and materials in 1953, 532 categories in 1957 and 689 categories in 1978.   Private distribution of goods and materials were strictly prohibited although the state materials agencies and the state commercial departments could not possibly handle every type of goods in a timely manner.   For example, many mountain products were rotting in mountains because they could not be shipped out on time.   As a result, the output of many mountain products declined by 70 to 80 per cent in 1978 compared to 1949.   For more discussion, see Yang, 1998, p.310.

3   Deng (1983, p.126) unequivocally stressed the reform of the economic system and the organizational system beside the technological reform when he spoke to the Ninth National Congress of the Chinese Trade Union in October 1978.

4   Chen Yun was a key party veteran.   He was elected into the CPC Central Committee in 1931 and into the CPC Politburo.   He entered the CPC Politburo Standing Committee as Deng Xiaoping in September 1956.   He was dismissed from his positions during the Cultural Revolution and was re-elected into the CPC Politburo Standing Committee in December 1978.   While Deng Xiaoping was mainly responsible for day-to-day party activities, Chen Yun had mainly engaged in the management of economic activities of the party state apparatus since 1944.

5   Chen Yun proposed to let the state-owned and collective economic entities play the principal role while allowing individual economic undertakings to play a subordinate role; to let the planned production play the principal role while allowing free production in the areas designated by the state plan to play a subordinate role; and to let the state markets play the principal role while allowing the free markets guided by the state to play a subordinate role.   Chen's economic model was criticized as the 'economic guideline of the revisionism' and 'rightist thought' in early 1960s.

6   He was a member of the CPC Politburo Standing Committee and Vice-Premier, responsible for the fiscal and economic policies in the late 1970s and the early 1980s.

7   In the political report of the CPC 12th National Congress in September 1982, the mandatory plans were meant to cover the state sector of the economy, including its production and distribution of capital goods and consumption goods essential for national welfare and the people's livelihood; and the guiding plans were meant to cover the collective sector.

8   Deng's pragmatism dates back to 1962 when he advocated letting peasants adopt whatever form of production, provided it could easily and swiftly restore and develop agricultural production, no matter whether it was based on the people's commune, the production brigade, the production team, or the household contract responsibility system.   He even proposed to legalize it if it was an illegal practice (Deng, 1989, p.305).

9   By the end of 1952 when the land reform ended, poor peasants and farm laborers nearly doubled their land holdings, middle peasants increased their holdings by nearly 15 percentage points, rich peasants' holdings were reduced by 11.3 percentage points, and landlords' holdings were cut down by 26.6 percentage points.   For more discussion, see Selden, 1979, p.35-9.

10   In 1961 and 1962, it was estimated 20 per cent of the Agricultural Production Teams adopted various forms of the household contract responsibility system.   Some provinces had a much higher percentage of production teams in practicing the production responsibility; for example, Anhui 80 per cent, Guizhou 40 per cent, and Ninxia and

Gansu 74 per cent. For more discussion of Mao's suppression of the peasants' innovation regarding agricultural production, see Li, 1998b, pp.623-32; Yang, 1996b, pp.42-97.

11   In October 1961 a survey was conducted of the 36 Production Teams that had adopted the household contract responsibility system and found they produced, on average, 26.9 per cent more grain than those that had not. For more discussion, see Li, 1998b, p.597.

12   In 1962 Liu Shaoqi, Chen Yun and Deng Xiaoping, members of the CPC Politburo, supported the idea of implementing the agricultural household contract responsibility system in the aftermath of the Great Leap Forward, which had led some twenty-seven million people to unnatural death. For more discussion see Li, 1998b, pp.594-632.

13   A group of households usually consisted of several or a dozen households, which was considered easier to manage than a production team that contained several dozens or even several hundreds of households.

14   He was a close associate of Deng Xiaoping and was transferred to Anhui in June 1977 after successfully rectifying, as the Minister of the Railway Ministry, the chaos of the Chinese railway transportation.

15   The contract is now on display in the Museum of the Chinese Revolution.

16   Dali L. Yang considered that the Great Leap Forward Famine had a great impact on the peasants' decision to adopt the household contract responsibility system. For more discussion, see Yang, 1996b.

17   Zhou Yueli was Director of the Rural Work Committee of the Anhui CPC Committee. For a discussion of Hua's opposition against the household contract responsibility system, see Ma and Ling, 1998, pp.127-8. For a discussion of Hua's enthusiasm for the agricultural collective model, the Dazhai Production Brigade, see Yang, 1996b, pp.124-6.

18   He orchestrated the discussion of the criteria of truth and was elected into the CPC Politburo in December 1978.

19   Since 1957 the Xiao Gang Production Team had never delivered any grain to the state but received grain from the state to feed its peasants. For more discussion, see Jiang and Fu, 1994, p.943.

20   The rural per capita income of Feng Yang County was 81 RMB *yuan* in 1978 and 368 RMB *yuan* in 1983. For more discussion, see Jiang and Fu, 1994, p.944.

21   For more discussion, see Yang, 1998, pp.187-9.

22   Sideline occupations and products refer to non-agricultural activities and products engaged and produced by rural households as a complement to their main agricultural activities and income, including hunting of wild animals, harvesting of wide vegetation and manufacturing of handicraft products, agricultural processed products and small commodities. From 1993, the category of sideline occupations have been cancelled, hunting of wild animals is classified into husbandry, and harvesting of wild vegetation and commodity industry run by rural households are grouped into the category of agriculture.

23   However, as the CPC Central Committee stressed the self-determination of peasants over whether or not to adopt the household responsibility system, there are still some villages that are still practicing collective production, such as the Da Qiu Village in Tianjin, the Liu Zhuang Village in Hunan Province, and the Hua Xi Village in Jiangsu Province.

24   It was the 1978 population figure. *Data source: China Statistical Yearbook 1999*, p. 111.

25   It was estimated that the total value of agricultural production (constant price) between 1978 and 1984 increased by 42.23 per cent, of which 46.89 per cent came from the raised productivity in direct connection with the adoption of the household contract responsibility system. The peasants' annual real income grew by 15.1 per cent and the agricultural population under poverty line reduced by two thirds. For more discussion, see Zhang, Huang and Li, 1998, pp.81-2.

26 From 1982 on, the CPC officially encouraged peasants to engage in non-agricultural activities, see the highlights of the CPC major new policy guidelines listed above. Certainly, these policy guidelines were based on the actual market conditions; in other words, the market also encouraged the transfer of the surplus agricultural labor into non-agricultural activities.

27 In Jiangsu Province where township and village enterprises developed more rapidly, 23.6 per cent of steel, 19.9 per cent of coal and 22.2 per cent of timber were transferred to township and village enterprises through extra-plan co-operation in 1978. For more discussion, see Yang, 1998, pp.193-5.

28 For more discussion of commodity distribution reform, see Wan, 1998, pp.133-55; Gui, 1998, pp.210-11. For more discussion of the pricing reform, see Taylor, 1996, pp.36-8.

29 On 5th March 1983, the CPC Central Committee and the State Council issued 'Instructions on the Development of Rural and Urban Retail Commercial and Service Industries'. On 25th February 1984, the State Council issued 'Regulations on Several Issues Concerning the Transporting of Goods for sale by Co-operative Commercial Enterprises and Individuals'.

30 *Data source*: *China Statistical Yearbook 1999*, p.553.

31 In 1978 there were only 150,000 self-employed individuals working in urban areas. In 1981 there were 1.83 million self-employed entrepreneurs in both rural and urban areas, and the number rose to 13.73 million in 1987. *Data source*: *China Statistical Yearbook 1997*, p.97; and Zhang and Ming, 1998, p.65.

32 There were six members and the other members of the Politburo Standing Committee referred to Yie Jianying, Chen Yun, Li Xiannian.

33 In the 1950s, China received technical and financial assistance in building and renovating 156 key industrial projects. For more discussion, see Feng, Mao, et al., 1996, pp.714-9.

34 The economic waves of the five successive industrial revolutions are shortening, from 50-60 years to around 30-40 years. For more discussion, see 'A Survey of Innovation in Industry', *The Economist*, 20th February 1999.

35 In May 1978 a government delegation headed by Vice-Premier Gu Mu had a tour of France, West Germany, Switzerland, Denmark, and Belgium. Vice-Premier Gu Mu reported the hard fact to the CPC Politburo.

36 It was estimated that a third of 18 million overseas Chinese came from Chao Shan, Guangdong Province. For more discussion, see Fong, Mao, et al, 1996, p.774.

37 The four special economic zones are Shenzhen SEZ, Zhuhai SEZ, Shantou SEZ, and Xiameng SEZ.

38 They include 'The Law of the PRC on Sino-foreign Joint Venture Enterprises' in July 1979, 'The Law of the PRC on the Corporate Income Tax of Sino-foreign Joint Venture Enterprises' in September 1980, 'The Law of the PRC on the Corporate Income Tax of Wholly Foreign-funded Enterprises' in December 1981, 'The Law of the PRC on Wholly Foreign-funded Enterprises' in April 1984, and 'The Law of the PRC on Economic Contracts Involving Foreign Interests' in July 1985. In 1982, the Constitution also added an article to legalize foreign investment in China.

39 For detailed discussion, see Jiang and Fu, 1994, pp. 856-65.

40 Chinese ministries, conglomerates, other provinces and cities rushed to invest in the SEZs in order to capitalize on the preferential policies of the SEZs. For example, in Hainan SEZ, the fifth SEZ set up in 1988, about half of the investment was made by domestic investors. For more discussion, see Feng, Mao, et al., 1996, pp.784-5.

41 They include joint ventures, co-operative operations, and wholly foreign-funded enterprises.

42   They include international lease, compensation trade, and processing and assembly projects.

43   *Data source: China Statistical Yearbook 1996, 1999*; Jiang and Fu, 1994, pp.845-55.

44   See Guo, 1998, pp.148-9; and *China Economic Times*, 22nd December 1998.

45   Major forms of official corruption in 1980s included abusing resource distribution power, levying illegal fees, engaging in profit-making business, embezzling public funds, and seeking and taking bribery.

46   For a discussion of the 1986-1987 student demonstrations, see Harding, 1987.

47   Fang Lizhi used to be Vice President of China Science and Technology University; Liu Binyan used be journalist of the *People's Daily*; and Wang Ruowang was a noted writer of Shanghai.

48   For more discussion, see Yang, 1998, pp.491-5; Harding, 1987, pp.191-201.

49   For more discussion, see Yang, 1998, pp.504-8.

50   For a detailed discussion of the 'leftist' conservative attack on economic reform and the open-door policy, see Yang, 1998, pp.332-3; Ma and Ling, 1998, pp.160-3.

51   For a detailed discussion of the opening following Deng's southern tour, see Guo, 1998, pp.159-63; Yang, 1998, pp. 264-5.

52   *Data source: China Statistical Yearbook 2002.*

53   *Data source*: MOFTEC.

54   *Data source*: UNCTAD, *World Investment Report* 1999.

55   In 2002, its import and export value reached 620.785 billion US dollars, 21.77 per cent increase over last year; its foreign direct investment amounted to 52.743 billion US dollars, 12.51 per cent higher than the previous year. *Data source*: MOFTEC.

56   At a press conference in Beijing on 1st November 2000, Chinese Foreign Ministry spokesman Zhu Bangzao said that the State Council's proposal on the ratification of the International Covenant on Economic, Social and Cultural Rights was favorably deliberated by the Standing Committee of the National People's Congress. Many members of the NPC Standing Committee suggested that the covenant relates to China's economic and social elements and should be passed at an early and proper date on the basis of comprehensive and detailed studies. *Xinhua Mews Service*, Wednesday, 1st November 2000, www.xinhuanet.com.

57   *China Statistical Yearbook 1999*, p. 609.

58   For more information, see *A Bridge Promoting Mutual Understanding, China's International Cultural Exchanges over the Past 20 Years*, (http://www.prc50.com/guoqing/cultural-htm) (26th October 1999).

59   The rule of law was endorsed by the CPC at its Fifteenth National Congress in September 1997. For more discussion, see Hao, 1999.

60   Over 70 per cent of the laws were proposed by the State Council and the majority of the local regulations were proposed by the local governments. For more discussion, see Gu and Wang, 1999, PP.246-59.

61   They regulate market actors, market activities and orders, macro-economy, foreign currencies, foreign investment, labor and management relations, regulating state-society relationship, and legislation.

62   They are the Administration Litigation Law, passed on 4th April 1989 and implemented on 1st October 1990, the State Compensation Law passed on 12th May 1994 and implemented on 1st January 1995, and the Administrative Reconsideration Law passed on 29th April and implemented on 1st October 1999.

63   Economic reform leads to a demand for political freedom, if it could result in a wide distribution of power resources. For further discussion, see Lipset, 1959. pp.*69-105*; and 1994, pp.1-22; see Inglehart, 1997; and also see Francis, 1999.

64   See *South China Morning Post*, Friday, 26th February, and Thursday, 4th March 1999.

65 It is estimated that the Chinese people have at least financial assets of over 9,480.4 billion RMB *yuan* (over 1,145 billion UUS dollars), including private saving deposit of 7,376.2 billion RMB *yuan* (2001), and private enterprise registered capital of 2,104.2 billion RMB *yuan* (June 2002). *Data source: China Statistical Yearbook 2002*; Chen, 2003.

66 Jiang Zemin touched the issue in his political report he delivered at the CPC 16th National Congress on 8th November 2002.   Dong Puqi, a well-known economist, stressed the importance of this issue, see *China Economic Times* 《中国经济时报》, 17th December 2002, p.1.

67 Guixiu Wang believed that there might be two factors which influenced Deng's withdrawal from the political reform. First, domestic and international situations were unfavorable for launching the political reform: the crackdown of the students demonstration in the Tiananmen Square on June 4th 1989 and the swift dismantling of the communist rule in the Eastern European countries and the Soviet Union. Second, the political reform was a complicated and long-term project, which could not possibly be completed in his lifetime, Deng was afraid. For more discussion, see Wang, 1999, p.34.

68 For more discussion of independence of the Judiciary, see *21ˢᵗ CN Business Herald* 《21 世纪经济报道》, 30th December 2002, p.6; *China Economic Times*, 15ᵗʰ November 2002, p.3.

69 For more discussion of this necessity, see Oksenberg, 1999.

70 The high speed of drafting and enacting laws is sharply contrasted with the weak enforcement of the laws in China. The problem of the weak law enforcement may be mainly attributed to people's weak sense of their legal rights, a complete lack of independence of the judiciary, the one-party monopoly of power and a marked lack of the absolute authority of laws in China, where the political institutional arrangement still holds power higher than law.   As a result, only about a third of the existing laws are being observed well and fairly well (Shi, et al., 1998, p.175) and the rural officials are selective as to which laws and regulations to observe (O'Brien and Li, 1999). However, drafting and enacting laws represent a first step towards the establishment of the unchallenged supremacy of laws in China. For more discussion, see Shi, et al., 1998, pp.159-218.

71 Namely, socialism, the dictatorship of the proletariat, leadership of the CPC, and Marxism, Leninism and Mao Zedong Thought.

72 The Article 100 of the 1982 Constitution of China.

73 'The Procedures on Liquidation of Enterprises with Foreign Investment'. For more discussion, see Chen, 2000.

74 They include such measures as decentralizing power from the center to the periphery, liberalizing commodity and labor markets, relaxing price control, restoring private ownership, and building a legal framework.

Chapter 6

Restoration of Private Enterprises and Property Rights

As discussed in the previous chapter, it is the restoration of the independent peasant producer that created an economic and material foundation for the rebirth of private ownership and private enterprises in China. It was unexpected by the CPC ruling elite that the agricultural reform and opening measures, which were meant to help sustain the planned economy, generated market forces and initiated the plan-market transition. Also unexpected, the private individual economy, in the form of specialised production households in the rural areas and self-employed producers and traders in the urban areas, developed into a ballooning private sector. When established as legal economic entities, private enterprises swiftly developed into an indispensable component of the economy, compelling the ruling elite to change their policies from restrictive control to open encouragement.

It took the CPC ruling elite 14 years to adopt a market economy to replace the planned economy, which represents a verdict on the state centralised distribution of resources. It took the ruling elite more years, nearly 20 years, to accept the private sector as an important component of the socialist market economy because the restoration of private enterprises based on private ownership challenges the essence of socialism. If foreign-funded enterprises were encouraged by the open-door policy on the grounds that foreign investment would bring capital, advanced technology, new equipment, and management expertise into China, the rebirth of Chinese domestic private enterprises was discouraged by the party and state apparatus until its contribution to the economy, in terms of job and wealth creation, could no longer be ignored. This chapter traces the development of private enterprises on the one hand and the revision of the ruling party's ideology on ownership on the other, trying to explain how the private enterprise has risen like a phoenix from the ashes, why the ruling elite had to revise the party ideology to accommodate the rebirth of private enterprises based on private ownership, and the implications for political developments in China.

A Tale of Socialism: Eliminating Exploiting Classes and Private Ownership

In retrospect, Mao's implementation of his vision of socialism in China since 1949 consisted of a series of campaigns and revolutions, which had two distinguishable stages: (1) eliminating exploiting classes and private ownership of capital goods that was considered by Marxists as the origins of evil; and (2) eliminating anyone, such as 'Rightists' and 'Capitalist Roaders', who dared to question Mao's socialist guidelines. The land reform in the early years of the Republic deprived the landlord of their land and property, effectively wiping out the landlord class. The socialist transformation campaign in 1953-1956 practically deprived peasants, handicraftsmen and national and petty bourgeois of their private ownership of capital goods, although differential policies applied to them.

During the early years of the People's Republic of China, the private capitalist sector occupied a very important place in the economy of the new People's Republic, accounting for 63.2 per cent of the gross industrial output value, 76 per cent of the wholesale trade, and 85 per cent of the retail trade (Zhu, Yao, Zou and Hu, 1998, p.67). Chinese national capitalist industrial and commercial enterprises underwent a two-stage socialist transformation: (1) from private capitalist enterprises into state capitalist enterprises in 1949-1952, and (2) from state capitalist enterprises into socialist state-owned enterprises in 1953-1956. The first-stage transformation was in fact a state-private corporatism with the private enterprises maintaining their ownership of capital goods and the state heavily engaged in ordering, purchasing and marketing the products of private enterprises. For example, 56 per cent of the private enterprises' output value were handled through the state purchase and marketing channels in 1952 (Zhang, Kong and Deng, 1993, p.543). The second-stage turned private enterprises into state-private joint ventures with the private enterprises handing over to the state their capital goods and the state paying private enterprise owners, as compensation, a fixed rate of interest on their capital share in the joint venture. By the end of 1956, all private enterprises ceased to exist through the state-private joint venture scheme based on the state policy of redemption.

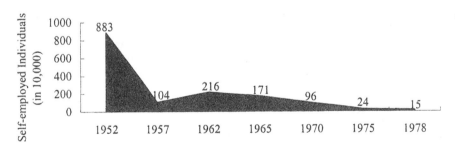

Figure 6.1   Squeezing Self-employed Individuals out of Business, 1952-1978

Source : China Statistical Yearbook 1997 and 1999 .

By the end of 1956, therefore, the CPC ruling elite had succeeded in replacing capitalist private ownership with socialist public ownership, wiping out exploiting classes and eliminating exploitation in China. Thereafter, Mao embarked on building his vision of socialism in China and eliminated anyone in his way, including intellectuals in 1957 and his colleagues in 1958 and 1966, who held different views on China's socialist construction. From 1957 to 1977 the state and collective sectors dominated China's economy. In 1978 there were only 150,000 self-employed people in urban areas (see Figure 6.1), working as shoe-repairers, bicycle-menders, small shop owners, and other community service providers, while in rural areas all the economic activities were brought under the collective umbrella.[1]

Unfortunately, Mao's socialist construction experiment, based on continual and endless class struggles, made Chinese people worse off than in 1957 (see Table 3.4), offering Deng Xiaoping an opportunity to launch a 'Second Revolution' to uplift Chinese people from poverty. Just like Mao Zedong's first revolution that relied on peasants to overthrow the KMT rule, Deng Xiaoping's 'Second Revolution' relied on hungry peasants to work out an economic development path that based on freedom to pursue wealth. This wealth pursuing freedom led naturally to freedom to hold private property including property of capital goods. Deng's economic development strategy, therefore, presupposed restoration of private ownership of capital goods in China.

The Origins of the Rebirth of Private Ownership: Rural and Urban Self-employed Producers and Traders

Before 1978 a successful small commodities market that involved private producers and traders would usually alert the party and state apparatus to the danger of the restoration of capitalism. If private producers and traders were found making profits, 'Capitalist Restoration' was the best excuse to close down the market and 'New Bourgeois' was the easy charge against those private producers and traders. For example, in 1971 there was a prosperous small commodities market in the Shi Shi County, Fujian Province, involving 318 registered self-employed industrial and commercial producers and traders and over 200 more without licenses. The small commodities market was considered by the regime as an example of 'Restoration of Capitalism' and closed down. Twelve private workshops were sealed up and five operators were arrested. One of them, Wu Xiayun, was sentenced to a seven-year imprisonment for his 'illegal' income of 7000 RMB *yuan* (about 2,845 US dollars).[2] In 1974 the Shi Shi small commodities market began to flourish again. Its prosperity eventually drew the attention of the central ruling elite in 1977. The Shi Shi County was labeled as an example of 'Restoration of Capitalism' again and a TV documentary was made to show the whole nation. The drama ended with the arrest of 11 'speculative profiteers' who had made a profit of 10,000 RMB *yuan* each and over 100 persons who had made a profit of over 1,000 but below 10,000 RMB *yuan* each. Therefore, before 1978, self-employed producers and traders consciously kept a low profile even if it was very prosperous and intentionally prevented it from expansion, afraid lest their business would become the target of the official prosecution.

The inauguration of economic reform following the discussion of the criteria of truth provided favorable conditions for the development of private industrial and commercial activities. As discussed in the previous chapter, the agricultural reform liberalized millions of peasants for possible industrial and commercial engagement and delivered extra millions of tons of agricultural produce into the society, which pressed the ruling elite to issue policy guidelines to promote private industrial and commercial activities. In the early 1980s agricultural specialized households and new economic associations were promoted by the party and state apparatus as a measure to increase production of commodities and services and to diverge extra agricultural labor force into industry and commerce. Many of agricultural specialized production households engaged in non-agricultural activities such as transportation, agricultural product processing, commerce, and small commodities manufacturing. According to statistics of the State Administration of Industry and Commerce, there were 988,000 rural households registered as self-employed producers and traders in 1981, with a total employment of some 1.2 million people and a registered capital of over 247 million RMB *yuan* (Zhang, 1999, p.207).

Considering the almost nonexistence of private self-employed producers and traders in the countryside before 1978, there was a considerable expansion of private industrial and commercial activities engaged by peasants within three years. As indicated in a 1984 survey, 62 per cent of the agricultural specialized production households surveyed were engaged in non-agricultural activities (Zhang, 1999, p.20). As specialized production households felt it difficult to expand business individually whenever business opportunity came by, they began to pool together their capital and labor together to set up private enterprises. As no party and state documents and policies recommended developing private enterprises that were tightly associated with private ownership and exploitation, a name was invented to call such economic entity as 'new economic associations of households'.[3]

At the same time, urban self-employed producers and traders also embarked on a fast government-sponsored development track. The party and state apparatus decided to promote the development of the individual economic sector in urban areas because the state sector could not provide full employment to the growing urban labor force,[4] coupled with millions of returned college and high school graduates who had been sent to the countryside to receive re-education from the peasants. In 1980 the CPC Central Committee held a national employment meeting, calling people to find employment through organizing economic entities and self-employment beside through state employment agencies. In July 1981, the State Council issued 'Policies and Regulations Regarding Non-agricultural Individual Economy in Urban Areas', requesting local governments to support and assist the development of individual economy[5] and allowing self-employed individuals to hire one to two hands and have up to five apprentices. In October 1981 the CPC Central Committee and the State Council jointly issued another document to confirm the development of other forms of economic ownership, including collective and private individual economy, while the public economy took the leading role. Its aim was clearly stated as (1) to promote economic construction, and (2) to increase employment. The CPC 12th National Congress of September 1982 also called for a further development of individual economy in rural and urban areas within the limits specified by the state, considering it as a necessary and beneficial complement to the public economy. In December 1982 the Fifth Session of the Fifth National People's Congress adopted an amendment to the Constitution, prescribing 'the individual economy of urban and rural working people, operating within the limits prescribed by law, is a complement to the socialist public economy. The state protects the lawful rights and interests of the individual economy'.

The ruling elite promoted individual entrepreneurship not only because it could create jobs and contribute to the economic development but also because it was considered as a non-exploiting economic entity based on private ownership of capital goods and personal labor although it could hire up to seven people, two hands and five apprentices. Nevertheless, it is a private economic form of organizing production and certainly involves exploitation when it hires labor although the upper limit is seven workers. The ruling elite wanted to place the individual private sector and exploitation associated with it under control, while making good use of its benefits to assist the economy.

However, the fast development of the individual economy went further than the legal prescriptions and official policies that were restrictive on individual producers and traders. The imposition of labor hiring quantitative restriction reflected a deep-rooted fear among the ruling elite and the general public who had been indoctrinated by Mao's class struggle doctrine for more than two decades that hiring labor meant exploitation and hiring more labor means more exploitation. However, some of self-employed producers and traders broke the quantitative restriction in order to expand their business, arousing a heated discussion of the issue of exploitation in the newspapers and testing the nerve of the party.

For example, Chen Zhixun was a specialized production household, contracting for looking after eight *mu* of fishponds in 1979, which were increased into 105 *mu* in 1980.[6] He hired one hand on a yearly basis and also several laborers on a temporary basis and made a profit of over 10,000 RMB *yuan* (US$5,865) in 1981, which was indeed unbelievably high income for a peasant in the early 1980s, prompting a discussion in the middle of 1981 in the media. Eventually, the public opinion reached a consensus that it needed not to be a fuss about the case even if it involved some exploitation.

However, the general public and the ruling elite were not so sure about another case that hired more than a hundred workers and had a yearly profit of over one million RMB *yuan*. Anhui Province produced another story-making news item in the early 1980s. In 1981 Nian Guangjiu, a self-employed producer and trader in Wu Hu City, nicknamed as 'Idiot', invented a special formula to roast melon seeds and named it after his nickname as 'Idiot Seeds'. Roasted Seeds was one of the three local products the city government wanted local self-employed producers and traders to develop as local specialities. The city government, therefore, sponsored special reports on the 'Idiot Seeds' in newspapers and on television. Together with its special taste, reduced price and advertising, 'Idiot Seeds' soon became a well-known special product in Anhui and other parts of China. Nian Guangjiu did not hesitate to expand its production and hired more workers to keep up the production. The labor force he hired increased from just three workers in 1981 to a sizeable labor force of 103 in 1983. The yearly output of 'Idiot Seeds' climbed from several tons up to several thousand tons. His profits also grew from just a thousand RMB *yuan* to more than a million *yuan*.

Since China practically extinguished private ownership and exploitation in 1956, China had never witnessed such a rapid expansion of private business, such a large scale of labor hiring, and such a large profit within such a short period of time and by one self-employed producer and trader. Was it a case of 'restoration of capitalism: exploitation'? People pondered this question over and over again. Local and provincial leaders were not quite sure how to deal with such a case and the central ruling elite were divided over it. Deng recommended taking a 'Wait and See' attitude towards such large self-employed producers and traders that hired more than eight laborers and his proposal was accepted by the CPC Politburo. Deng's 'Wait and See' position was formally institutionalized into a CPC Central Committee document in January 1983,[7] stating 'As to those (self-employed producers and traders) that have hired more laborers than the state policy allows, their practice should not be promoted, openly publicized, nor rashly banned; instead, they should be guided towards developing into various forms of the co-operative economy' (Zhang, 1999, p.36). The document clearly showed both the ruling elite's tolerance towards those self-employed producers and traders that hired more than eight laborers and their preference that such private economic entities would eventually develop into the category of the co-operative economy rather than a private sector that is based on private ownership and exploitation.

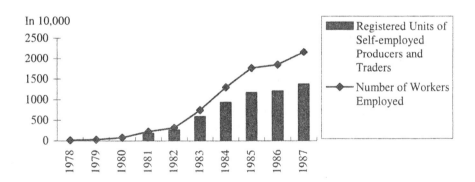

Figure 6.2 Development of the Private Individual Economy, 1978-1987

Source: Adapted from Zhang and Ming, 1999, p.93.

On 22 October 1984 Deng Xiaoping took another opportunity to persuade his conservative colleagues, members of the CPC Central Advisory Committee who were party veterans, to accept his 'Wait and See' position towards the development of private economy such as the 'Idiot Seeds' case because he did not believe it would harm socialism. Deng now had some achievements under his belt to prove the validity of his words.   One such achievement was the success of the agricultural reform that he had strongly promoted and another was that Hong Kong would be returned to China on his 'One Country Two Systems' formula.

With Deng's direct intervention, from 1983 to 1986 the party and state apparatus did not issue, any documents that categorically banned any self-employed business from hiring more than eight laborers.   In February 1984 the State Council issued a regulation to offer financial support to peasants and their new economic associations if they wanted to buy tractors and ships for transportation business.   It was a symbolic posture towards private producers and traders considering that the state banks only gave self-employed individuals credit share below one per cent of their total loans.   Nevertheless, when the barriers of the labor hiring quantitative restriction and the fear of exploitation were removed, the private economy witnessed a fast development (see Figure 6.2).

From 1982 to 1985, the private individual economy witnessed a dramatic development, with its registered units and persons employed increasing annually, on average, by 63 per cent and 71 per cent, respectively.   Deng's 'Wait and See' position, which was later honored by the CPC Central Committee, stimulated a three-digit boost to the private individual economy in 1983, with the registered units and the workers employed swelling by 126 per cent and 133 per cent over the previous year, respectively.

By the end of 1987 the private individual economy already employed over 21 million people, generating an output value of 30.6 billion RMB yuan and handling a total retail volume of 74.4 billion RMB *yuan* (Zhang and Ming, 1999, pp.65-6). The momentum of individuals getting rich seemed unstoppable and self-employed people would seek various ways to expand business and increase their wealth.   One way was to hire more hands and some of them even broke the quantitative restriction.   For example, in 1983 only 509 self-employed individuals and specialized production households hired laborers in four counties and cities of Hubei Province, employing 3,246 workers and in 1985 the two figures redoubled to 2,543 and 15,838, respectively.   In Liaoning Province there were 5,220 registered units of self-employed individuals and specialized production households that hired 40,478 laborers in 1983 and both the registered units and the workers hired increased by 257 per cent and 228 per cent in 1984 and again by 95 per cent and 90 per cent in 1985, respectively.   In three counties of Hebei Province, the number of self-employed individuals and specialized production households that hired over 50 laborers grew from 49 in 1983 to 159 in 1984.   On the whole, the business expansion of the individual economy was on the increase in the 1980s.[8]

Another approach was to form new economic associations among several households, which was private in nature but set up on the co-operative or share-holding principles, receiving more support from the party and state apparatus.   It developed quite rapidly in southeast coastal areas.   For example, agricultural new economic associations registered a faster development than the collective enterprises and other forms of enterprises, in the Jinjiang County, Fujian Province, before private enterprises were first officially accepted by the CPC Central Committee in 1987 (see Figure 6.3).

A third way of expanding private business was to forge a corporatist liaison with the local party and state establishment, setting up a private enterprise but registering it as a collective or co-operative enterprise of the local village committee, the township government, or the city residents committee. This corporatist liaison offered private enterprises 'Red Caps', which would give them some privileges of collective enterprises. For example, Hebei Province conducted a survey in 1988 and found that between 5 to 10 per cent of the surveyed enterprises wore 'Red Cap'. As a result, the registered private enterprises were far below the actual number of privately owned enterprises. In 1989 there were 6,532 registered private enterprises but in 1988 the estimated number was already 13,900 (Zhang, 1999, p.50).

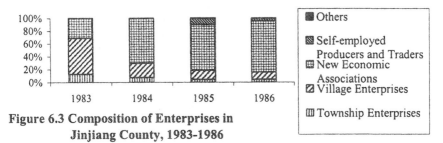

Figure 6.3 Composition of Enterprises in Jinjiang County, 1983-1986

Source: Adapted from Zhang and Ming, 1999, p. 34.

Therefore, even before the party and state apparatus officially allowed the existence of private enterprises, many rural and urban self-employed producers and traders made use of the existing policies, regulations and the tolerance of the party and state apparatus, breaking the quantitative labor hiring restriction, or running their private business in the name of the co-operative or collective enterprises. It was estimated by the State Administration of Industry and Commerce that in 1987 there were already 225,000 de facto private enterprises in China, employing 3.6 million workers, 51 per cent of which were registered as individual producers and traders, hiring 1.84 million laborers, 27 per cent as co-operative enterprises, employing 0.96 million workers, 22 per cent as collective enterprises employing 0.8 million workers (Zhang, 1999, p.51).

The 'Red Cap' phenomenon had its deep-rooted psychological, political and economic reasons. First, 'Red Cap' could provide a certain degree of political safety to owners who harbored a deep psychological fear of wearing a 'Bourgeois Cap', because they would still vividly remember the costs of being an exploiting class, the target of class struggles since 1949. Second, the central ruling elite did not take tough measures against such 'Red Cap' practices, probably because these 'Red Cap' enterprises were at least under direct control of the party and state apparatus. Third, such 'Red Cap' enterprises could have much easier access to policy bank loans, low price capital materials, and state technology and information support services. And fourth, more 'Red Cap' enterprises meant not only more local economic development and jobs but also more local government revenue since their management fees were collected by the local governments as its extra budgetary income, which could be used by local leaders for miscellaneous purposes. Even after private enterprises were legalized in 1988 there were still many owners of private enterprises who preferred to keep their 'Red Caps'. In 1995 the State Administration of Industry and Commerce conducted a survey of 178,000 collective enterprises in 16 provinces and found that 20.8 per cent of them could be called private enterprises, if the criteria of private enterprises was that 51 per cent of the investment came from private sources. According to this discovery, the actual number of private enterprises in China would be double the number of registered private enterprises (Zhang, 1999, p.51).

By 1987 the domestic private sector, including the self-employed producers and traders and the 'Red Cap' enterprises, had already become an indispensable component of the economy, employing some 23.36 million people. Besides its job creation, which the central ruling elite welcomed, the private sector also delivered products and services to the society that were usually ignored by the state-owned enterprises.

The Private Sector as a Complement to the Socialist Economy

The success of the agricultural reform and the fast development of the domestic private sector became ammunition for the reform-minded ruling elite to push forward the economic reform. In January 1987 the CPC ruling elite reached a consensus at the CPC Politburo meeting concerning the status of the private enterprises and issued a document 'To Further the Agricultural Reform'. Noticing the innate problem of income distribution, the document accepted for the first time the private enterprises as a complement to the socialist economy. Compared with Deng's 'Wait and See' attitudes, the document represented an important step forward towards legalising private ownership, outlining the party policy guidelines: (1) to allow private enterprises to exist, promoting their benefits to society while controlling their bad effects; (2) to anticipate the existence of a few private enterprises for a foreseeable future, both during the development of a commodity economy and the preliminary stage of socialism; and (3) to call on the state apparatus first to formulate temporary rules and then through legal procedures to institutionalise regulations regarding their business scope and registration, to formulate taxation laws that would both regulate income distribution and encourage production expansion, and to work out measures for labour protection and a guarantee of legal rights of each party involved in a private enterprise.

However, the document did not provide any ideological justification for the CPC's tolerance towards private enterprises and exploitation associated with them. It was the CPC 13th National Congress, held in October 1987, that produced a positive conclusion on the nine years' economic reform based on Deng's development strategies and guidelines. This was summarised as the theory of the preliminary stage of socialism, a new operative ideology of the CPC justifying the restoration of private ownership and the development of private enterprises. Zhao

Ziyang, Secretary General and a protégé of Deng Xiaoping, delivered a political report to the Congress, expounding the new operative ideology. Endorsed by the Congress, the political report became the CPC's guidelines for the preliminary stage of socialism.

The idea of the preliminary stage of socialism was mentioned, in its various forms, by the CPC ruling elite and in CPC documents on quite a number of occasions, conveying different meanings. When Marshal Ye Jianying talked about the childhood of socialism on 29th September 1979,[9] he pointed out its immaturity and fragility, which made it easy to fall prey to political conspirators such as Lin Biao and the Gang of Four. The preliminary stage was first mentioned in a CPC document[10] in June 1981, but the emphasis was on China's beginning of socialism to fend off anti-socialism sentiments in the aftermath of the Cultural Revolution. It appeared in two party documents[11] in September 1982 and September 1986 when the concerned issue was on how to build spiritual civilisation during the preliminary stage. Although Deng Xiaoping did not use the term 'preliminary stage of socialism' until August 1987, he pointed out on several occasions that China was not qualified for its claimed socialism since its productivity and people's living standards had been kept low between 1958 and 1978, arguing 'poverty is no socialism and socialism should eliminate poverty' (Deng, 1993, pp.10-11, p.116, p.138, p.237). Therefore, Deng considered the fundamental task was to develop productivity and the economic reform was aimed at liberalising and developing productivity, which he called 'the Second Revolution' (Deng, 1993, p.113). As early as 1978 and 1979, Deng (1983, p.131, p.149) stressed that China's modernisation strategies, guidelines and methods should be based on its actual social and economic conditions, a pragmatic approach dramatically different from Mao's socialist construction based on his class struggle model of socialism.

Beside accepting Deng's economic development as the first priority of the party during the preliminary stage, which would last, at least, 100 hundred years after the socialism transformation of 1953-1956, and confirming Deng's strategy of developing productivity through promoting individual prosperity prior to common prosperity, the political report revised the concept of Chinese socialism in two areas: (1) the ownership system; and (2) the income distribution system.

During the preliminary stage, the public ownership, including state-owned and collective enterprises, is the principal economic ownership of the economy and other forms of ownership, including co-operative, individual-owned, foreign-funded, and private enterprises – the curse of bourgeois exploitation – are accepted as supplementary to the public ownership. The CPC encouraged these supplementary economic entities to have an appropriate development, that is, without weakening the principal role of the public ownership. Accordingly, distribution is no longer based on labour input only, but also on capital (interests), investment (dividends), and surplus value (profits). These ideological revisions represented an emergence of a new operative ideology of the CPC that acknowledged the restoration of private ownership and its contribution to the economic development and the improvement of people's living standards during the preliminary stage of Chinese socialism, while maintaining its fundamental conviction that socialism should eliminate exploitation and ensure common prosperity.

If the CPC was trying to realize socialism before 1978 through a strategy of first turning 'haves' into 'have-nots' and then bringing everyone to common prosperity at the same time in the future, since 1978 it has adopted a different strategy of turning 'have-nots' into 'haves' in batches, spreading prosperity over the population section by section. Naturally, the implementation of the new strategy presupposed the restoration of private ownership and the development of the private sector, which had been practiced by self-employed producers and traders and peasants since 1978. However, the new operative ideology helped the CPC ruling elite to justify their new economic strategy while upholding the basic socialist principles: elimination of exploitation and common prosperity, which will be realized when the preliminary stage ends. On 12th April 1988 an amendment was added to the Article 11 of the Constitution, stipulating:

> The state permits the private sector of the economy to exist and develop within the limits prescribed by law. The private sector of the economy is a complement to the socialist public economy. The state protects the lawful rights and interests of the private sector of the economy, and exercises guidance, supervision and control over the private sector of the economy.

On 25th June 1988 the State Council issued 'Provisional Regulations of the People's Republic of China on Private Enterprises'. [12] From then on, private enterprises began to have some legal protection although they were allowed to play a complementary role to the public sector. Private enterprises embarked on a steady development even in the aftermath of the June 4th incident of 1989.

The Non-state Sector as an Important Component of the Socialist Market Economy

Since 1988 Chinese domestic private enterprises have become legally part of the economy and have experienced a rapid development in the 1990s. Figures 6.4 and 6.5 display an upward curve, signifying a rapid expansion of private enterprises since 1989. On average, between 1989 and 1999 private enterprises have recorded 35.5 per cent annual growth in numbers of units, 31.7 per cent in employment, 68.3 per cent in registered capital, 49.1 per cent in output value, and 56.5 per cent in consumer goods retailing value. In particular, private enterprises witnessed a robust expansion following Deng's southern coastal tour of 1992, with their registered capital, output value and consumer goods retailing value, maintaining a growth rate of over 100 per cent and their number of units and employment increasing by over 60 per cent in 1993, 1994 and 1995.

The individual economy of self-employed producers and traders also experienced a similar expansion, which is shown in Figures 6.6 and 6.7. Compared with the development of private enterprises, the individual economy displays low entrance costs and a robust development in retailing business while private enterprises show a faster increase in capital input and a strong development in manufacturing and service industries.

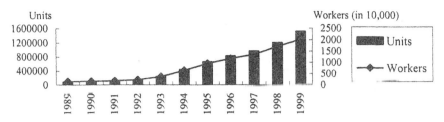

Figure 6.4 Private Enterprises, Size and Employment, 1989-1999

Source: Zhang and Ming, 1999, p.60; Zhang, Ming and Liang, 2002, pp.6-12.

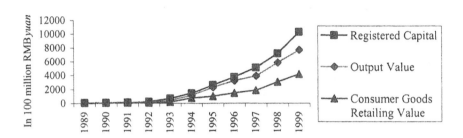

Figure 6.5 Private Enterprises, Registered Capital and Performance, 1989-1999

Source: Zhang and Ming, 1999, p.60; Zhang, Ming and Liang, 2002, pp.6-12.

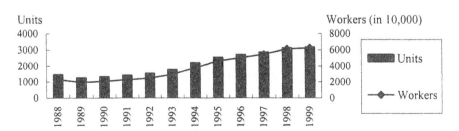

Figure 6.6 Individual Economy, Size and Employment, 1988-1999

Source: Zhang and Ming, 1999, p.66; Zhang, Ming and Liang, 2002, pp.31-4

Since private enterprises gained legal status, the Chinese people's imagination and energy were further motivated to work hard and to seek and accumulate more wealth. This primitive motive 'to get rich' is the basic drive underpinning the robust development of the private sector, increasingly compelling the ruling elite to concede more and more rights to private enterprises. Another major reason why the ruling elite decided to restore and develop the private sector is that the party and state apparatus could no longer provide full employment to the growing labor force. The official unemployment figure has kept on rising (see Figure 6.8) and the actual unemployment rate may be much higher, between 5 to 8 per cent, i.e. between 12 to 14 million, if including those functionally laid-off workers of the state owned enterprises (Ma and Ling, 1998, p.329).

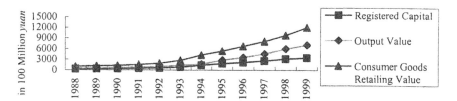

Figure 6.7 Individual Economy, Registered Capital and Performance, 1988-1999

Source: Zhang and Ming, 1999, p.66; Zhang, Ming and Liang, 2002, pp.31-34

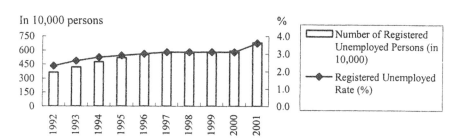

Figure 6.8   Unemployment in Urban Areas, 1992-2001

Source: *China Statistical Yearbook 1997, 1999, 2002.*

The performance of the state-owned enterprises looks disappointing (see Figure 6.9), considering the reform in this sector was started as early as the agricultural reform. The party and state apparatus has devised a series of reform measures in an attempt to revitalize the public sector. The following is a brief summary of the official measures to reform the state-owned enterprises:[13]

- In 1979, the profit-retention scheme was tried in some parts of China to allow the enterprises to retain part of their profits as employee welfare, enterprise funds and development and research funds;
- In 1979, the profit-contracting approach was tried in parts of China, by which the enterprise could negotiate an individual profit-sharing contract with the state, and the latter would grant the former a set of management decision powers; then, the enterprise would divide its profit responsibility among its workshops which would further re-divide their profit responsibility among work units and even workers, much like the agricultural household contract responsibility system;
- In 1983, the tax-for-profit reform was started in parts of China, which forced the enterprises to accept their legal obligation to pay taxes as independent legal persons to the state treasuries rather than submitting profits to the state as dependent subordinates.   Under this arrangement, they enjoyed more autonomy but also more legal financial responsibilities;
- In 1984, based on the experience of the experiments of the above reform approaches, the management by contract system was standardized and implemented throughout China;[14]
- In 1992 the modern enterprise system experiment was launched in large and medium-size state-owned enterprises, hoping to set up standardized corporations and firms through the ties of assets, and large competitive enterprise groups that are cross-regional, inter-trade, multi-ownership, and multi-national; at the same time small state-owned enterprises could be sold or leased to the private sector; and in 1995 the reform strategy was summarized as 'Grasp the big and let go the small';[15]
- In 1997 the public ownership took various forms, such as the state-owned, the state-controlled share-holding companies, the joint stock co-operative enterprises, and those enterprises funded by social public funds.

In the late 1990s, the performance of the state-owned enterprises started to improve with the total profit rising but still looked disappointing as the total lost remained over 60 billion RMB *yuan* (See Figure 6.9).

Starting from the beginning of the 1990s, therefore, the party and state apparatus appeared to have no other choice than to promote the development of the non-state sectors, including individual owned, foreign-funded, and private enterprises, to provide new jobs and to keep up economic growth.   Although government policies and legal protection are necessary conditions for sustaining the expansion of private enterprises, it is the economic efficiency of private enterprises that has kept the private sector growing.   For example, the private enterprise's ratio of pre-tax profits to total capital and its per capita pre-tax profit were much higher than the state-owned enterprises except in the electricity power and gas production and supply (see Table 6.1).

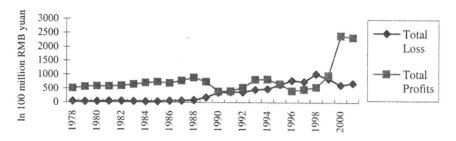

Figure 6.9 Performance of State-owned Industrial Enterprises, 1978-2001

Source : *China Statistical Yearbook 1997, 2002* ; various issues of Statistical
Communiques.

Table 6.1 Economic Efficiency of State-owned and Private Enterprises, 1996

Sector	Ratio of Pre-tax Profit to Total Capital (Percentage)		Per Capita Pre-tax Profit (RMB *yuan*)	
	State-owned Enterprises	Private Enterprises	State-owned Enterprises	Private Enterprises
Mining and Quarrying	13.6	128.6	5800	13900
Manufacturing	12.5	62.9	5400	6700
Electricity Power & Gas	11	115.8	20700	6800
Building	11.8	74	2400	9700

Source: Zhang and Ming, 1999:140-141.

Against the economic background of the 1990s, the ruling elite began to relax
restrictions on the private sector. In 1992 the CPC 13th National Congress
endorsed the political report delivered by Jiang Zemin on 12th October 1992, which
outlined a market economy to replace the planned economy. Although the private
sector, including individual owned, private, and foreign-funded enterprises was
still allowed to play a complementary role to the public sector, state-owned and
collective enterprises in the market economy, the report proposed three policies
concerning the private sector: (1) the public sector and the private sector should be
encouraged to develop together over a long period of time; (2) the public sector
and the private sector could form various forms of associations between them
totally out of their free will; and (3) some small state-owned enterprises could be
leased or sold to collective enterprises and private individuals. These three policies
represented an official launching of a second wave of state-private joint ventures
although such practices had existed for over a decade.

Compared to the first wave of joint state-private ventures in 1953-1956, which was aimed at setting up a socialist public economy through eliminating private ownership and exploitation, the second wave of joint state-private ventures was intended to help the state to reduce its debt burden[16] and to shift the responsibility of looking after the concerned workers through encouraging the private sector to take over some portions of the public sector. In March 1993 the First Session of the Eighth National People's Congress endorsed the idea of leasing or selling small state-owned enterprises to collective enterprises or private individuals. In reality, the majority of such small state-owned enterprises were being transferred into private hands. In other words, the ruling elite were prepared to get rid of the majority of the money-losing state-owned enterprises through merging them with the private sector or selling them to the private sector.

To a certain extent, the official policy to promote state-private economic co-operation came at a right time when self-employed individuals and private enterprises had accumulated a sizeable capital and some experience in management (see Figures 6.4, and 6.5; and also see Figures 6.6, and 6.7). On the other hand, the ruling elite gave up the strategy of relying only on the public resources to reform the state-owned enterprises as Vice Premier Zhu Rongji lamented in December 1996 that more state investment meant more losses (Ma and Ling, 1998, p.344). Instead, the ruling elite began to mobilize private resources to assist the reform of state-owned enterprises. Although such state-private co-operation had already existed as indicated above, the proclaimed policy would certainly further encouraged the private sector to transfer its capital and management expertise to the public sector. For instance, Zhu Cheng City, Shandong Province, had sold 274 public-sector enterprises, including 237 collective enterprises and 37 state-owned enterprises, to private hands, by July 1994. Chen Guang, CPC Secretary General and Mayor of Zhu Cheng City, was given a nickname 'Chen Mei Guang'. 'Mei Guang' (卖光) in Chinese means 'sold out', suggesting Chen Guang was good for nothing except for selling out the public assets.[17]

The transformation of the public enterprises, including collective and state-owned enterprises, mainly takes one of the following forms: (1) to turn them into limited liability or joint stock limited companies through bringing in domestic private or foreign investment; (2) to turn them into joint stock co-operative enterprises through selling their net assets to workers and private hands, who jointly own the new enterprises; (3) to lease them to private hands or non-state enterprises; (4) to merge them with private or other non-state enterprises; (5) to sell them to private hands or other non-state enterprises; or (6) to bankrupt them.

By the end of 1995 the party and state apparatus had decided, based on experience of the state-owned enterprise reform, on a reform strategy of 'Grasping the big and letting go the small'. The state intended to focus its attention on revitalising 1,000 big state-owned enterprises because they occupied 40 per cent and 51 per cent of the total assets and the net assets of the state-owned enterprises respectively, providing 52 per cent of the tax revenue and generating 66 per cent of the profits although their number was only 0.3 per cent of the total state-owned enterprises.[18] Since then the transformation of small state-owned enterprises spread rapidly throughout China. The form of joint stock co-operative enterprise is usually the first choice of small state-owned enterprises under transformation, particularly village and township enterprises. By the end of 1996 there had already been 3 million joint stock co-operative enterprises in rural areas, accounting for three quarters of the total in China. In Shandong Province, for instance, 41.6 per cent of village and township enterprises had transformed into joint stock co-operative enterprises, 32.8 per cent in Jiangsu Province, 25.9 per cent in Zhejiang Province, and about 20 per cent in Guangdong Province.[19] In some areas over 50 per cent of small state-owned enterprises had been transferred into non-state enterprises by the end of 1997. For example, over 3,700 small state-owned enterprises, out of some 5,000 small state-owned enterprises, in Shichuan Province had been sold to the private sector in 1997 (Ma and Ling, 1998, p.382).

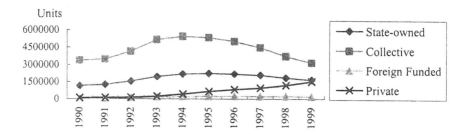

Figure 6.10 Expansion of Non-state Enterprises, 1990-1999

Source: Zhang, Ming, and Liang, 2002, p.6.

In essence, the transformation of small state-owned enterprises along this line represented a major retreat of the public sector from the economy, inviting the private sector to fill the vacancy (see Figure 6.10). Therefore, it attracted strong attacks from the 'leftist' conservative force within the CPC and the society. Four articles that sharply criticized economic reform and the open-door policy were published in overseas media and began to circulate in China between early 1995 and early 1997.

What the articles argued against was the market-oriented reform, including the agricultural reform, the open-door measures, the restoration of private ownership, the development of the private sector and the state-owned enterprises reform strategy of 'Grasping the big and letting go the small'. They concluded that a domestic bourgeois class had already emerged economically; with the further development of the private sector, the bourgeoisie would seek to change their present subordinate role to a leading role both economically and politically. Therefore, the formation of the bourgeoisie was the potential threat to the proletariat dictatorship in China, leading to, with the support of the international bourgeoisie, the replacement of the proletariat dictatorship by the bourgeois dictatorship in China. The emergence of the private sector and the bourgeoisie provided favorable conditions for hatching bourgeois world outlook and the bourgeois liberalization, which escalated corruption and crimes particularly since 1992. The articles even claimed that there were economic, political and ideological representatives in the party and state apparatus, forming a league of the bourgeois interests within the establishment, which was the leading force in the 'peaceful evolution of capitalism' in China. Their prescription for preventing such a restoration in China was to always keep the private sector at a subordinate position in relation to the public economy.[20] Although the authors of the four articles are unknown, they did stimulate an open ideological debate among Chinese intellectuals on the market-oriented reform and opening measures in the late 1996 and the early 1997. In response to Deng's call 'No disputing but getting things done',[21] Chinese newspapers and magazines tried not to publish confrontational ideological discussions among Chinese intellectuals on the reform and opening measures.

In the early 1997 the media broke its taboo and on 10th February 1997 a magazine based in a Beijing institute published a report on a seminar that had been attended by over 20 professors, experts and academics on 18th January 1997, criticizing an article written by Li Youwei, Party Secretary General of Shenzhen City.[22] It accused Li Youwei of advocating privatization, cultivating a new bourgeois class, and demanding to change the nature of the CPC and concluded that a party cadre like Li Youwei was no longer up to the requirements of a party member, let alone an alternate member of the CPC Central Committee. Thereafter, successive anti-reform articles appeared in three Beijing based magazines: *Zhong Liu Magazine*《中流》, *Current Ideological Trends* 《当代思潮》 and *Search for Truth* 《真理的追求》.[23]

However, these articles could not stop the 'get-rich' tide of the nation generated by the market-oriented reform and open-door measures. The ruling elite paid little attention to these anti-reform articles but kept up the reform momentum with a hope of maintaining a high rate of economic growth and reducing the loss of the state-owned enterprises. In March 1996 Vice Premier Zhu Rongji spent three days in Zhu Cheng City, inspecting cases of the transformation of state-owned enterprises in the City. He was impressed by the City's experiment of turning state-owned enterprises into joint stock co-operative enterprises through selling the net assets of the state-owned enterprises to workers and private hands. He made it unequivocally clear that he did not care about whether such new enterprises were called share-holding or joint stock co-operative enterprises, or whether they belonged to the public ownership or the private ownership, so long as the state loss could be stopped and the bank loans could be paid back. He wished the other state-owned enterprises would follow their example (Wei and Chen, 1998, p.634).

Jiang Zemin, Secretary General of the CPC Central Committee, took the opportunity to speak to the students of the provincial and ministerial training class of the CPC Central Party School at their graduation ceremony on 29th May 1997 to give his views on the next round of the economic reform, and to see provincial and ministerial level leaders' reactions about his reform policies he was going to submit for deliberation and consideration to the CPC 15th National Congress that was scheduled to be held in September 1997. Jiang Zemin argued that it would be pointless to talk about Marxism without considering China's current times and actual conditions, and he advocated seeking those forms of public ownership that would best promote productivity. At the CPC 15th National Congress, Jiang not only succeeded in confirming Deng Xiaoping's ideas as the ideological guidance principles of the CPC but also had his policy proposal on the restructuring of the ownership system accepted, which was summarized as follows:

- During the preliminary stage of socialism, other forms of ownership should be encouraged to develop while maintaining the principal role of public ownership;
- The principal role of public ownership is reflected more in the controlling power and the competitiveness of the public sector than its weight in the economy;
- Separation of the system of public ownership from the realization of public ownership, and the choice of the forms to realize the public ownership should be based on Deng's 'Three Criteria of Benefits', that is, raising the national comprehensive capabilities, improving people's living standards, and promoting productivity;
- The non-state economy is an important component of the economy;
- Confirming the strategy of reforming small state-owned enterprises through internal restructuring, integrating, merging, leasing, operational contracting, joint stock co-operative system, and selling state assets.

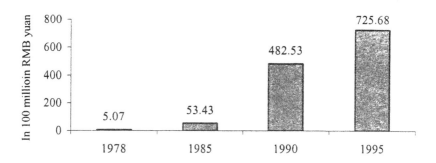

Figure 6.11 Revenue Contribution of the Private Sector, including Foreign-funded Enterprises, 1978-1995

Source: *China Financial Yearbook 1996*; Zhu, Yao, Zhou and Hu, 1998, p.245.

The ruling elite reached a consensus on the development of the private sector and the transformation of small state-owned enterprises into other forms of ownership, not because Jiang's argument was so convincing that his colleagues accepted his policy proposal, but because the representatives of the Congress understood very well there was no way to go back but to forge ahead along the market-oriented reform strategy. The contribution of the private sector to the economy could not be ignored. Besides its job creation and its provision of products and services to the society, the private sector's contribution to the state revenue has kept on a steady increase since 1978 (see Figure 6.11).

In 1995 the private sector generated a tax payment of 72.568 billion RMB *yuan*, accounting for 11.6 per cent of the total state revenue. The average annual increase in its revenue payment between 1978 and 1995 was 35.8 per cent while those of the state-owned enterprises and the collective enterprises were 9.5 per cent and 13.5 per cent, respectively. Although the state-enterprises contributed 71.2 per cent of the state revenue in 1995, their profits were included in their contribution and the state had to allocate over 60 billion RMB *yuan* to cover the losses of the state-owned enterprises (see Figure 6.9). The state-owned enterprises took in 76.1 per cent of bank loans while the private sector only 3.6 per cent.[24] Thus, the 1995 revenue contribution of the private sector was much more meaningful.

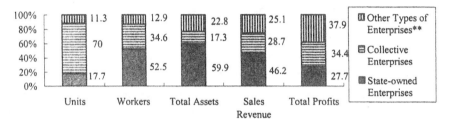

Figure 6.12 Main Indicators of Industrial Enterprises by Ownership, 1997*

* Only those non-state enterprises with an annual sales income of over 5 million yuan are included.
** Other types of enterprises referred to non-state enterprises, including domestic private enterprises, foreign funded enterprises, and enterprises funded by overseas Chinese from Hong Kong, Macao and Taiwan.

Source: Enterprise Bureau, State Economic and Trade Commission, *China Economic Times*, 11 March 1998.

And in 1997 the private sector had already occupied an undeniable position in the economy and the performance of the private industrial enterprises was far better than both the state-owned enterprises and the collective enterprises when considering the private sector had fewer units, employed fewer workers, input less capital, and had a smaller sales revenue (see Figure 6.12). Before the socialist transformation, the private sector handled over 60 per cent of the total retail sales of consumer goods in 1952 and after twenty years of economic reform, the private sector again accounted for over 60 per cent of the total retail sales of consumer goods (see Figure 6.13).

Therefore, the CPC ruling elite only accepted the reality of the private sector. Only to further develop the private sector, the ruling elite realized that they might have a better chance to maintain the economic growth and to improve people's living standards. Heading the state-owned enterprise reform, the ruling elite had to rely on the resources of the private sector to reform the ailing public sector, through letting go small state-owned enterprises while getting hold of the big ones. If the ruling elite could have revitalized the state-owned enterprises, maintained a high rate of economic growth, and improved people's living standards without restoring private ownership and private enterprises, they might never have agreed to the restoration of private enterprises.

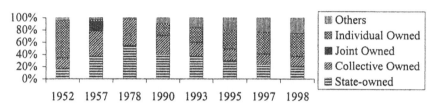

**Figure 6.13 Total Retail Sales of Consumer Goods
by Ownership, 1952-1998**

a) The retail sales of the joint-owned units in 1952-1958 referred to those of the joint state-private units. Since 1958, it referred to those of the enterprises of various forms of domestic joint ownership and the Sino- foreign joint ventures.
b) The retail sales of the individuals in 1952-1957 included those of the private enterprises.
c) Since 1993, other types of ownership have included private, share holding, foreign funded enterprises and enterprises funded by the entrepreneurs from Hong Kong, Macao and Taiwan. The retail sales to the non-agricultural residents by the agricultural residents have also been included.

Source: China Statistical Yearbook 1999 .

Economic and Political Implications

The restoration and subsequent rapid development of the private sector has generated fundamental changes in China. The discussion in this section focuses on the changes in the economic, civil-social and ideological environments that are constraining policy choices of the ruling elite.

As discussed in the previous sections, the rapid development of the private sector has sufficiently changed the economic structure, breaking the dominance of the public sector in the economy and the society as well. There are several ways to measure the transformations. The private sector is now an indispensable component of the economy, handling over 60 per cent of the consumer goods retailing (see Figure 6.13.), generating over 58 per cent of the industrial output value (see Figure 1.1), and employing about 30 per cent of the rural and urban workers (see Figure 6.14). Since 1980 the private sector has maintained an annual output value growth of 20-30 per cent much higher than the public sector 5-10 per cent; about 50 per cent of the export in terms of value comes from small and medium private enterprises; and the private sector now accounts for over 60 per cent of the GDP.[25]

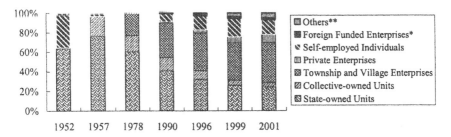

Figure 6.14 Employment by Ownership, 1952-2001

Note: Figures since 2000 on workers and staff refer to fully employed workers and staff, while figures for previous years refer to total workers and staff.
*Including units with funds from Hong Kong, Macao, and Taiwan
**Others include share-holding and joint-owned units, limited liability and share-holding corporations.

Source: *China Statistical Yearbook, 1999, 2002*.

The private sector will expect more expansion in the years to come owing to several factors. First, as indicated in Table 6.1 and Figure 6.12, private enterprises are more efficient than state-owned enterprises, indicating strong potentials for further expansion. Second, as China has joined the WTO and is expected to open its door wider to the outside world, the ruling elite have quickened steps to get rid of money losing medium and small state-owned enterprises and to transform them into non-state enterprises, in a bid to reduce the losses of the public sector and regroup resources to bolster up the big ones. By December 2000 more than 40,000 medium and small state-owned enterprises had changed hands, according the State Administration of Industry and Commerce; and the number of private enterprises had reached 1,7 million, with a total capital of 1,250 billion RMB *yuan*, increasing by 77 per cent and 143 per cent compared to 1997, respectively.[26] Third, in order to meet the requirement of the WTO on equal treatment of all enterprises, China began a national review of its laws and regulations, repealing those that were in contradiction with the principles and rules of the WTO, especially those that discriminate against private enterprises. The Ministry of Foreign Trade and Economic Co-operation instructed local governments to abolish those regulations that were restricting private trading companies, giving them equal treatment as state-owned trading companies.[27]

The ruling elite began to expect such expansion of the private sector in the second of half of the 1990s. In December 1996 Zhu Rongji, Vice Premier, commented that there would be no danger even if the share of the public sector in the gross national industrial output value declined to 60 per cent, so long as the public sector could control the economic lifelines.[28] Two years later, the private sector narrowed the gap by eight percentage points. Some Chinese economists are more positive about the expansion of the private sector. According to Zhang Zuoyuan (Zhang, 1998, p.40), an economist based in the Chinese Academy of Social Sciences (CASS), the GDP share of the state sector (excluding the collective enterprises) could be as low as some 20 per cent without causing any problem to the regime.

Secondly, the rapid expansion of the private sector has produced some 30 million new bourgeois or petty bourgeois – owners of private enterprises and individual producers and traders, transforming a society of common poverty into one of high disparity. China's Gini Index rose from 0.16 in 1978 to 0.415 in 1995 and to 0.456 in 1998, higher than that of the United States.[29] How fast the private sector has accumulated capital can be glimpsed from the results of two surveys. The Sociology Institute of CASS and All China Association of Industry and Commerce conducted three respective surveys of private enterprises in 1993, 1995, and 1997. Their 1993 survey found that every private enterprise, on average, had a net capital of 323,000 RMB *yuan* and the owner received an average annual income of 50,000 RMB *yuan* (Yang, et al., 1997, p.35). Their 1997 survey found the two figures climbed to 1,153,000 and 104,070 RMB *yuan*, respectively (Zhu, Yao, Zhou and Hu, 1998, pp.131-66). The capital accumulation of private enterprises and the income of the owners had increased between 1993 and 1997 at an average annual rate of 37.4 per cent and 21.1 per cent, respectively.

In 1995 China had 2,655 private enterprises with a registered capital over 5 million RMB *yuan*, 20 of which had assets of over 100 million RMB *yuan*. It was estimated that in 1995 China had about one million persons who had a savings deposit of over one million RMB *yuan*, accounting for a third of the total savings deposit of 3,000 billion RMB *yuan*. The 10 per cent richest of the population owned over 40 per cent of the total savings deposit while the 10 per cent poorest only 3 per cent; and the gap between the rich and the poor has been enlarging at an annual rate of 10 per cent. At the same time there were still 34 million peasant and several millions of urban dwellers living under the poverty line.[30] China has now a stratification of four major social classes: the political and economic elites,[31] comprising about seven million people, or one per cent of the total workforce; a new middle-class[32] of about 111.3 million people, or 15.8 per cent of the total workforce; the working class,[33] rural-urban migrants, and the peasantry, some 480 million people, or about 69 per cent of the total workforce; and the 'off-post' group: unemployed and pauperized rural population, making up some 100 million people, about 14 per cent of the total workforce.[34]

Economically speaking, the newly rich have a large say in the allocation of private economic resources. Whether or not billions of private savings are channeled to investment or to consumption is to be decided by the savers and the society, rather than by the state (He, 1998, p.156). One example is that the government failed to persuade people to spend more on consumption in the late 1990s even after it had slashed the interest rates of savings deposit six times: for example, the interest rate for one year savings deposit was cut down from 9.18 per cent in May 1996 to 3.78 per cent in December 1998, which is indicated by the continual positive growth in savings and the depressed consumer price (see Figure 6.15). The continued growth in savings may be explained by the fact that the income of the newly rich has kept rising (Yang, et al., 1997, p.35) and that it is this social group of people who are more likely to have surplus money for savings. The depressed consumer price may be contributed to the fact that the rural income has declined substantially, adversely affecting the purchase power of the low-income rural residents of some 800 million.

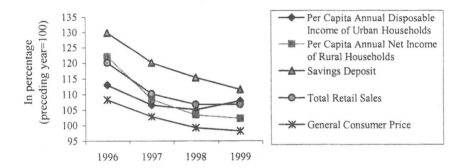

Figure 6.15 Indices of Per Capita Income, Savings Deposit of Households, Total Retail Sales, and General Consumer Price, 1996-1999

Source : China Statistical Yearbook 1999 ; Statistical Communique of the people's Republic of China on the 1999 National Economic and Social Development .

Politically, the newly rich are very concerned with politics, especially the party and state policy institutionalization concerning the private sector. The majority of the owners of private enterprises interviewed indicated their intention to set up their own association to promote and protect their interests. Some of them are voicing, through the media, meetings of local and national people's congresses and people's political consultative conferences, their political demands for equal treatment as the state-owned enterprises, implementation of the existing laws and regulations on promoting the private sector, amendment of the Constitution.[35] As more and more people are gaining economic independence of the party and state apparatus, Chinese people enjoy far more freedom in economic activities than 20 years ago, and this trend is shown by the continual rising of China's rating on the Fraser Institute Economic Freedom Index from zero in 1975 to 5.6 in 1997. Economic freedom may lead to political demands. With more and more people joining the middle-income class with growing private assets, they are likely to become more assertive in protecting their private assets.[36]

The party and state apparatus has involved some private entrepreneurs in the policy deliberation processes at various levels of people's congresses and political consultative conferences. Over 5,400 owners are deputies to local and provincial people's congresses and eight are deputies to the Ninth National People's Congress. More than 8,500 owners are deputies to local and provincial political consultative conferences and 46 are deputies to the Ninth National People's Political Consultative Conference (Jiang, 1999, p.109).

According to a document issued in 1989 by the CPC Central Committee, owners of private enterprises are barred from joining the CPC. However, in 1995 the Wuhan municipal government sponsored a survey of 380 owners of private enterprises, discovering 28.4 per cent of those interviewed were CPC party members (Zhu, Yao, Zhou and Hu, 1998, p.470). The three national surveys of 1993, 1995 and 1997 also found 13.1 per cent, 17.1 per cent and 16.6 per cent of owners interviewed were CPC members.[37] The 1997 survey found 24.1 per cent want to join the CPC. The CPC 16th National Congress endorsed officially the admission of the newly rich into the party.[38] This indicates that the ruling elite are adapting to the changing environment, which is a meaningful change in the membership structure of the CPC that vows to eradicate private ownership and exploitation.

Thirdly, the rapid expansion of the private sector has been the most important factor, if not the only factor, in remolding or revising the operative ideology of the CPC. As indicated in the previous sections, because of the rapid development of the private sector and its growing contribution to the maintenance of a continual economic growth, the basis of the legitimation of their rule, the ruling elite had no option but to upgrade the status of the private sector from a supplementary role to an important component of the economy, shifting their strategy from keeping the private sector in designated areas to allowing it to develop together with the public sector, changing the CPC's fundamental anti-private and anti-exploiting rhetoric, and welcoming a new round of state-private joint incorporation. These policy shifts and strategy changes are direct products of the adoption of a new operative ideology of the CPC. The invention of the preliminary stage of socialism opened the way to developing private enterprises – carriers of exploitation. The ideological justification for various ways of realizing the public ownership started a second round of promoting state-private joint ventures with the private sector taking over small and medium state-owned enterprises, which is considered as the third ideological emancipation since 1978.[39]

Although the third ideological emancipation has paved the way for further expansion of the private sector, it actually did a better job to blur the distinction between public and private ownership than to answer such questions as what is private ownership and why it is needed in China. As indicated above, the transfer of small and medium state-owned enterprises into private hands is, in essence, a form of privatization, while the ruling elite and their controlled media prefer to call it diversification of the public ownership. Although in these newly transformed share-holding enterprises, local governments take the minority shares and the management and the workers control the majority (Zhang, Huang and Li, 1998, p.31), they are considered 'public', not 'private' (Wei and Chen, 1998, p.101). For the ruling elite, such twisted explanation would give them more convincing justification for getting rid of money-losing state-owned enterprises without any danger of being accused of privatization. The society was, therefore, misled to pay more attention to the salability rather than the fairness of the state-private transaction. Professor Qing Hui, who suggests that the transformation of state-owned enterprises into non-state enterprises is privatization, has warned that there are cases of unfair practices in transferring public assets into private hands.[40]

The key issue is that the ruling elite would like to blur the boundary of the public and the private ownership in order to justify selling state-owned assets. Some well-known economists have provided new theoretical explanations for the emergence of different forms of ownership since 1978. Two theories have gained popularity with the ruling elite, both of them providing a dichotomy between the public and the private ownership with the contents of their private ownership categories being different from each other. One theory is to look at the public ownership under socialism as the social ownership, which can be extended to cover every form of ownership in China except the private ownership, including the state ownership, the working people's collective ownership, the working people's co-operative ownership, the social individual ownership, the socialist community ownership, the socialist civil society ownership, the socialist co-operative ownership, and the socialist corporate ownership. The share-holding form of enterprises, a hybrid of various forms of the social ownership, is regarded as one major form of social ownership. [41]

Another theory offers an opposite approach to categorize forms of ownership, providing a dichotomy between the state-run economy and the civil-run economy. The state-run economy refers to those economic entities owned and run by the state or managed by the government. The civil-run economy refers to all economic entities that do not belong to the state-run economy, including the private economy and other forms of public ownership except for the state-run ones, including township enterprises, co-operative economic units, and those economic units owned by communities, civil societies and various funds (Xiao, 2000). These two theories provide some theoretical rationale to the ruling elite who advocate the diversification of public ownership without privatization, because the diversification, according to their theories, enlarges the scope of public ownership rather than the private sector.

In reality, the shrinking of the public sector and the expansion of the private sector seems inevitable and both the ruling elite and academics are seeking new justifications or theories to prepare for the ultimate revelation that the private sector will become a principal component of the economy.

For example, Xiao Liang (Xiao, 1997) proposed one notion that the economic basis of the socialist superstructure should be taxation rather than public ownership. His logic is that more economic development leads to more resources for taxation, that more taxation means a more solid economic basis and a stronger national economic power. His argument provides some theoretical justification for a further retreat of the public sector.

The ruling elite are also seeking some ideological justification for the ultimate revelation that the private sector will become a principal component of the economy. In February 2000 when he was making an inspection tour of Guangdong Province, Jiang Zemin launched his 'Three Represents' theory, which demands the CPC always represent the development trends of China's advanced productive forces, the orientation of China's advanced culture, and the fundamental interests of the overwhelming majority of the people. In June 2000 Jiang Zemin advocated 'Three Innovations': the system innovation, the science and technology innovation, and the theory innovation. The party theoreticians wrote a series of commentaries to elaborate the 'Three Innovations'.[42] As for the theory innovation, people should be encouraged to speak out 'new words'.[43] For the system innovation, practice and the people's initiatives should be respected.[44] And for the science and technology innovation, the whole society should treat talented persons kindly.[45] All these advocacy amounts to one conclusion that the CPC needs new thinking in the face of the rapidly changing domestic and international environments and what the CPC is doing represents China's advanced productive forces, advanced culture, and the majority's interests. In November 2002 Jiang Zemin's 'Three Represents' theory was formally endorsed by the CPC 16th National Congress, which indicates that CPC ruling elite and decision-makers are successively adapting to the changing world and are prepared to advocate and adopt new operative ideology.

The rapid development of the private sector is producing three marked changes in the civil-social and economic environments that may exert strong influence on the formulation of a new operative ideology or the revision of the fundamental ideology of the CPC: (1) the emerging of a new bourgeois class; (2) an enlarging disparity between the newly rich and the poor; and (3) a growing demand for more legal protection for private property. The rapid development of the private sector is producing a new bourgeois class, as was warned in the first of the four articles that criticized economic reform and the open-door policy. Over 30 million newly rich cannot be overlooked and more and more people will join the 'haves' as the private sector continues to grow. The ruling elite do not have any available ideological guidelines to deal with the emerging bourgeois class because it is the taboo of the CPC to talk about the existence of a bourgeois class, which has been established by Deng Xiaoping, the architect of the economic reform. In the middle of 1980s, Deng Xiaoping promised, on several occasions, that the economic reform and opening measures would not lead to a disparity between the rich and the poor in China and would not produce a bourgeois class, and that the CPC would not allow a bourgeois class to emerge in the first place (Deng, 1993, p.64, p.172). Deng declared that if reform policies would lead to a rich-poor disparity, China's reform must be a failure (Deng, 1993, p.111, p.138). It seems that the ruling elite will have to break the taboo, to make a necessary revision of the CPC's ideology to deal with the phenomenon of the bourgeois class, and to formulate policies to effectively deal with the problem of the growing disparity.

The rapid development of the private sector is also generating a growing demand for more legal protection for private property. The constitutional amendment proposal to stipulate that private property is as inviolable as public property was turned down in the early 1999 because the issue involved is in direct contradiction with the fundamental ideological principle of the CPC that vows to eliminate private ownership and exploitation. However, the owners of private enterprises have never given up their hope and have started to work their way from bottom up. It was reported that a county of Zhejiang Province has adopted a regulation on protecting private property.[46] In terms of the output value of private enterprises, Zhejiang Province ranked first in the whole nation and its private sector delivered about a quarter of the provincial revenue in 1997.[47] If more and more local counties adopt the private protection regulation, the backward institutionalization will eventually reach the national level, the National People's Congress.

As more and more people become rich and more and more private property has been accumulated, more private property owners will be pressing for more legal protection for their property in their local regions where their economic resources can influence the local policy institutional process. This institutional development will press the ruling elite to face such sensitive issues as: Is the bourgeoisie or the 'haves' only a temporary phenomenon in the preliminary stage of socialism or a permanent sight throughout the socialism, or how long the private ownership and exploitation will be tolerated, only during the preliminary stage of socialism or throughout the whole period of socialism?

In fact, what happened in a county of Zhejiang Province is an ideological crisis more than a constitutional crisis in technical terms. A series of mind emancipation[48] have given freedom back to the Chinese people to worship themselves and to pursue happiness and wealth and accumulate private assets. With private property substantially growing, private property owners will naturally step up demands for more legal protection for their property.

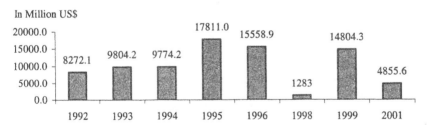

Figure 6.16 Errors and Omission of Balance of Payments, 1992-2001

Source : China Statistical Yearbook 1999, 2000, 2002.

Therefore, changes in the operative ideology of the CPC has led to pressure for a change in the party's fundamental ideology, just as Moore (1950, pp.421-2) argued 'shifts in operative ideology were likely, sooner or later, to provide changes in the officially promulgated doctrine'. The ruling elite are being compelled to face the dilemma: to bring the CPC's operative ideology closer to the CPC's fundamental ideology or to bring the latter closer to the former (Feng, 1995, p.209), to change the superstructure to suit the prevailing economic basis or to scale the economic basis backward to suit the present superstructure (Yang, 1998, p.575). If the central ruling elite sanction the local elite who support the private property protection and outlaw the local protection for private property, they will certainly cause a confidence crisis among private property owners, which may not only slow down the local economic development but also lead to more capital flight out of China. Even under the tight control of foreign currencies, China's capital flight was very serious in the late 1990s (see Figure 6.16). With China joining the WTO and its currency, RMB, becoming fully convertible in the near future, even a hint of policy change towards the private sector would cause a massive capital flight.

It seems that the ruling elite have no option but to provide more and more legal protection to the private sector in order to maintain the economic development momentum. Even when China finishes the journey of the preliminary stage of socialism proclaimed by the CPC in around 2050, it seems most likely that the country will still need the private sector to boost its economic development because China will still be a medium-developed country at that time, far behind the advanced industrialized countries. Therefore, China has a long distance to cover before its economic and social development is on a par with that of the advanced industrialized countries. When China has become an advanced industrialized country, there may be no need or no way to distinguish the private sector from the public sector.

Conclusion

The analysis of the institutionalization of the private ownership and the development of private enterprises indicates that after restoration of the independent producer status of the peasants, the ruling elite's policy decision and institutionalization have been influenced by the changes in the civil-social and economic environments (see Figure 2.2). Since Chinese peasants became independent producers again, more and more quantities of agricultural products and extra labor force have become available to the society. Agricultural specialized production households were encouraged by the ruling elite to produce and distribute small commodities that had been neglected by the state plan. In urban areas individual producers and traders were also encouraged not only for the reason of providing more goods and services to the society but also for the failure of the state to provide full employment to the blooming urban labor force.

The original logic behind the decision to encourage individuals to engage in small-scale manufacturing and commerce was that as long as the economic contribution of individual producers and traders were made supplementary to the planned economy by means of limiting the number of workers they could employ, their bad effects, exploitation and income disparity, could be placed under control while their benefits, extra goods and services and more employment, could be happily harvested.

However, when people were given back their freedom to pursue wealth and accumulate private property, individual producers and traders simply ignored the labor force employment restriction whenever business opportunities lured them to expand business and offered them more income. The tension between the fast development of the individual economy and the official policy was brought to the surface in 1983 and 1984 when one self-employed person made a million RMB *yuan* within one year through expanding his business and employing over 100 workers. This relaxing party policy stimulated a fast development of the individual economy and also facilitated new joint state-private enterprises to operate in 'Red Cap' until the official policy to encourage such joint ventures emerged in 1992 and confirmed in 1995.

The rapid development of private enterprises in the name of self-employed producers and traders eventually made the rebirth of private enterprises an undeniable fact so that the ruling elite accepted the private enterprise as one of the economic entities in 1987 although it was given a supplementary role to play. The private sector witnessed ever since a robust development and has played a significant role in the economy. How significant a role it played may be inferred from the intention of the ruling elite to tap resources of the private sector in reforming the ailing state-owned enterprises in the early 1990s. 1995 was an important landmark in China's economic transformation in that it marked the official debut of the second wave of joint state-private corporatism. If the first wave of joint state-private corporatism in 1953-1956 was to turn private enterprises into public ones, eradicating the private ownership and exploitation, the second wave was to turn public enterprises into private ones, eradicating the money-losing state-owned enterprises. As a result, the private sector gained another opportunity for rapid expansion and development, playing a more important role in the economy. In 1997 the ruling elite had to acknowledge its role and accepted it as an important component of the economy in a bid to make more use of the resources of the private sector in transforming the public sector.

The restoration and rebirth of private enterprises and the subsequent and rapid development of the private sector has led to significant changes in the four institutional environments: economic, civil-social, constitutional and ideological environments (see Figure 2.2). First, no longer a unified public ownership command economy, China's economy has been transformed into a mixture of state-owned, collective, private, foreign-funded, and share-holding economic entities, with the public sector shrinking from its dominant role and the private sector expanding into a dominant role. Second, no longer a society of equal poverty, China has developed into a society showing a growing disparity between the rich and the poor, with a growing number of people becoming new bourgeois. Third, no longer a dogmatic ideology of Marxism and Leninism, the operative ideology of the CPC has been revised according to the actual conditions of China, deviating from its fundamental ideological principles, elimination of private ownership and exploitation. Fourthly, the building of a market-economy has led to a transition, although at a slow pace, from the rule of the party to the rule of law.

In retrospect, changes in the party operative ideology in 1978 set in motion changes in the economic and civil-social environments that, in turn, pressed for further changes in the ideological environment. The subsequent changes in the ideological environment further stimulated changes in the socio-economic and constitutional environments. It is a chain of influences–changes–influences, driven by people's eagerness to become rich and promoted by the policy decisions of the ruling elite to keep up the economic growth momentum and to improve people's living standards. It seems certain that these chain reactions will continue for the foreseeable future in China. Xiao Liang (Xiao, 1997) proposed a possible justification for the prospective shrinking of the public sector and the aggressive expansion of the private sector, arguing that the economic base of socialism is taxation. So long as the economy is growing, the sources of taxation will grow as well and more tax revenue can be collected. Therefore, the state's economic foundation will become firmer and state power will be stronger. With enough revenue the state may be in a better position to make some compensations and corrections to the side effects of the market efficiency – unfair income distribution. The results of these government corrections may produce a socialist market economy with market mechanisms plus social justice and equality (Ma and Ling, 1998, p.421). The public ownership and the public sector's share in the economy, therefore, should no longer be the power basis of the ruling elite.

Beside these economic structural pressures, the ruling elite are facing increasing pressure from the owners of the private sector to make private properties as inviolable as the public property. When more and more local congresses and governments are beginning to provide this legal protection for private properties, the central ruling elite will have to consider a constitutional amendment to offer national legal protection for private properties if they do not want to destabilize the economy.

Therefore, changes in the CPC operative ideology on private ownership and private enterprises are indeed leading to pressures for changes in the constitutional environment, which may hold the key to a meaningful democratic reform of the political system. When China has its constitution amended to stipulate that private properties is as inviolable as public property, it represents the beginning of revising the CPC's socialist fundamental ideology. It is a realist and pragmatic approach to the democratic reform, which offers the CPC ruling elite an opportunity to salvage socialism through legal means. Evidence of the institutional analysis suggests that China is moving closer to democratization, not because the revised socialist ideology will eventually promote such a transition, but because property rights are considered by many researchers as the most important market institution and have a closely intertwined relationship with the institutional structures of a modern democracy.[49] In this sense, the rapid development of the private sector in China may be a salient case to prove that more economic freedom in an authoritarian regime will eventually lead to a demand for political freedom,[50] although the ruling elite and the party's socialist ideology may hold up the democratic tide temporarily.

Notes

1   In the first half of the 1970s when the Cultural Revolution seriously disrupted the industrial production, further deteriorating the shortage of commodities, some peasants pooled their capital and labor and set up private cooperative enterprises but registered

them as collective enterprises. They were usually called 'Red Cap' private enterprises, using the bank account number of the production brigade or the people's commune and paying, in return, to the collective organization a yearly management fee.

2 Calculated at the exchange rate of one US dollar = 2.46 RMB *yuan*. *Data source: China Statistical Yearbook* 1997, p.588.

3 The new economic association of households was an informal share-holding system. Each member input agreed shares of capital, labor, or even technology (calculated as shares) into the economic association, which distributed its profits, in return, to its members according to their shares. However, in reality, such economic associations were very loose in organization, some of which were cooperatives in nature, others were partnership entities, and still others were just labor contract projects.

4 It was estimated between 1980 and 1985 there were 37 million urban adults seeking employment, while the public sector had already employed over 100 million workers; most of the state-owned enterprises were over-staffed.

5 The individual economic in China refers to those economic activities engaged by self-employed individuals with less than eight workers.

6 *Mu* is a unit of area and one *mu* equals 0.0667 hectare.

7 It is 'Current Issues of the Rural Economic Policy', approved and issued by the Politburo of the CPC Central Committee on 2nd January 1983.

8 For more discussion, see Zhang, 1999, pp.32-4.

9 He gave a speech to mark the 30th anniversary of the People's Republic of China.

10 'Resolutions on Several Historic Issues of the CPC since 1949' was adopted by the Sixth Plenum of the CPC 11th Central Committee on 27th June 1981.

11 The political report of the CPC 12th National Congress on 1st September 1981 and 'Resolutions on the Guidelines for Building Socialist Spiritual Civilization' adopted by the Sixth Plenum of the CPC 12th Central Committee on 28th September 1986.

12 'Provisional Regulations of the People's Republic of China on Private Enterprises 《中华人民共和国私营企业暂行条例》' came into effect on 1st July 1988.

13 Summarized from the policies and documents of the party and the state regarding the reform of state-owned enterprises.

14 Taylor (1996, p.47) suggests that the management by contract system may be a crucial stage on the road to the privatization of state enterprises. The joint stock method, that is, 'corporativization' of state enterprises, may be a solution to privatizing the Chinese state enterprises (Taylor, 1997, p.159; 1996, p.47-51).

15 The basic idea is that the state should only focus on big enterprise groups and merge, lease, contract out, sell, or bankrupt small state-owned enterprises.

16 The average assets-liability ratio of state-owned enterprises was around 65 per cent in the 1990s. The state banks had provided 2,000 billion RMB *yuan* loans to the state-owned enterprises, about 20 per cent of which were believed to be bad loans.

17 For more discussion, see Wei and Chen, 1998, pp.621-35.

18 By 1998 the State Council had designated 120 state-owned enterprises groups as the pilot project, sending chief inspectors who were responsible to the State Council to supervise the operation of these designated enterprises groups, with each chief inspector looking after one to three enterprises groups.

19 For more discussion, see Wei and Chen, 1998, p.174.

20 For more discussion of the four articles, see Ma and Ling, 1998, p.242-353.

21 During his southern coastal tour of 1992, Deng Xiaoping (1993, p.374) admitted 'No disputing is my invention'. His exact words are as follows: 'No disputing is to win valuable time for action. Disputing will make things complicated and waste our time but can accomplish nothing. No disputing, to be bold to have a try and make a move.

The agricultural reform has been done this way and the urban reform should be done this way as well.'

22   It is one of the first four special economic zones. Li Youwei wrote the article when he was receiving training at the CPC Central Party School in December 1996, arguing for the coexistence of the public sector and the private sector and the necessity to develop the private sector during the preliminary stage of socialism. He suggested that common prosperity could be basically achieved when the majority of the proletariat becomes a working class with assets (a middle class), with the rich exploiting class and the poor proletariat being the minority of the two extremes. He argued that the private sector is part of the socialist economy and the superstructure should be adjusted to suit various forms of ownership of capital goods.

23   For a discussion of these articles, see Ma and Ling, 1999, p.367-403.

24   Data source: *China Statistical Yearbook* 1997, p. 622.

25   For more discussion, see Chen, 2003.

26   For more discussion, see 'China Promotes Private Business to Improve SOE's Performance', http://www.chinatopnews.com, 21st December 2000.

27   http://www.chinesenewsnet.com, 1st January 2001.

28   In 1995, the share of the state-owned enterprises was 34 per cent, that of the collective enterprises 36 per cent. For more discussion, see Ma and Ling, 1999: 344.

29   *World Development Indicators*, World Bank, 1998; Li and Hou, 2000.

30   For more discussion of the income and wealth disparity, see Zhu, Yao, Zhou and Hu, 1998, p.96; Yang et al., 1997, p.34; He, 1998, p.232; and Li and Hou, 2000.

31   The political elite consist of top state officials, high- and middle-ranking local officials, and functionaries of large state-owned, non-industrial institutions, and most of them have been turning into a property-holding class. The economic elite are composed of the owners of large or medium private companies.

32   The new middle-class, assessed by income and status, is divided into two groups, on the top rungs are well-paid intellectual workers, managers of middle and small enterprises in the state sector, private owners of middle and small firms, white-collar employees of firms with foreign investment, employees of state monopolies, comprising a total of about 29.3 million people, some 4 per cent of the total workforce; and on the lower rungs are specialized technicians, scientific researchers, lawyers, teachers in higher education and middle schools, rank-and-file employees in the arts or media, average functionaries in government, middle- and lower-level management in state enterprises, upper-level self-employed and traders, comprising about 82 million people, or 11.8 per cent of the total workforce.

33   The working is composed mainly of employees of state enterprises.

34   For a detailed discussion of class stratification in China, see He, 1998, p.218-44; and also He, 2000.

35   For more discussion, see 'A Special Report on the Economic Treatment of the Non-state Sector', *China Economic Times* 《中国经济时报》, 27th March 1998.

36   Although no one would like to set a static figure on the income of the middle class emerging in China, most researchers agree that the annual per capita income of the middle class is presently between 25,000 and 35,000 RMB *yuan*. Now some 18 per cent of the labor force can be included in the middle class and it is estimated that this figure may reach 35 per cent in 2020. For more discussion, see *21st Business Herald*, 30th December 2002, p.49; *China Economic Times*, 15th November 2002, p.5.

37   The three surveys were conducted by the Sociology Institute of China Social Science Academy and All China Association of Industry and Commerce. For more discussion, see Zhang and Ming, 1999, pp.131-66.

38 On 14th November 2002, an amendment to the Constitution of the CPC was approved at the closing session of the Party's 16th National Congress, which is meant to reinforce the Party's class foundation and to expand its mass base through opening its door to any advanced element of other social strata, including the newly rich.

39 The discussion of criteria of truth and the confirmation of practice as the only criterion of testing theories, orchestrated by Hu Yaobang in early 1978 with full support of Deng Xiaoping, is considered the first ideological emancipation, breaking 'the cult of personality' and granting the reformers a mandate to pursue reform measures they would think worth trying. The acceptance of market mechanisms following Deng Xiaoping's southern tour of 1992 is considered the second ideological emancipation, discarding 'the cult of the plan economy' and offering the reformers a clear target of establishing a market economy. The third ideological emancipation has disbanded 'the cult of the public ownership'. For more discussion of the three rounds of ideological emancipation, see Ma and Ling, 1998, p.424-5.

40 A professor of Qing Hua University, Qing Hui headed a research project on the transformation of township enterprises in Jiangsu Province in 1997 and found many workers were strongly against the unfair procedures of public-private enterprise transformation, calling for playing fair and preventing individuals from seeking personal gains. For more discussion, see Bai, 1998, pp.230-7, p.268; Ma and Ling, 1998, pp.384-5; and also see Taylor, 1996, pp.47-51, 1997, p.159.

41 Yu Guangyuan, a famous economist in China, proposed the notion of the social ownership in 1997. For more discussion, see Ma and Ling, 1998, p.417-419.

42 A series of articles were written by the newspaper commentators and published in July and August 2000 in *The Study Times* 《学习时报》, the newspaper of the Party School of the CPC Central Committee.

43 *The Study Times,* 7th August 2000.

44 *The Study Times,* 14th August 2000.

45 *The Study Times,* 21st August 2000.

46 It was commented that if the local regulation were in contradiction with the Constitution, it would be null and void. However, the researchers believed that it might promote economic prosperity in the county while it would cause confusion in the local judicial work. For more discussion, see *Comprehensive Understanding of 'State Innovation System' and Building an Overall 'China (State) Innovation System'* 《全面理解" 国家创新体系" 含义，构建完整" 中国（国家）创新体系"》, 2000.

47 Fifty per cent of the private enterprises are located in the southeastern coastal provinces and cities, including Guangdong, Zhejinag, Shandong, Jiangsu, Shanghai, Hebei, and Liaoning. The demand for legal protection must be more urgent in these areas.

48 Licheng Ma and Zhijun Ling believe that there have been three rounds of mind emancipation. The first one broke 'the cult of personality' in 1978; the second one smashed 'the cult of planned economy' in 1992; and the third broke 'the cult of public ownership'. What and when is the next round? For more discussion, see Ma and Ling, 1998, p.424-426.

49 The other important market institutions in this sense include contract law and commercial codes, financial markets, and respected judicial systems. For further discussion, see John D. Sullivan, executive director of CIPE, 'Market Institutions and Democracy', *Center for International Private Enterprise* (CIPE), 25 September 1999; and An interview with Hernando de Soto by the CIPE, 'Securing Property Rights: the Foundation of markets', *Center for International Private Enterprise,* 25 September 1999.

50   After ranking 161 nations on their economic freedom, Mr. Brian Johnson, a policy analyst at the heritage Foundation in Washington, concludes: 'These countries that are most economically free generally are also the most politically free. Similarly, these countries that are most economically repressed also tend to be the most politically repressed'. James Gwartney, an economist at Florida State University, Tallahasee, figures political freedom and economic freedom advance each other, observing 'Political reform precedes economic reform and makes it more lasting, or economic reform, with its higher income levels, leads to a demand for political reform'. For more discussion, see David R. Francis, 'Political freedom translates into economic freedom', *The Christian Science Monitor,* Thursday, February 43, 1999.

PART IV
CHANGES IN THE MASS PUBLIC
ORIENTATIONS

Chapter 7

Mass Public Orientations and Implications for Policy Institutionalization

As discussed in Chapters Five and Six, in order to achieve economic development, the post-Mao ruling elite have been forced to adopt pro-market working ideology, promoting market-oriented values such as contracts, market competition, and property rights. At the same time, they have made greater efforts in guiding mass orientations towards their authoritarian values: no multiparty election, no separation of the three powers, sticking to the one-party dominance of the people's congress, which were laid down by Deng Xiaoping in the 1980s (Deng, 1993, p.220, pp.240-1). Have they succeeded in doing so? Or have Chinese mass attitudes become less authoritarian, more liberal and pro-democratic as predicted by modernization theory that economic freedom may lead to political freedom and economic development may lead to changes in mass orientations [1] towards democratic values (Francis, 1999; Inglehart, 1997, pp.162-7)?

If Chinese mass attitudes are found shifting towards liberal and pro-democratic values, they will add another dimension of change to the social institutional environment, which is more dynamic in influencing policy institutionalization than such structural changes in the institutional environments as social class differentiation and the market systemic transformation.

This Chapter first gives a brief review of the concept and empirical studies of political culture, analyzing two empirical studies of Chinese political culture, the 1990 and 2000 opinion surveys, and then discusses their implications for policy institutionalization of China under transition.

Theories and Practices

Modernization theorists believe changes in mass attitudes towards more assertive, independent, liberal, tolerant, and self-seeking attitudes are associated with modernization and economic development, a process of value change from authoritarian to libertarian values. Such shifts in attitudes and value change are eroding the legitimacy of authoritarian regimes, pressing for democratic reforms, and eventually leading to their collapse. In the late 1980s the ruling elite of South Korea experienced strong pressure from the mass public for democratic reforms in the form of a strong labor movement, opposition movements, and activism among students, intellectuals, women, and church groups (Inglehart, 1997, p.179; Flanagan and Lee, 2000, pp.626-59). The Chinese ruling elite felt the same challenging pressure in the spring of 1989 but resolved to force the removal of student demonstrators out of Tiananmen Square on 4th June 1989. If the Chinese public attitudes had been shifted towards liberal democratic values,[2] the Chinese ruling elite might have opted for a more conciliatory solution to the student demonstrations at Tiananmen Square.

Opinion shift and value change may reach a point when soldiers will no longer fire on demonstrators to uphold the authoritarian rule, such as the downfall of Ferdinand Marcos in the Philippines and the failure of the 1991 coup against Mikhail Gorbachev in the former Soviet Union (Flanagan and Lee, 2000, pp.626-59).

Unfortunately, the role of public opinion in the economic and political transformations does not always receive the same recognition as the role of the political elite. Deng Xiaoping's talks during his 1992 tour of Chinese southern coastal areas were highly appraised as breaking the deadlock of China's market-oriented economic reform while Chinese people's strong opinion support of further economic reform did not receive such publicity.[3] The democratic image of Yeltsin on top of a tank defending the White House against the military coup in August 1991 was highly regarded while the popular support he was appealing for and did receive was not given much credit.[4] It is less likely that without a climate of mass attitudes favorable to China's market transition and Russian democratic transition, both Deng and Yeltsin could have had the way as they wished. Many researchers are calling to bring 'mass publics' back to the focus of transitional studies that are usually elite-centered (Maher, 1997, p.79; Inglehart, 1997, p.167).

Although inquiries of the importance of political culture can date back to Plato and Aristotle, it is Almond and Verba (1963) who pioneered empirical studies of political culture in the 1960s. Their original research was to unveil historical puzzles why democracy survived in some countries (Britain and the United States), and why it collapsed in others (Germany, Italy and Mexico). Their findings strongly indicated that beliefs, feelings and values significantly influence political behavior, and that these beliefs, feelings and values are the product of both childhood socialization and adult political socialization and experiences (Almond, 1989, p.29). Gabriel Almond defines political culture as:

- substantive content, which is further divided into three sub-branches: the system culture of a nation, consisting of the distributions of attitudes towards the national community, the regime, and the authorities; the process culture, including attitudes towards the self in politics (parochial, subject, or participant), and attitudes towards other political actors (e.g. trust, co-operative competence, hostility); and the policy culture, consisting of the distribution of preferences regarding the outputs and outcomes of politics, the ordering among different groupings in the population of such political values as welfare, security, and liberty;
- varieties of orientation towards these system, process and policy objects, which may be cognitive, consisting of beliefs, information and analysis;

affective, consisting of feelings of attachment, aversion, or indifference; or evaluative, consisting of moral judgments of one kind or another; and

● the systemic relations among these components, in other words, one known mass attitudes towards one political object or outputs of politics in a given population may predict their views on another object or outputs (Almond, 1989, p.27-8).

Kristen Hill Maher believes that there are some specific orientations that—if widespread in a given society – increase the likelihood of substantive and stable democracy developing, including (1) support for multiparty competition and non-violent conflict resolution, (2) external efficacy, (3) support for the rule of law and democratic constitutionalism, (4) political tolerance, (5) a value of individual liberty, or a 'rights orientation', (6) interpersonal trust and co-operative social relations, and (7) a participatory orientation and internal efficacy (Maher, 1997, p.93).

One of the major claims made by practitioners of political culture is that there is reciprocal interaction or influence between political culture and political structure or institutions (Almond, 1989, p.29; Maher, 1997, p.82).

In the 1970s Archie Brown and Jack Gray did a comparative study of political cultural in USSR, Yugoslavia, Poland, Hungary, Czechoslovakia, China, and Cuba, finding that these communist regimes failed to create a new socialist man despite the fact that these communist regimes made an unusually overt and conscious attempt to create new political values to replace the old ones through communist processes of socialization and education (Brown and Gray, 1977, pp.270-1).

Mao Zedong is notorious in making continual efforts to transform mass attitudes according to his visions of socialism and communism. However, he failed to make permanent changes in the orientations of Chinese people; otherwise, Deng Xiaoping's call 'Getting rich is glorious', a bourgeois disposition condemned by Mao, could not have gained currency so soon among the general public, awakening their deep desire for wealth. It is a good example of the ruling elite promoting a specific traditional orientation among the general public in the post-Mao era. The restoration and development of the private sector is a case of the mass orientation influencing the ruling elite to accept the results of the 'getting rich' drive. They are examples of the reciprocal influence between the general public and the ruling elite, or between Chinese mass orientations and political institutions in the post-Mao era.

Chinese political culture is usually portrayed as anti-democratic, containing such attributes as authoritarianism, passivity, ignorance of politics, fear of politics, and intolerance (Gray, 1977, pp.197-230; Nathan, 1986, p.120; Nathan and Shi, 1992; Huntington, 1991a, p.105, p.300 and 1991b; He, 1992; White, 1993, p.243). Evidence regarding the nature of Chinese political culture used to be drawn from documentary research, interviews and field observation. A more reliable way to detect real patterns of mass attitudes is to conduct public opinions surveys. In the 1980s, Chinese researchers began to conduct opinion surveys and many of them touched on political-cultural topics. For example, in 1990, Andrew J. Nathan and Tianjian Shi conducted a national survey in China, assessing approximately fifty political-cultural variables, providing a statistically accurate and comprehensive picture of the mass attitudes of 1990.[5]   Jib Chen, Yang Zhong and Jan William Hillard (1997) conducted an opinion survey in Beijing in 1995 and found high popular support for the regime. Since their questionnaire was designed to find the level of popular support for the regime, their survey failed to generate data about the political orientations of the survey population. The interpretation value of their survey is limited.   Also in 1995 Daniel V. Dowd, Allen Carlson and Shen Mingming (1999) carried out a survey in Beijing and their data suggested no apparent public pressure for democratization in Beijing. However, their findings might not represent the true picture of mass orientations of the Beijing residents since their survey methodology is questionable.   Respondents were asked to choose only one value that they considered most important from a list of political values. Their survey might fail to collect information on the true attitudes of those respondents who might consider several values were equally important but were asked to select only one as most important.   Their data collected this way, therefore, cannot show reliable patterns of Beijing mass attitudes. We consider Nathan and Shi's survey is significantly important in that it is not only a scientifically valid national sample survey but also provides a comprehensive and reliable picture of Chinese political culture in 1990.

The 1990 and 2000 Surveys

In December 1990, Nathan and Shi conducted a nation-wide opinion survey in China in co-operation with the Social Survey Research Center of People's University of China. The 1990 survey interviewed 3,200 adults and collected 2,896 questionnaires (with a response rate of 90.5 per cent) throughout China, except for Tibet, to provide a statistically accurate picture of mass attitudes. Their survey data indicated that the short-term prospects for democracy in China were dim because the party and state apparatus enjoyed a 'safety cushion' and 'the reservoir of confidence' – low levels of government impact, system affect, and tolerance among the Chinese people, especially among the less educated and less privileged.   However, their data suggested that the long term prospects for democracy in China were promising because 'the more urban and educated sectors showed more democratic attitudes, supporting expectation as derived from modernization theory that China's culture will move closer to the patterns characteristic of democratic countries as the economy grows'.[6]

During the last decade, particularly since the market economy was chosen as the economic reform target in 1992 and since the rule of law was accepted as the legal reform target in 1997, China has witnessed most of its dramatic economic, social, and political changes discussed in previous chapters.   Its 2001 urban population accounted for 37.66 per cent of the total, 11.25 percentage points higher than in 1990 and its urban annual per capita disposable income and rural annual per capita net income reached 829 and 286 US dollars respectively, compared to 316 and 144 US dollars in 1990.[7] According to the modernization theory, therefore, it may be more likely that more Chinese hold liberal and democratic attitudes than ten years ago.

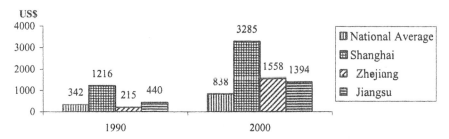

Figure 7.1 Per Capita GDP of Shanghai, Zhejiang and Jiangsu, 1990-2000

Note: Zhejiang's 1991 Per Capita GDP is used; all the figures are calculated from the data of the following sources at the exchange rates: US$1=4.784 in 1990; USD$1=5.323 in 1991; US$1=8.277 in 2000, respectively.

Source: 1) *China Statistical Yearbook 1996 &1999; Shanghai Statistical Yearbook 1996; Jiangsu Statistical Yearbook 1996*; 2) *Statistical Communiqué of PRC on the 2000 National Economic and Social Development*; 3) *Communiqué of PRC on the Key Data of the Fifth Population Census (No. Two)*; 4) *Statistical Communiqué of Shanghai on the 2000 Municipal Economic and Social Development*; 5) *Statistical Communiqué of Jiangsu on the 2000 Provincial Economic and Social Development*; 6) *Zhejiang People's Government Report on the 2000 Provincial Economy.*

We put the suggested conclusion of the 1990 survey to test by replicating the 1990 survey in the summer of 2000.[8] The 2000 survey covered Shanghai, Jiangsu Province and Zhejiang Province. Bordering on each other and located in the Yangtze Delta, they are among the most prosperous and dynamic regions of China. In 1998 their total GDP and import and export value already accounted for 20 per cent and 23.5 per cent of the national figures, respectively.[9] Their per capita GDP of 1990 and 2000 is displayed in Figure 7.1. In 1990 Shanghai and Jiangsu had a higher per capita GDP than the national average while Zhejiang had a much lower per capita GDP, only 63 per cent of the national average. In 2000 all the three regions registered a much higher per capita GDP than the national average with Zhejiang displaying a faster growth than Shanghai and Jiangsu.

If the mass attitudes of these three regions are found more liberal and pro-democratic than the Chinese mass attitudes of 1990, a tentative conclusion may be suggested that China's political culture is moving closer to the patterns characteristic of democratic countries as its economy keeps growing, although the conclusion is subject to further tests.

The 2000 survey used the same questionnaire of the 1990 survey with limited modification in one question. Besides, we also added a number of questions to test mass attitudes on the development of the private sector in China.

The 2000 survey was conducted in co-operation with East China University of Politics. The sampling size of the 2000 survey was 1,650 adults, to be divided into two groups: (1) a general public group of 1,500 adults selected from three areas: Shanghai, Jiangsu Province and Zhejiang Province (500 cases from each region); and (2) a specified group of 150 adults selected from the owners and managerial level personnel of the private enterprises operating in the three regions. The inclusion of a separate sample from the private sector will allow us to see whether the new bourgeoisie, private entrepreneurs, are pro-authoritarian and may become obstacles to democratization as suggested by some researchers.[10] A stratified multistage area sampling procedure was employed to select the sampling from the general public. The primary sampling units employed were counties for the rural domain and cities for the urban domain. The secondary sampling unites were townships in rural areas and districts and streets in urban areas. The third stage of selection was villages in the rural areas and residents' committees in the urban areas. For both domains, households were used at the fourth stage of sampling. A simple random sampling procedure was employed to select the sampling from the private enterprises operating in the three regions but the majority of cases come from Shanghai private sector.

Among the ordinary sample (1479 cases), 73.5 per cent are urban residents and 25.6 per cent are rural residents. Fifty-four per cent of the ordinary sample used to be rural residents before the age of 18 years, indicating a rapid urbanization in the three regions. Seventy-six per cent of the sample are between 18 and 49 years old, 13.4 per cent between 40 and 49, 8.4 per cent between 50 and 59, and 2.2 per cent over 60. The education level of the ordinary sample is 4.5 per cent are illiterate, 11.4 per cent some primary education, 63.4 per cent some secondary education, and 18.3 per cent some college education. Among the category of some college education, 9.3 percentage points are contributed by those respondents who have received some college education from evening colleges, broadcasting college programs, and professional college programs. In the three regions, such informal college education is very popular and most of these programs are non-degree programs. Those respondents who reported they have received some college education may have finished only one such course.

Students of East China University of Politics and Law were employed as field interviewers. In total, 1,650 adults were interviewed and 1,625 questionnaires (1,479 from the ordinary sample and 146 from the private sector sample) were collected, which represents a response rate of 98.5 per cent.

Findings of the 2000 Survey

Although we have collected mass attitudes in the three regions on a wide range of issues as the 1990 survey, discussions within this chapter will focus on the findings of the survey on the following dimensions of mass attitudes: (1) the perceived impact of government, (2) feelings of political efficacy, (3) political tolerance, (4) attitudes towards government's handling of issues, (5) political, social and procedural attitudes, and (6) attitudes towards the private sector. As benchmarks of analysis, the findings of the 1990 survey are displayed in brackets.

The Perceived Impact of Government

The 2000 survey employed the same questions as the 1990 survey to measure the respondents' awareness of the impact of government, one of the cultural requisites considered necessary to generate an interest in politics and a desire to participate in the political process (Nathan and Shi, 1992).

The results are displayed in Table 7.1. On average, over 60 per cent of the respondents of the 2000 survey stated both national and local governments have an impact (Great effect / Some effect) on their daily life, while the 1990 survey found that only about 23 per cent said so. Not only more urban dwellers but also more rural residents felt the impact of the national government on their daily life (see Figure 7.2).

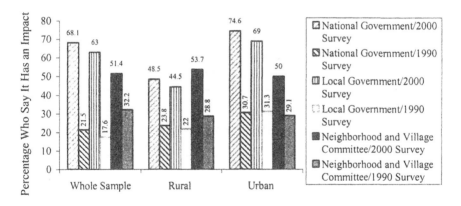

Figure 7.2 Perceived Impact of Government by Type of Household Registration

Source: the 1990 and 2000 surveys.

Not only more people with some college education were perceiving the impact of the national government on their daily life but also more people with none education and some primary education felt the impact (see Figure 7.3), suggesting that the government is losing the 'safety cushion' among the less educated people. The majority are now associating government administration with the quality of their daily life, which may be a logical basis for a political demand for more accountability of the government.

Table 7.1 Perceived Impact of National and Local Government and Neighborhood or Village Committee on Daily Life

(in percentage, figures in brackets are results of the 1990 survey)

	Village / Neighborhood Resident Committee	Local Government	Central Government
Great effect	13.8	11.1 (5.4)	27.3 (9.6)
Some effect	37.6	51.9 (18.4)	40.8 (11.7)
No effect	44	35.5 (71.6)	29.3 (71.8)
Other	1.9	-- (--)	-- (--)
Do not know	2.7	1.5 (4.6)	2.6 (6.7)
N=1479 (N=2896)			

The questions used in the two surveys: 'Now let's discuss the village committee/neighborhood resident's committee. How much effect do you think its activities have on your daily life?' 'Now let's discuss the local government. How much effect do you think its activities have on your daily life?' and 'Now let's discuss the national government in Beijing. About how much effect do you think its activities have on your daily life?'.

Source: the 1990 and 2000 surveys.

Table 7.2 Perceived Impact of National and Local Government and Neighborhood or Village Committee, by Regions

(Percentage who say it has an impact.)

	Village / Neighborhood Resident Committee	Local Government	Central Government	Number of Cases
Shanghai	47.4	66.6	75.4	500
Jiangsu	51.8	69.3	69.1	488
Zhejiang	55	53.2	59.9	491

Source: the 2000 survey.

Those from the private sector sample felt the impact of government on their daily life more intensely than those from the ordinary sample (see Figure 7.4), perhaps because private enterprise owners have to deal with various government agencies on a regular basis. Their business activities are not only being regulated by both national laws and regulations and local regulations and rules, but also being affected by helpful or predatory local officials.

On the whole, the perceived impact of both national and local governments on people's daily life in Shanghai, Jiangsu and Zhejiang is higher than in Italy and Mexico (see Figure 7.4). Fewer respondents from the general sample felt the impact than citizens of the most developed democratic countries: the United States, the United Kingdom and Germany, while the perceived government impact among the respondents from the private sector sample is at a quite similar level as among citizens of the three democracies.[11]

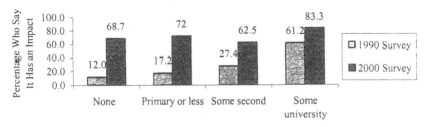

Figure 7.3 Educational Differences in the Perceived Impact of the National Government on Daily Life

Source: the 1990 and 2000 surveys.

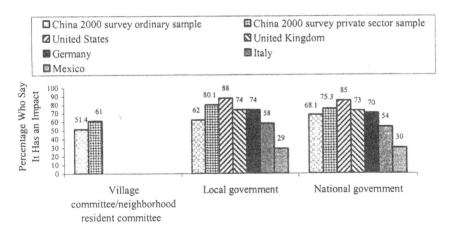

Figure 7.4 Perceived Impact of Government by Countries

Source: Almond and Verba, 1963; Nathan and Shi, 1992; the 1990 and 2000 surveys.

Among the three regions, Shanghai is more developed than Jiangsu and Zhejiang and the perceived impact of the central government among the Shanghai mass public is higher than that among the general public in the other two regions. However, the reverse pattern of the perceived impact of the village / residence committee on their daily life appears (see Table 7.2). This suggests that more economic development of a region seems to generate an increasing perception of the national government's impact on their daily life and a decreasing mass perception of the impact of the grass-root government.

The degrees of the perceived impact of the government on the daily life of the urban and rural communities are different. More rural respondents (53.7 per cent) were feeling the impact of the village committee/neighborhood resident's committee on their daily life than the urban respondents (50 per cent) while more urban respondents (69 per cent and 74.6 per cent) were reporting the impact of the local and national governments on their daily life than the rural respondents (44.5 per cent and 48.5 per cent). This suggests that the rural grass-root government has a greater impact on the daily life of the rural residents while the local and national governments have a great impact on the daily life of the urban residents.

Political Efficacy

The sense of political efficacy is considered by many researchers as a powerful determinant of people's involvement in politics and an important indicator of the health of a democratic system.[12] As in the 1990 survey, the 2000 survey took political efficacy as composed of two components, internal efficacy, consisting of beliefs about one's competence to understand and participate in politics; and external efficacy, referring to beliefs about the responsiveness of the government.[13]

The 2000 survey used the same questions as the 1990 survey to measure political efficacy in Shanghai, Jiangsu and Zhejiang and the results are indicated or noted in Tables 7.3 and 7.4. On the whole, internal efficacy in the three regions is much higher than that revealed by the 1990 survey (see Table 7.3). Quite similar to the 1990 survey, more respondents claimed to be able to understand work unit issues and fewer respondents believed they could become a good leader in their work unit or village. When turning to national affairs and the national government, however, a reverse pattern has emerged where many more respondents of the 2000 survey were more confident in their ability to serve as government leaders than in their ability to understand national affairs.

The private sector sample respondents also displayed a similar reverse pattern of internal efficacy on national issues. However, there are some differences in the degrees of their self-estimation of their ability to understand issues and to act as a leader. More respondents from the private sector sample than from the ordinary sample have registered their confidence in their ability both to understand their work unit affairs (76.7 per cent) and to be a good leader at their work unit or village (69.2). Fewer from the private sector sample (50 per cent of them) were confident in their understanding of national issues as well as others but more (91.1 per cent) believed in their ability to become a government leader. It seems people from the private sector are more eager to be in politics than the general public, reflecting a deep desire to control their own destiny – to make more money and to protect their accumulated property.

Table 7.4 highlights the results of a similar but differently worded question, requesting respondents to measure their understanding of important issues facing the nation, the local government, and the work unit. It is surprising to see such a drastic increase in the 2000 survey respondents' self-perceived understanding of the three issues 'very well' or 'relatively well', on average, by over 30 percentage points more than the figure of the 1990 survey on each issue.

Table 7.3 Internal Efficacy

(Figures in brackets are results of the 1990 survey)

Percentage who report they:	Understand work unit affairs as well as others	Understand national affairs less well than others	Can be as good a unit leader as any others	Can be as good a government leader as any others
Strongly agree	17.8 (17.6)	3.7 (16.5)	19.3 (8.4)	81.7 (6.1)
Agree	48.9 (29.7)	19.6 (32.4)	27.7 (14.1)	7.8 (10.7)
Not sure	17.8 (5.5)	19.4 (4.7)	19.2 (4.2)	4.5 (3.3)
Disagree	5.9 (24.6)	42.5 (23.3)	17.9 (29.9)	4.5 (27.3)
Strongly disagree	3.4 (8.0)	11.6 (8.6)	3.1 (24.8)	0.7 (32.3)
Do not know	6.2 (14.6)	3.2 (14.3)	12.8 (18.6)	0.8 (20.2)
N=1479 (N=2896)				

Actual text of the question: 'Do you strongly agree, agree, disagree or strongly disagree with the following statements:
I think that my understanding of the situation in our work unit is no worse than other people's.
I think that my understanding of national affairs is not as good as ordinary people's.
I think that I would not be a worse work unit leader than other people.
I think that I would not be a worse government leader than other people'.

Source: the 1990 and 2000 surveys.

Comparing the understanding of the village, local and national issues 'very well' or 'relatively well' among the rural respondents and the urban respondents, the rural people seem to be more parochial with 76.8 per cent of them understanding the village issues very well or well but only 49.7 per cent and 23.9 per cent of them understanding the local and national issues very well or well, respectively. The pattern of the internal efficacy of the urban residents seem to be both parochial and metropolitan with 78.5 per cent, 53.6 per cent and 67.7 per cent of them reporting a good understanding of the work unit, local and national issues very well or well, respectively. Comparing to the findings of the 1990 survey, the internal efficacy of the urban residents increases much faster than that of the rural residents while the internal efficacy of the rural residents on the national issues grows much slower than on the village issues.

Table 7.4 Understanding of National-level, Local, and Work Unit Affairs

(Figures in brackets are results of the 1990 survey)

Percentage who say they:	National Affairs	Local Affairs	Work Unit Affairs
Understand very well	5.6 (0.9)	5.7 (1.9)	32.3 (15.4)
Understand relatively well	51.0 (17.0)	47.1 (18.0)	45.8 (31.9)
Understand poorly	34.0 (37.5)	33.4 (32.7)	11.8 (23.0)
Do not understand at all	6.9 (41.5)	6.1 (44.8)	6.5 (25.9)
Others	-- (--)	-- (--)	3.7 (--)
Do not know	2.5 (3.1)	7.6 (2.7)	0 (3.9)
N=1479 (N=2896)			

Actual text of the question: 'Regarding the important international and domestic issues facing our country, how well do you think you understand them? How about the important issues facing the city (county, or district)? How about the important issues facing your work unit (village), do you understand them very well, relatively well, not very well, or not at all?'

Source: the 1990 and 2000 surveys.

Figure 7.5 shows the findings of the 1990 survey and the 2000 survey on the respondents' understanding national and local affairs 'very well' or 'relatively well' with comparable figures from *The Civic Culture*. It is a little surprising to find that more respondents of the 2000 survey than citizens of the five democratic countries claimed they understood national issues well and the figure for their self-claimed understanding of local issues is higher than that of Italians and Mexicans. Respondents in the private sector sample were even more positive than those from the ordinary sample on both national and local issues and claimed to have a better understanding than citizens of all the five democracies on national issues and were roughly on a par with Americans and Germans on local issues.

It is interesting that the claimed understanding of national issues by Chinese respondents in the two surveys is always higher than their claimed understanding of local issues, while the opposite is true with the self-estimation of citizens of the five Western democracies. Considering that Chinese respondents' rating of their ability to become government leaders is also higher than their rating of their ability to understand national affairs, it suggests that more people in the three regions than in the five nations are interested in participating in national politics.

When comparing the internal efficacy among the general public in the three regions, an interesting picture emerges (see Table 7.5). The gap between the perceived understanding national affairs and the perceived ability to become a national leader among the Shanghai and Jiangsu respondents is 25.2 and 20.7 percentage points respectively, but the gap among the Zhejiang respondents is 60.4 percentage points. Considering Zhejiang Province economic development speed has been faster than Shanghai and Jiangsu in the 1990s, does the extraordinary gap suggest that faster economic development boosts people's desire to participate in national politics while exerting a lesser influence on people's perceived ability of understanding national affairs? A person's ability to understand takes time to acquire and learn through education and experience but the desire to do something may be more likely subjective to changes in his social and economic environments.

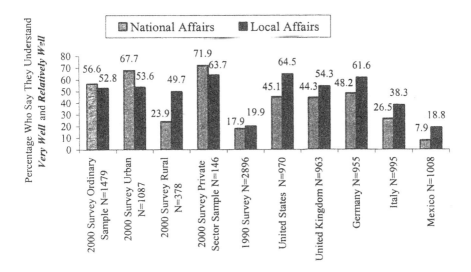

Figure 7.5 Understanding of National and Local Affairs

Actual text of the question used in *The Civic Culture*: 'Thinking of the important national and international issues facing the country--how well do you think you can understand these issues?'.

Actual text of the question used in China: 'Regarding the important international and domestic issues facing our country, how well do you think you understand them?'.

Source: Almond and Verba, 1963; Nathan and Shi, 1992; the 1990 and 2000 surveys.

The same question of the 1990 survey is used to measure the external efficacy of Chinese people, asking about the respondent's expectation of equal treatment at a government office. Findings are illustrated in Figure 7.6 and Table 7.6. Since official corruption has not only run out of control but also been upgraded from individual corruption to system corruption in the 1990s, it is not a surprise to find that fewer respondents expected equal treatment in 2000, more than 20 percentage points less than in 1990. People's expectation of a fair government in the three regions, therefore, is far behind the average level of the five democratic countries. However, the respondents from the private sector sample expected equal treatment approximately at the same level as those of the 1990 survey, indicating a stable working relationship between the private sector and the state administration.

Table 7.5 Internal Efficacy by Regions

(Percentage who agree or disagree)

Region	Understand work unit affairs as well as others (agree)	Understand national affairs less well than others (disagree)	Can be as good a unit leader as any others (agree)	Can be as good a government leader as any others (agree)	Number of cases
Shanghai	65.4	59.4	47	84.6	500
Jiangsu	67.8	65.4	43.8	86.1	488
Zhejiang	66.8	37.5	59.9	97.9	491

Actual text of the question: 'Do you strongly agree, agree, disagree or strongly disagree with the following statements:
I think that my understanding of the situation in our work unit is no worse than other people's.
I think that my understanding of national affairs is not as good as ordinary people's.
I think that I would not be a worse work unit leader than other people.
I think that I would not be a worse government leader than other people'.

Source: the 2000 survey.

Education is generally considered to have a positive impact on people's expectation of fair government, which is shown by the increase in the expectation of equal government treatment with the rising levels of education in four of the five democratic countries (see Figure 7.7). The 1990 survey depicted a curvilinear shape in the relationship between education and output effect, with the impact of education on people's expectation of equal treatment being positive up to the primary school level and turning negative beyond this level. The 2000 survey shows a V-shape of the relationship. Those with some primary education are 17.6 per cent less likely than those with no education to expect equal treatment. Beyond the primary education level the impact of education becomes positive. In comparison with the 1990 survey, people's expectation of equal treatment declines by 37.3 per cent at the level of some primary education and by 18.6 per cent at the level of some secondary education.

The low rate of expectation of equal treatment from the government among the less educated people indicates that the ruling elite are losing the cushion for their authoritarian rule – 'the reservoir of confidence in the government among less-educated Chinese' revealed by the 1990 survey.

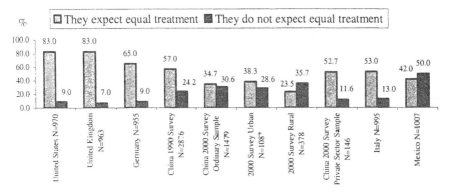

Figure 7.6 Expectation of Treatment by Government Bureaucracy, by Nation

Actual text of the question used in *The Civic Culture*: 'Suppose there were some questions that you had to take to a government office – for example, a tax question or housing regulation. Do you think you would be given equal treatment – I mean, would you be treated as well as anyone else?'.

The text of the question used in China: 'Suppose there were some issues that you had to take to a government office. Do you think you would be given equal treatment – I mean, would you be treated as well as anyone else?'.

Source: Almond and Verba, 1963; Nathan and Shi, 1992; the 1990 and 2000 surveys.

Table 7.6 Expectation of Treatment by Governmental Bureaucracy

(Figures in brackets are results of the 1990 survey)

Percentage who say:	Ordinary Sample	Private Sector Sample
They expect equal treatment	34.7 (57.0)	52.7
They do not expect equal treatment	30.6 (24.2)	11.6
Depends	15.0 (0)	20.5
Other	-- (9.1)	--
Do not know	19.7 (9.8)	15.1
	N=1479 (N=2876)	N=146

Actual text of the question: 'Suppose there were some issues that you had to take to a government office. Do you think you would be given equal treatment – I mean, would you be treated as well as anyone else?'.

Source: the 1990 and 2000 surveys.

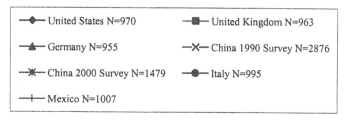

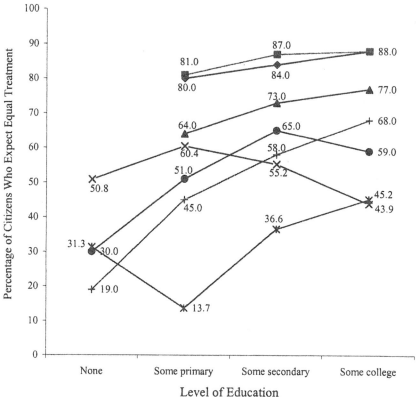

Figure 7.7 Expectation of Equal Treatment by Government Authorities, by Education

Source: Almond and Verba, 1963; Nathan and Shi, 1992; the 1990 and 2000 surveys.

Political Tolerance

Political tolerance is considered a fundamental basis for democratic contestation and regime legitimacy and is required to ensure the equality of citizens and minority rights. [14] The question presented to interviewees in the 1985 ISSP survey was 'There are some people whose views are considered extreme by the majority. Consider people who want to overthrow the government by revolution'. The 1990 survey adapted the question to the Chinese setting by stating 'There are some people whose ideology is problematic, for example, they sympathize with the Gang of Four. (1) If such a person wanted to express these kinds of ideas in a meeting, should he/she be allowed? (2) If such a person wanted to express these kinds of ideas as a teacher in college, should he/she be allowed? (3) If such a person wanted to publish articles or books to express these kinds of ideas, should he/she be allowed?'. [15]

In the 1990s the image of the Gang of Four was fading out of people's mind and becoming little relevant to the mass public, while Western values were being considered by the CPC as sources of spreading bourgeois liberalization in China. In other words, acquiring Western values is associated with developing bourgeois liberalization for Western-style democracy: free election, freedom of association and speech, and check and balance of power. We adapted, therefore, the question again to the Chinese conditions by replacing 'they sympathize with the Gang of Four' with 'they are leaning towards the Western values and concepts'. Findings are shown with the 1985 ISSP survey figures for the four developed democratic countries (see Figure 7.8).

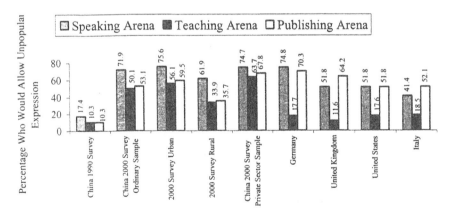

Figure 7.8 Political Tolerance

Source: the 1985 ISSP survey; Nathan and Shi, 1992; the 1990 and 2000 surveys.

The level of the tolerance of the three regions is quite high, although the urban respondents are more tolerant than the rural respondents. The 2000 survey suggests that people from Shanghai, Jiangsu and Zhejiang are more tolerant than citizens of the four democratic countries in the 'Teaching Arena' (see Figure 7.8). Considering that Chinese people are extremely concerned about their younger generation's education, this high level of tolerance in educating their youngsters indicates an anticipation of a more tolerant society in the future. In the 'Speaking Arena', they are more tolerant than Britons, Americans and Italians and in the 'Publishing Arena' they are more tolerant than Americans and Italians. The 2000 survey has revealed the same pattern of the relationship between tolerance and education as the 1990 survey: the less educated are less tolerant. However, the tolerance gap between those with some primary education and those with some college education has significantly narrowed (see Figure 7.9). That the less educated people are becoming more tolerant reinforces our previous suggestion that the regime is losing its safety cushion among the less educated mass public.

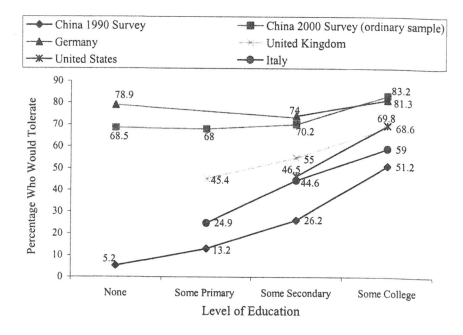

Figure 7.9 Tolerance for Speaking at Meeting, by Education and Country

Source: the 1985 ISSP suvey; Nathan and Shi, 1992; the 1990 and 2000 surveys.

The tolerance for speaking at a meeting among the respondents from Shanghai, Jiangsu and Zhejiang is 81.8, 73.6 and 60.1 percentage points, respectively, suggesting again that more economic development and urbanization leads to more tolerance among the population.

Attitudes towards Government's Handling of Issues

The 2000 survey used the same question as the 1990 survey to measure popular attitudes towards 20 issues.[16] The survey results are displayed in Table 7.7. Over half of the 2000 survey respondents were not satisfied with the government handling of ten issues while the 1990 survey respondents showed dissatisfaction with the government on only two issues, indicating that the public is becoming more critical of the government and expecting the government to do more to solve these problems. Although the government has delivered many more economic benefits to the public in the 1990s than in the previous decade, more people simply believe that the government should have done much better. Most of these issues, such as corruption, unemployment, inequitable income distribution, bureaucratism, and inadequate government investment in education, were among the prominent complaints that had aroused the 1989 demonstrations throughout China. Over 70 per cent of the 2000 survey respondents were dissatisfied with the government's handling of the three issues: corruption, unemployment and environment protection, suggesting a lost of confidence in the government's tackling of these problems.

Price control, population control and opening are the three issues on which the largest number of respondents thought the government has done enough, suggesting the mass public expect the government to continue the present policies regarding these issues. The public relative satisfaction with the government's handling of these issues may be explained by the facts that the prices have been kept under control, actually declining in the late 1990s (see Figure 6.15), that the population growth has been curbed as indicated in the 2000 fifth population census,[17] and that China was seeking to join WTO to increase its integration with the world community.

Over 10 per cent of the respondents considered the government has done too much on two issues – encouraging the development of private enterprise and population control, indicating many people are unhappy with government policies on these issues. While in the 1990 survey, only one issue, population control, received over 10 per cent 'too much' response. Private enterprise is the issue on which the largest number of respondents considered the government has done too much, suggesting that quite a few people are unhappy with the side effect of the development of private enterprises – the increasing gap between the rich and the poor. Although nearly half of the respondents selected 'just right' and were satisfied with the government performance on population control, the government policies on population control were still unpopular among a significant portion of the respondents.

There are some different focuses of complaints between the respondents of the ordinary sample and those of the private business sample. The general public are more concerned about economic welfare issues than the people from the private business sector, with the former over 10 per cent more than the latter complaining about the government's handling of these issues except environment protection. The majority of the respondents from the private sector sample (63.7 per cent) considered the government should have done much more to help private enterprises and ranked it as its second priority issue, while only 32.5 per cent of the respondents from the general public registered complaint on this issue and ranked it as their 18th priority issue, because there were many other economic welfare issues demanding their concern.

Table 7.7 Attitudes towards Government's Handling of Issues

(In percentage, figures in brackets were results of the 1990 survey)

Issues[18]	'Not Enough Attention'		'Just Right'	'Too Much Attention'	'No Interest'[19]
Complaints					
Oppose corruption	74.1	(53.8)	14.5	2.2	9.2
Oppose bureaucratism	61.1	(46.8)	19.5	6.1	13.2
Oppose crime	51.1	(47.1)	36.4	2.2	10.2
Price control	32.3	(55.7)	50.5	2.2	15.1
Economic welfare					
Environment protection	77.8	(33.6)	11.2	1.5	9.5
Unemployment	73.8	(37.8)	13.3	1.2	11.6
Income distribution	66.3	(42.5)	11.2	4.3	18.2
Consumer protection	60.5	(33.6)	22.8	2.5	14.2
Housing	60.0	(34.2)	18.4	3.1	18.4
Education	56.7	(42.1)	24.6	6.1	12.7
Subsidies	50.6	(27.9)	26.4	3.9	19.2
Population control	29.1	(24.7)	49.8	13.9	7.2
Reform					
Political Reform	42.4	(17.6)	20.5	5.3	31.8
Economic reform	39.3	(17.9)	22.6	7.2	31.0
Private enterprise	32.5	(18.2)	25.7	15.5	26.5
Anti-bourgeois liberalization	31.7	(21.2)	33.1	10.5	24.7
Foreign policy					
Taiwan	48.6	(17.0)	27.7	4.2	19.5
Defense	31.4	(9.8)	33.3	2.8	32.5
Opening	31.2	(12.6)	43.7	7.5	17.5
Foreign aid	20.1	(5.7)	26.6	8.9	44.3

N=1479 (N=2876)

Source: the 1990 and 2000 surveys.

Table 7.7 is a statistical order of issue priority assigned by respondents to each issue according to the percentage points of 'not enough' responses, delivering a clear message that the majority of the mass public are dissatisfied with the government performance on most of the issues. However, it cannot tell the internal pattern of responses towards these issues. Factor analysis can provide statistically reliable explanations on how issues are associated in the public mind through identifying clusters of issues that are related to one another in the response patters of the respondents. Table 7.8 categorizes such internally related clusters of issues into four agendas: Complaint Agenda, Reform Agenda, Economic Welfare Agenda, and Foreign Policy Agenda.

Table 7.8 Factor Analysis of Issue Priority[a]

	Complaint Agenda	Reform Agenda	Economic Welfare Agenda	Foreign Policy Agenda
Oppose corruption	**0.74**			
Oppose crime	**0.74**			
Price control	**0.69**	0.38		
Oppose bureaucratism	**0.69**			
Population control	**0.65**		0.32	
Education	**0.64**			
Environment	**0.55**		0.39	
Consumer protection	0.48	0.30	0.43	
Economic reform		**0.84**		
Political reform		**0.83**		
Private enterprises	0.34	**0.64**		
Antibourgeois liberalization	0.46	**0.51**		
Housing		0.37	**0.77**	
Income distribution			**0.59**	
Unemployment	0.47	0.31	**0.51**	
Subsidies			0.38	0.38
National defense		0.36		**0.74**
Taiwan	0.43			**0.69**
Opening	0.47	0.34		0.48
Foreign aid		0.42		0.46
Percentage of variance	47.1	8.8	6.6	5.9
Eigenvalue	9.4	1.8	1.3	1.2

[a] The factors are derived from a principal axis analysis of responses to the issue priority question in oblique rotation. Loading scores below 0.3 are suppressed since the usual practice in interpreting factor analyses focuses on items with loading scores above 0.5.

Source: The 2000 survey.

Table 7.8 shows a picture of the close association of the interrelated issues in the responses patterns of the respondents. Factor One includes corruption, crime, price control, bureaucratism, population control, education, environment, and consumer protection. Since these issues represent an interrelated set of issues that require a better performance and administration of the regime and bear direct impact on people's daily life, we label Factor One as the Complaint Agenda. Factor Two displays a coherence of issues, including economic reform, political reform, private enterprise, and antibourgeois liberalization, that demand certain changes in the existing laws, regulations and rules if better economic results can be expected, and we call Factor Two as the Reform Agenda. Facto Three includes housing, income distribution, unemployment and subsidies that imply direct impact on people's economic and social welfare, and therefore, we name Factor Three as the Economic Welfare Agenda. Factor Four covers national defense, Taiwan, opening and foreign aid that concern China's foreign relations. In the factor analysis of the 1990 survey, opening cohered in the Reform Agenda. In our factor analysis, it is included in the Foreign Policy Agenda. Perhaps in the mind of the mass public, opening measures have been sufficiently enshrined into the Constitution, laws and regulations, and any further measures to broaden opening to the outside world mainly represent implementation of the existing rules rather than constituting a new reform.

Table 7.9 Correlations between Respondents' Attributes and Issue Agendas*

	Complaints Agenda	Reform Agenda	Economic Welfare Agenda	Foreign Policy Agenda
Household registration[a]	0.21	0.22	-0.32	0.08
Sex[b]	0.28	0.22	0.23	-0.17
Age[c]	-0.14	-0.15	-0.16	0.14
Education[d]	0.42	0.39	-0.43	0.25
Family income[e]	0.19	0.18	-0.2	0.11
Party member[f]	0.2	0.16	-0.15	0.11
Occupation[g]	0.23	0.27	-0.24	0.12
State unit[h]	0.25	0.25	-0.31	0.12
N=1479				

* All correlations are significant at the .001 level.
[a] Household registration: 1 if urban household registration, 0 if rural household registration.
[b] Sex: 1 if male, 0 if female.
[c] Age: 1 if older, 0 if younger.
[d] Education: by years of formal schooling.
[e] Family income: by RMB *yuan*.
[f] Party member: 1 if member of Communist Party of China, 0 if not.
[g] Occupation: 1 if white collar, 0 if other.
[h] State unit: 1 if respondent reported working at state organization or state-owned enterprise, 0 if working at collective or other kind of enterprises.

Source: the 2000 survey.

The factor analysis of the 2000 survey identifies 16 issues with loading scores above 0.5 while the factor analysis of the 1990 survey identified 11 issues. This may suggest that the mass public in the three regions are cognitively sophisticated, displaying more mature patterns of their orientations towards different issue agendas that may have different impacts on their daily life.

Table 7.9 displays correlations of selected respondent attributes with the respondents' tendency to give high priority to each issue agenda. The size of the correlation coefficient is a measure of how strongly the attribute influences a respondent's tendency to be concerned with the issues of each agenda. Compared to the findings of the 1990 survey, there is exactly the same pattern as it was ten years ago. All the correlations are statistically significant, with education being the most powerful predictor of the respondents' issue priorities, to be followed by occupation, household registration and sex.

Table 7.10 Multiple Regression Analysis of Respondents' Attributes on Issue Agendas

	Complaints Agenda		Reform Agenda		Economic Welfare Agenda		Foreign Policy Agenda	
	Co-efficient	Beta	Co-efficient	Beta	Co-efficient	Beta	Co-efficient	Beta
Household registration[a]	0.04	0.05	0.09	0.08**	-0.33	-0.16***	-0.01	0.01
Sex[b]	0.25	0.17***	0.17	0.13***	-0.14	-0.05***	0.17	0.11***
Age[c]	-0.03	-0.04***	-0.03	-0.06***	0.03	0.15***	0.02	-0.07***
Education[d]	0.03	0.27***	0.02	0.22***	-0.03	-0.22***	0.05	0.17**
Family income[e]	-0.03	0.05	-0.03	0.06**	0.02	-0.01*	0.02	0.07**
Party member[f]	0.18	0.09***	0.14	0.07***	-0.16	-0.04***	0.23	0.09***
Occupation[g]	0.04	0.04	0.26	0.12***	-0.09	-0.02**	0.09	0.28
State unit[h]	0.08	0.07**	0.08	0.07**	-0.11	-0.05***	7.02	0.05
Constant	-0.48		-0.44		0.62		-0.09	
R Squared		0.14		0.14		0.26		0.1

N=1479

* =significant at the .1 level; ** =significant at the .05 level; *** =significant at the .01 level.
[a] Household registration: 1 if urban household registration, 0 if rural household registration.
[b] Sex: 1 if male, 0 if female.
[c] Age: 1 if older, 0 if younger.
[d] Education: by years of formal schooling.
[e] Family income: by RMB *yuan*.
[f] Party member: 1 if member of Communist Party of China, 0 if not.
[g] Occupation: 1if white collar, 0 if other.
[h] State unit: 1 if respondent reported working at state organization or state-owned enterprise, 0 if working at collective or other kind of enterprises.

Source: the 2000 survey.

Table 7.10 presents a multiple regression analysis of respondents' attributes on issue agendas. The standardized regression coefficients (betas) measure the relative strength of each variable in affecting respondents' choice of issue agendas.

Again, the pattern is nearly the same as it was ten years ago. Different variables affect adherence to different agendas. Education is the strongest factor that influences the choice of issue agenda consistently over all four agendas. Sex is the second strongest factor influencing respondents' choice of agendas, with men being more concerned with Complaint, Reform and Foreign Policy Agenda issues and women more concerned with Economic Welfare Agenda issues; to be followed by the variables, household registration and age, that influence adherence to the Economic Welfare agenda, with rural residents, less educated, less better off, non-party members and older people placing relatively high priority on this agenda, while the better educated, the young, urban residents, party members and those working in the state sector are more concerned with Complaint and Reform Agenda issues.

Table 7.11 Attitudes towards Government's Handling of Issues by Permanent Household Registration

(Percentage who say 'Not enough attention')

Issues	Rural	Urban
Complaint Agenda		
Oppose corruption	53.7	80.9
Consumer protection	40.7	66.9
Oppose bureaucratism	47.1	65.5
Education	32.8	64.9
Oppose crime	42.3	53.6
Reform Agenda		
Political Reform	28.8	47.3
Economic reform	28.6	43.3
Economic Welfare Agenda		
Unemployment	56.9	79.4
Income distribution	38.4	75.5
Housing	52.1	62.4
Subsidies	40.5	53.7
	N=378	N=1087

Source: the 2000 survey.

Although the general complaint levels of the rural respondents over the government's handling of the 20 issues are much higher than those of the 1990 survey respondents, they are over 10 percentage points lower than those of the urban respondents on the following issues (see Table 7.11). That the urban dwellers tend to be more critical of the government's handling of such issues as jobs, incomes, subsidies, education and housing is perhaps due to the fact that they used to be secured by the state as welfare products. Certainly, urban dwellers are expecting the government to do more to solve these problems but that does not necessarily mean that the urban dwellers wish to return to the old ways of doing things; otherwise, the majority of them would not want the government to further the political and economic reforms. On those problems of corruption, bureaucratism and crime that urban residents are feeling more intensely than rural people, that does not mean that these problems are more serious in urban areas than in rural areas. Perhaps, urban dwellers are better educated, better informed, or more liberal, or all of these factors influence their perception of these problems, or simply, results of urbanization.

Political, Social and Procedural Attitudes

The 2000 survey used the same six statements to test attitudes towards democracy[20] and the pattern of responses is displayed in Table 7.12. It also used the same six questions to test attitudes towards women (social liberalism) and two questions to test attitudes towards criminal procedure (procedural liberalism)[21] and the pattern of responses is shown in Tables 7.13 and 7.14.

Table 7.12 Opinions on Democracy

(in percentage, figures in brackets are results of the 1990 survey)

Issue	Pro-democracy	Anti-democracy	Don't Know
More democracy will lead to chaos (disagree)	76.2 (37.7)	9.5 (22.4)	14.3 (39.9)
Multiple parties will cause political chaos (disagree)	64.0 (29.5)	18.1 (35.7)	17.1 (34.7)
Different thinking will lead to chaos (disagree)	72.0 (32.2)	17.1 (43.0)	10.9 (24.8)
Heads of cities should be elected (agree)	87.5 (67.8)	3.8 (21.6)	5.9 (10.6)
China needs more democracy now (agree)	77.3 (54.8)	11.8 (6.0)	11.0 (39.3)
China's democracy depends on CPC's leadership (disagree)	19.1 (1.7)	72.3 (76.1)	8.6 (22.2)
N=1479 (N=2876)			

Source: the 1990 and 2000 surveys

Attitudes of the respondents are much more pro-democratic than those of the 1990 survey on all the statements except the last one: 'China's democracy depends on CPC's leadership'. Although more respondents in 2000 did not agree with the statement (19.1 per cent, compared to 1.7 per cent in the 1990 survey), the majority (72.3 per cent) still believed in the capability of the CPC to initiate a democracy-oriented political reform. Another obvious difference is that fewer respondents have chosen 'Don't Know', indicating the respondents are more confident than those of the 1990 survey when facing such politically sensitive questions.

However, there is a marked difference in the patterns of attitudes towards democracy among the rural and urban respondents of the three regions. Their majorities share quite similar views on most of the democratic issues except for 'Multiple parties will cause political chaos (disagree)' and 'Different thinking will lead to chaos (disagree)'.   On these two issues of democracy, the urban respondents are more pro-democratic than the rural respondents, although, on the whole, around 40 to 60 per cent of the rural respondents still show pro-democratic orientations, more pro-democratic than those respondents of the 1990 survey (see Table 7.13). This mixed pattern of orientation of the rural respondents may be due to their personal political experience of the election of the village committee members, a quasi-democratic election, where individual candidates are allowed but the majority of candidates are CPC members.

Table 7.13 Opinions on Democracy by Permanent Household Registration

(in percentage)

Issue	Rural	Urban
Multiple parties will cause political chaos (disagree)	38.9	73.5
Different thinking will lead to chaos (disagree)	43.2	81.7
	N=378	N=1087

Source: the 2000 survey.

Generally speaking, social attitudes of the three regions are quite similar to those revealed by the 1990 survey (see Table 7.14). However, the respondents are more conservative than those of the 1990 survey on three particular questions: 'If your unmarried son wanted to marry a divorced woman, would you approve?' 'If your immediate supervisor was a woman, would you feel annoyed?' and 'Do you care if you do not have a son?'. It is interesting to find a mixed pattern of social attitudes of the mass public in the three regions towards women.   Chinese traditional attitudes considered that women should stay at home looking after their husbands and children, that divorce was not socially acceptable, and that it was unacceptable to parents when their unmarried son wanted to marry a divorced woman.   After over 20 years of economic reforms and opening to the outside world, mass attitudes on divorce and women's income and education in the three regions have become liberal while those attitudes on marrying a son to a divorced woman, having a woman supervisor and having no son become less liberal. Nowadays, women's income is an indispensable part of the family income and their education is an important factor on how much money women can bring back home.   Does this suggest that the propensity to change social attitudes may be associated with economic benefits that such changes can bring to family?

The mass public of the three regions displayed quite similar patterns of social attitudes except on 'allowing son to marry a divorced woman', on which only 8.8

per cent of the mass public of Jiangsu answered 'yes', much lower than their counterparts from Shanghai and Zhejiang.

Table 7.14 Social Attitudes

(in percentage, figures in brackets are results of the 1990 survey)

Issue	Liberal	Conservative	Don't Know
Would you allow son to marry a divorced woman (yes);	23.0 (46.0)	48.7 (38.5)	15.9 (15.6)
Do you mind if supervisor is a woman (no);	56.7 (81.2)	16.0 (5.3)	7.2 (13.5)
Wife's educational level should be lower than husband's (no);	70.1 (70.3)	21.1 (17.4)	8.8 (12.3)
Wife's income should be lower than husband's (no);	72.0 (75.0)	22.4 (15.5)	5.5 (9.5)
Do you care if you do not have a son (no);	45.7 (63.8)	22.4 (27.1)	3.1 (9.1)
Should couple be able to divorce (yes);	73.2 (55.0)	12.0 (33.8)	14.8 (11.2)
N=1479			

Source: the 1990 and 2000 surveys.

It is a little amazing to see the rural respondents displayed more or less similar orientations towards most social issues as their urban counterparts except on one issue. On 'Do you care if you do not have a son?' 34.9 per cent of the rural respondents answered 'No' while 35.2 per cent 'Yes'. This mixed pattern indicates that a third of the rural adults are departing with, perhaps, the most deep-rooted traditional view that one must have at least a son to continue your line of blood. Since the population growth pressure mainly comes from the rural areas where over three-quarters of the population live, this attitudes shift towards liberal values among the rural adult population may contribute greatly to the declining population growth in the 1990s indicated in the Fifth National Population Census.

Procedural liberalism in these three regions is relatively strong (see Table 7.15). Especially, a large majority of the respondents showed strong support for judicial independence from the government and the party, indicating the public is complaining about the present political system that is nourishing rather than curbing official corruption. One major reason for the failure of the political system to bring official corruption under control is its lack of separation of power and lack of effective supervision and check on power. More urban respondents were pro-democratic, 81.1 per cent versus 53.2 per cent, than their rural counterparts who answered 'No' to the question 'Judge should solicit opinions of local government'. This orientation difference among the rural and urban respondents may have a lot to do with urbanization.

Table 7.16 displays findings on which sections of the public hold democratic and liberal values through correlating the strength of pro-democratic and liberal attitudes with the same respondent's attributes. It shows the same pattern of correlations as shown in Table 7.9. Education is the first strongest correlation, to be followed by type of household registration, work, sex and family income. Those who are better educated, urbanites, male, young tend to be more liberal on all three dimensions.

Table 7.15 Attitudes towards Due Process

(In percentage, figures in brackets are results of the 1990 survey)

Issue	Pro-Due Process	Ignore Due Process	Don't Know
Punish without legal procedure	57.4 (43.2)	36.9 (40.7)	5.5 (16.1)
Judge should solicit opinions of local government	73.9 (22.6)	15.9 (57.3)	10.2 (20.1)
N=1479			

Source: the 2000 survey

Table 7.16 Correlation between Respondents' Attributes and Degree of Democratism

	Political	Social	Procedural
Household registration[a]	0.26	0.24	0.24
Sex[b]	0.29	0.17	0.19
Age[c]	-0.27	-0.69	-0.09
Education[d]	0.5	0.4	0.35
Family income[e]	0.22	0.16	0.18
Party member[f]	0.15	0.14	0.17
Occupation[g]	0.26	0.2	0.22
State unit[h]	0.3	0.23	0.24
N=1479			

All correlations are significant at the .001 level.

[a] Household registration: 1 if urban household registration, 0 if rural household registration.
[b] Sex: 1 if male, 0 if female.
[c] Age: 1 if older, 0 if younger.
[d] Education: by years of formal schooling.
[e] Family income: by RMB *yuan*.
[f] Party member: 1 if member of Communist Party of China, 0 if not.
[g] Occupation: 1if white collar, 0 if other.
[h] State unit: 1 if respondent reported working at state organization or state-owned enterprise, 0 if working at collective or other kind of enterprises.

Source: 2000 survey.

The multiple regression displayed in Table 7.17 shows that all the variables significantly affect respondents' choice of democratic/liberal attitudes. The strongest is education, to be followed by age, sex, household registration, and party membership. However, the 2000 pattern of effects of the variables on respondents' choice of democratic attitudes is a little different from that of the 1990 survey. In 1990, respondents who were better educated, male, younger, more urban, and members of the party tended to be more tolerant and less authoritarian in their values. In 2000, respondents who were better educated, male, younger, and more urban, displayed quite similar orientations as the respondents of the 1990 survey. Respondents who were better paid and members of the party tended to be procedural liberal in their values while those who were less paid and non-members of the party began to be more pro-democratic in their values. In other words, the 2000 survey data suggests that not only those who are better educated, more urban and younger, but also the less privileged under the political system are expecting a democracy-oriented political reform.

Table 7.17 Multiple Regression Analysis of Respondents' Attributes and Degree of Democratism

	Political		Social		Procedural	
	Co-efficient	Beta	Co-efficient	Beta	Co-efficient	Beta
Household registration[a]	0.11	-0.11***	0.33	0.085***	0.145	0.10***
Sex[b]	0.38	-0.01***	0.23	0.055***	0.145	0.11***
Age[c]	-0.22	-0.35***	-0.03	-0.065**	0.005	-0.02
Education[d]	-0.1	0.07***	0.10	0.275***	0.045	0.24***
Family income[e]	-0.2	-0.15**	-0.02	-0.005	0.005	0.05**
Party member[f]	-0.01	-0.16**	0.25	0.035**	0.155	0.07***
Occupation[g]	0.02	-0.15**	0.08	-0.005	0.095	0.05*
State unit[h]	0.07	-0.13***	0.08	0.005	0.075	0.05*
Constant	1.21		2.89		0.155	
R Squared		0.09		0.17		0.155
N=1479						

* =significant at the .1 level; ** =significant at the .05 level; *** =significant at the .01 level.
[a] Household registration: 1 if urban household registration, 0 if rural household registration.
[b] Sex: 1 if male, 0 if female.
[c] Age: 1 if older, 0 if younger.
[d] Education: by years of formal schooling.
[e] Family income: by RMB *yuan*.
[f] Party member: 1 if member of Communist Party of China. 0 if not.
[g] Occupation: 1if white collar, 0 if other.
[h] State unit: 1 if respondent reported working at state organization or state-owned enterprise, 0 if working at collective or other kind of enterprises.

Source: 2000 Survey

Attitudes towards the Private Sector

In order to measure people's attitudes towards the private sector in China, the 2000 survey has included two groups of questions. One group measures people's attitudes about the government's handling of the private sector and the other group detects how people look at the effects of the development of the private sector. Findings are displayed in Figures 7.10 and 7.11.

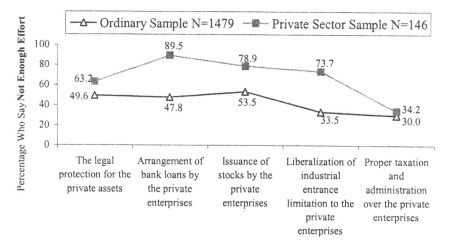

Figure 7.10 Attitudes toward Government's Handling of the Private Sector

The text of the question used in the survey: 'The private economy has become an important part of our socialist economy. For each of the following problems that I mention regarding how to develop the private economy, please tell me on which problems you think the government has spent too much effort, on which problems it has spent the appropriate effort, and on which problems it has spent not enough effort'.

Source: the 2000 survey.

On the whole, the complaints of the government's handling of these issues are much stronger in the private sector than in the general public. Nearly half of the respondents from the ordinary sample considered the government has not done enough on the legal protection of private assets, arrangement of bank loans by the private enterprises and issuance of stocks by the private enterprises, and about 30 per cent held the same opinion on next two issues (see Figure 7.10).

The majority of the respondents from the private sector sample were not satisfied with the government's handling of all the issues except taxation and administration. Relatively speaking, complaint about the government's handling of taxation and administration was the lowest in both groups of respondents.

Among the private sector group, the strongest complaint was on the second issue: arrangement of bank loans by the private enterprises, which corresponds with the reality that the private sector has only taken a fraction of China's annual total short-term loans, 0.58 per cent in 1994, 0.59 per cent in 1995, 0.7 per cent in 1996 and 0.78 per cent in 1998.[22]

Figure 7.11 shows findings of attitudes of the respondents towards the further development of the private sector, who 'agree' to the five statements. The attitudes of the two samples were divided on the first two statements and proximately the same on the next three statements. Over half of the respondents of the ordinary sample were worrying about the growing disparity between the rich and the poor and nearly half of them were concerned about possible social unrest and instability because of the growing disparity while only around 20 per cent of those from the private sector were sharing their worries on these two issues. The majority of both groups of respondents were showing positive attitudes towards further development of the private sector, which they believed will raise labor productivity, strengthen the comprehensive power of the country and raise the people's living standards.[23] In other words, policies designed to boost the private sector will be welcomed although the general public show concern about more inequality and possible social unrest.

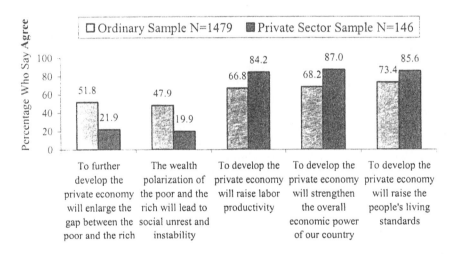

Figure 7.11 Attitudes toward the Private Sector

The text of the question used in the survey: 'Do you agree with the following views and opinions?'.

Source: the 2000 survey.

Conclusion: Implications for Policy Institutionalization

In summary, there are some meaningful differences between the attitudes of people from Shanghai, Jiangsu Province and Zhejiang Province in 2000 and those of the Chinese public in 1990. Firstly, fewer people from the three regions have avoided answering those questions that are politically sensitive (see Table 7.12) and that would show respondents' critical comments on the government handling of corruption, unemployment, income distribution, and other socio-economic, reform and foreign policy issues (see Table 7.7). This difference between the expressed attitudes of respondents of the 1990 and 2000 surveys indicates that fewer respondents of the 2000 survey have maintained such traditional and authoritarian values as conformity, submission and deference to authorities, signifying a process of people's value change under way.

The public disappointment with the government's handling of issues has grown substantially in the last decade. In 1990, 30 per cent of the respondents were dissatisfied, on average, with the government's handling of each of the 20 issues while in 2000, 48.4 per cent were showing their dissatisfaction (see Table 7.7). Besides, a large majority of people were focusing their disappointment on the government's handling of environment protection, corruption, unemployment, income distribution, and bureaucratism, most of which may develop into a crisis leading to democratic movements like the 1989 anti-corruption and anti-authoritarian-rule demonstrations if not properly and effectively dealt with.

The majority of people in the three regions feel more significantly the impact of national and local government on their daily life (see Table 7.1). More of the less-educated people and rural residents also felt the government impact on their daily lives (see Figures 7.2 and 7.3). This suggests that the majority of people now associate government administration with the quality of their daily life, which may be a logical basis for a political demand for more accountability of the government.

The public internal efficacy is surprisingly higher than in 1990. Particularly, the self-claimed ability to become a good national leader has 34.6 percentage points higher than the self-claimed ability to understand national issues (see Table 7.3). This abnormal gap between one's estimation of ability to understand and to act may be a strong indication of people's loss of confidence in and contempt towards the ruling elite rather than displaying their overestimation of their leadership ability.

The public external efficacy, that is the expectation of equal treatment by government bureaucracy, by contrast, has declined significantly since 1990. Even the less-educated people expected less fair government (see Table 7.6; Figure 7.6). In other words, the majority of people in 2000 have lost their trust in the government.

The public political tolerance, by contrast, has greatly increased, with over half of people willing to tolerate different views on Teaching and Publishing Arenas and over 70 per cent tolerate on Speaking Arena (see Figure 7.8). What is extraordinary, is that the majority of the less-educated people are becoming tolerant on Speaking Arena, (see Figure 7.9).

Social attitudes of the mass public in the three regions in 2000 were more liberal on 'divorce' and similar to those of the Chinese public in 1990 on 'wife's educational level' and 'wife's income'. More people in 2000 were becoming less liberal on three questions: 'Would you allow your son to marry a divorced woman?' 'Do you mind if supervisor is a woman?' and ' Do you care if you do not have a son?' (see Table 7.14).

Procedural liberalism among the mass public in the three regions is much stronger than in 1990. Particularly, a large majority (73.9 per cent) supported the independence of the judicial branch while only 22.6 per cent of the respondents did so in 1990. This strong shift in the public attitudes may be explained by the growing dissatisfaction of the public over the government's handling of official corruption, by the increasing awareness among the less-educated and less-privileged of the impact of the government on their daily lives, and by the declining expectation of equal treatment by the government bureaucracy. The stronger procedural liberalism displayed by the 2000 respondents suggests that the mass public are becoming less authoritarian, expecting to see the installment of the rule of law in China.

The majority of the respondents tended to be pro-democratic on all the statements except the last one, the CPC's leadership in China's democratization, while in 1990 only two issues, 'election of city leaders' and 'more democracy now', were endorsed by over half of the respondents (see Table 7.12). These mixed patterns of mass attitudes towards democracy may suggest the majority of people are holding orientations towards a democratic polity but wish to see an evolutionary transition under the leadership of the CPC. This disposition towards the CPC is contingent upon the performance of the CPC to deliver economic benefits to the mass public. In other words, if any issue of the Complaint Agenda (see Table 7.7) develops into a crisis, the public pro-CPC opinion on the statement 'China's democracy depends on CPC's leadership' may dissolve swiftly.

About half of the respondents hoped the government would do more to facilitate the further development of the private sector on legal protection, bank loans, and stock listing (see Figure 7.10). The majority supported the government's policy to further develop the private sector but with strong reservation on its side effects – the growing gap between the rich and the poor and possible social unrest and instability (see Figure 7.11).

The urban respondents tended to be less authoritarian, more liberal and more pro-democratic than their rural counterparts, indicating that urbanization has played an important role in shaping people's orientations towards liberal and democratic values.

The data of the 2000 survey has found the majority of the new bourgeoisie, private entrepreneurs, are no less liberal, pro-democratic and pro-procedural than the general public. No evidence from the data supports the view that the new rich may become obstacles to democratization as suggested by some researchers; rather, it suggests that the new rich may opt for a democratic transition if the prospective democratic polity can provide more legal protection for their business and private properties.

In conclusion, the data of the 2000 survey suggests that the ruling elite have failed to enforce their authoritarian values on mass orientations and confirms the conclusion of the 1990 survey that 'China's culture will move closer to the patterns characteristic of democratic counties as the economy grows'. The data of the 2000 survey suggests that the political culture of these three regions is quite supportive and conducive to democratization if the ruling elite initiates a democratic transition now. Within such an environment of mass attitudes favorable to liberal and democratic values, the ruling elite may find it increasingly difficult to maintain their one-party authoritarian rule because those who are the less privileged under the political system are becoming less authoritarian, more liberal and pro-democratic in their values:

- those who are less educated and less paid are beginning to feel the impact and alienation of the regime; and
- those who are less paid and non-members of the party are beginning to show more tolerant and pro-democratic values.

In a word, the regime is losing the 'cushion of safety' among the less privileged that was indicated in the data of the 1990 survey. Although the data of the 2000 survey does not warrant a conclusion that China will certainly embark on a democratic transition soon, the data does provide evidence that the political and cultural orientations of the mass public in the three more developed regions, are shifting towards more liberal and pro-democratic values conducive to democratization. It is reasonable to believe that people of the less developed regions may develop liberal and pro-democratic attitudes as China keeps on its present momentum of economic, social and political transformation, bringing prosperity to these less developed regions. These shifts in mass public orientations towards liberal and pro-democratic values represent a meaningful change in the civil-social environment (see Figure 2.2), further narrowing the discretionary power of the ruling elite in policy institutionalization while increasing the leverage of society to influence the former's policy choices.

Notes

1 'Orientations' refers to a broad range of beliefs, values, and assumptions that people hold about social and political life. Such orientations may be cognitive, affective, or evaluative. They are general in the sense that they may structure many more specific attitudes or opinions.

2 The 1990 World Values Survey found a high subjective well-being index (42, which is mean of: percentage of 'Happy' responses minus percentage of 'Unhappy' responses, and percentage of 'Satisfied' responses minus percentage of 'dissatisfied' responses). For more discussion, see Inglehart, 1997. p.359. Another separate survey of 1990 discovered a widespread ignorance of the government's impact on daily life, a reservoir of confidence in the government among less-educated Chinese, and low tolerance levels among the Chinese public. These mass opinions may have provided a social 'safety cushion' to the authoritarian regime. For more discussion, see Andrew J. Nathan and Tianjian Shi, 'Cultural Requisites for Democracy in China: Findings from a Survey,'

Journal of the American Academy of Arts and Sciences, Vol.122, No.2 (Spring 1992), pp. 95-123.

3   A 1990 survey revealed strong mass support for economic reform in China: 93 per cent of the respondents considered the economic reform delivered beneficial effects while 48 per cent reported negative effects; and only 29 per cent of the respondents favored direct government control. The survey covered four counties (two in the north and two in the south), involving 1,270 ordinary people and 252 local cadres. For more discussion, see Chhibber and Eldersveld, 2000, pp.350-73.

4   Just one year before the collapse of the Communist rule in the former Soviet Union, the 1990 World Values Survey found a surprisingly low level of subjective well being (-1); see Inglehart, 1997, p.359. Another survey conducted in the European USSR discovered that over 60 per cent of the respondents supported for democratic reform, see Duch, 1993, p.599.

5   Andrew J. Nathan is Professor of Political Science at Columbia University; Tianjian Shi is assistant Professor of Political Science at the University of Iowa. For a discussion of their findings, see Nathan and Shi, 1992; and also see Nathan and Shi, 'Left and Right with Chinese Characteristics, Issues and Alignments in Deng Xiaoping's China', *World Politics*, 48(4), (July 1996), pp.552-50.

6   Nathan and Shi, 1992, p.116.

7   Many analysts predict that China's urbanization may reach 60 per cent of its population in 20 years if it maintains an annual growth rate of 1.5 per cent, see *China Economic Times*, 8th November 2002, p.9. US dollars figures are calculated at the exchange rates: US$1=4.784 in 1990 and US$1=8.277 in 2001, respectively.
Data source: China Statistical Yearbook 1999, 2002.

8   Nicholas Rees, Jean Monnet Professor of European Institutions and External Relations, University of Limerick, Bernadette Andreosso-O'Callaghan, Jean Monnet Professor of Economics and Director of Euro-Asia Center, University of Limerick, and Yanlai Wang, a research associate at the Euro-Asia Center, jointly organized the 2000 survey in co-operation with East China University of Politics and Law.

9   *Data source: China Statistical Yearbook 1999*, National Bureau of Statistics, People's Republic of China, Beijing: China Statistics Press, 1999, pp.63, p.592.

10   The suggestion that the new bourgeoisie are pro-authoritarian is based on interviews rather than on random sample surveys. Therefore, their conclusion is questionable. For their interviews and conclusion, see He, 2000b; also see Pearson, 1997, pp.162-5.

11   It is compared to a series of surveys conducted in the five countries in 1959-1960 and 1985 respectively, when they were democratic at the time of their survey. See Nathan and Shi, 1992; Almond and Verba, 1963; and also see *International Social Survey Program* (ISSP), *Role of Government – 1985 Codebook* ZA-NO. 1490 (Ann Arbor, Mich.: ICPSR, University of Michigan).

12   See among others, Nathan and Shi, 1992; Nie, Powell, and Prewitt, 1961; Milbrath and Goel, 1977, pp.58-9; Dalton, 1988, p.50; and Weatherford, 1992.

13   Craig, Niemi, and Silver, 1990, p.290.

14   See among others, Nathan and Shi, 1992; Diamond, Linz, and Lipset (eds), 1989, pp.16-7; Gibson, 1992.

15   ISSP is a continuing program of cross-national collaboration conducted in Australia, Germany, the United States, Great Britain, Austria, and Italy. It brings together pre-existing national social science projects and co-ordinates research goals by adding a cross-national perspective to the individual national studies. See *International Social Survey Program* (ISSP), *Role of Government – 1985 Codebook* ZA-NO. 1490 (Ann Arbor, Mich.: ICPSR, University of Michigan); Nathan and Shi, 1992.

16   The question used in the two surveys is 'Nowadays, our government is facing many problems, and to solve these problems is not easy. For each of the following problems that I mention, please tell me on which problems you think the government has spent too much effort, on which problems it has spent the appropriate effort, and on which problems it has spent not enough effort'.

17   The average annual population growth rate is 1.4 per cent between 1981 and 1991 and 1.07 per cent between 1990 and 2000. *Data source: China Statistical yearbook 1996; Communiqué of PRC on the Key Data of the Fifth Population Census (No. One).*

18   Issues are: Subsidizing basic necessities of life; Protecting the environment; Population control; family planning; Raising the education level; National defense; Foreign aid; Solving the housing problem; Solving the employment problem; Solving the problem of inequitable income distribution; Protecting consumers' rights; Political system reform; Economic system reform; Encouraging the development of individual or private enterprises; Opposing bourgeois liberalization; Opposing bribery and corruption, and rectifying party work style; Opposing crime; Price control; Opposing bureaucratism; Opening to the outside world; Reunifying with Taiwan.

19   No interest equals 'don't know' plus 'no answer'.

20   The statements were presented in an agree-disagree format:
   • If there are too many political parties in a country, it will lead to political chaos.
   • If people's ideas are not united, there will be chaos in society.
   • Broadening the scope of democracy in our country now would affect stability.
   • It is now very necessary to broaden the scope of democracy in our country.
   • The realization of democracy in our country depends upon the leadership of the party.
   • Some people believe heads of cities (counties) should be elected by the people, others believe they should be appointed by the higher authorities. What do you think?

21   The questions were asked in an agree-disagree format:
   • Do you care if you do not have a son?
   • A couple has been married many years, but their feelings all along were incompatible, and the wife has fallen in love with another man. Some people think that under this type of situation, it should be permitted for the couple to divorce; some people think it should not be permitted for them to divorce. What is your opinion?
   • If your unmarried son wanted to marry a divorced woman, would you approve?
   • If your immediate supervisor were a woman, would you feel annoyed?
   • The educational level of a wife should not be higher than her husband's.
   • The salary of a wife should not be more than her husband's.
   • Ruthless criminals should be punished immediately, without having to follow complicated legal procedures.
   • When trying a major case, the judge should solicit the opinions of the local government.

22   Although we do not have figures of medium-term and long-term loans, we believe the private enterprises' share of medium-term and long-term loans must be smaller since it is more difficult for them to arrange for such loans. *Data source: China Statistical Yearbook 1997 and 1999.*

23   These last three statements are the three principles advocated by Deng Xiaoping in the late 1980s, against which all new policies should be measured and rated for their soundness and appropriateness.

PART V
PROSPECTS FOR A DEMOCRATIC TRANSITION

Chapter 8

Conclusion

The main objective of this book is to investigate whether there is any evidence to suggest that economic freedom will lead to political freedom, that social and economic development and transformations will lead to democratization, and that China is moving closer to democracy. This book suggests an institutional analytic framework for examining the transitional case of China, which has been based on transitional theories and the new institutionalism, comprising political actors, institutions and six policy institutional environments. In the previous chapters, the institutional analytic framework is applied to three case studies: (1) agricultural reform and the open-door policy, (2) the restoration of private enterprises and property rights, and (3) the political and cultural orientations of the mass public.

The major findings from the case studies on the dynamic interactions between political actors, institutions and policy institutional environments indicate that changes in one institutional environment often lead to changes in other institutional environments, and that changes in the institutional environments have an influence on the institutional behavior of the post-Mao ruling elite, who tend to be less authoritarian, more pragmatic and more responsive to the institutional environments. The evidence of the case studies rejects the null hypothesis and supports the alternative hypothesis, suggesting that China is moving closer, on the continuum of regime change (see Figure 2.1), towards democracy, as institutional building in the economic arena or environment has been spreading into the ideological, civil-social, constitutional and political environments (see Figure 2.2), although it is not a democratic transition conventionally recognized by transitional theorists because it lacks an immediate regime change.

This chapter provides a summary of the findings of the case studies examined in the previous chapters. First, the patterns of change in the institutional environments will be measured against the six institutional environments (see Figure 2.2) and on the continuum of regime change (see Figure 2.1). Second, the institutional behavior of the ruling elite will be examined in the context of changes in the institutional environments. Third, the prospects for democratization in China will be assessed, as well as any possible reversion, although less likely, to a Maoist authoritarian regime.

Patterns of Change in the Institutional Environments

The case studies of agricultural reform, the open-door policy and the restoration of private property ownership have produced evidence to support Linz and Stepan's claim that the five arenas or macro institutional environments are interactive and dependent, with each having an effect on the other (Linz and Stepan, 1996, pp.7-15). The Chinese ruling elite wanted to reform the economy and to open up to the rest of the world with a clear intention to uphold the planned economy at the inauguration of the economic reforms and open-door policy. The unfolding of a chain of causes and effects in institutional changes have led the ruling elite to change reform strategies and to undergo institutional adaptation to the changing environments and to maintain the momentum of economic development (see Chapter 5).

In response to both international and domestic economic and political environments, the reform-minded ruling elite initiated the discussion on the 'criteria of truth' and won the support of the majority of the CPC decision-makers in making changes in the ideological environment. This institutional change gave Deng Xiaoping and his reform-minded associates a mandate to interpret and work out what kind of political ideology is needed for modernization and economic development (see Chapter 4). The economic-development priority has replaced Mao's class struggle priority in the operative ideology of the ruling party. 'Getting rich' and 'letting some people and some places become prosperous first' have been accepted as the new strategy to conduct economic development. This ideological breakthrough may be regarded as the end of the cult of personality, which is regarded as the first ideological liberalization or emancipation of the mind in China since 1949 (Ma and Ling, 1998, p.424). However, the majority of the ruling elite were not prepared for the all-round reform of the command economic system. The breakthrough in the economic reform did not come from the top but from the bottom up: those peasants who had suffered chronic hunger revived the practice of the household contract responsibility system. They succeeded in pressing the ruling elite to restore peasants' independent producers and to dismantle the people's commune as a collective production organization. The institutionalization of the household contract responsibility system in party documents and the constitution was not completed until 1993 when an amendment was added to the constitution that endorsed the household contract responsibility system and abolished the agricultural collective organization (see Chapter 5). However, the impact of agricultural reform also reached other institutional arenas or environments.

The changes in the agricultural institutions not only led to production of an increasingly larger quantity of agricultural products, but also made more and more agricultural laborers redundant. In order to facilitate distribution of agricultural products and labor resources, the ruling elite started to issue policies supportive of the private individual economy. Their strategy was to contain the development of the private sector, as a supplement to the public economy, by limiting the number of workers a self-employed producer and trader could employ. As it presupposed private ownership of capital goods in individual enterprises, this policy change challenged the socialist claim to eliminate private ownership. Therefore, reform of the economic management of production led to a change in the socialist ideology. The ideological change meant that people could pursue wealth and accumulate private assets. Many individual enterprises soon developed, whether in 'red cap' or in the name of collective enterprises, into private enterprises that broke the official labor employment limit, by hiring more than seven workers.

Although the domestic private sector was restricted by the government, it developed and expanded, not only producing more products and services to society but also creating more jobs at a time the government could not possibly provide full employment to the growing urban labor force. The ruling elite had no option but to officially recognize the role of private enterprises by restoring private ownership right in China. The theory of preliminary socialism was invented to justify such a deviation from the orthodox ideology of socialism (see Chapter 6).

Compared to the domestic private enterprises, foreign private entrepreneurs received much better treatment in terms of market entrance, tax reductions, and access to bank loans.[1] Special economic zones were created to attract foreign investment, not only offering foreign-funded enterprises the above preferential treatment but also creating a semi-market environment to make them feel like operating in their parent countries. This later experiment of market institutions in special economic zones provided the reform-minded ruling elite with some confidence and rationale to press for the establishment of a market economic system in China. By 1992 when Deng made a tour of the southern coastal areas calling for a market economy, domestic market forces had already achieved a significant development with the rapid expansion of economic activities of independent farmers and private enterprises (see Chapter 6). That is why, after the ruling elite decided to go for a market economy, the transition from the command economy to a market economy was started quite smoothly.

As the market economy is a rule-governed economic system, the government was required to respond by developing new laws for the construction of a market economy in China. Market institutions are usually considered closely interrelated with democratic institutions that uphold the principles of freedom of choice, free enterprise, and private property rights.[2] With the completion of laws necessary for a market economy, China is providing more legal protection to the general public and the private sector, eroding the authoritarianism of the regime (see Chapter 5). The institutional analysis suggests that institutional building in the economic arena is leading to institutional building in the ideological, civil-social, constitutional and political arenas or environments (see Figure 2.2), with a gradual shift of institutionalization towards Type B and Type A processes (see Table 3.1).

All of these structural changes in the economic, ideological and constitutional arenas or environments have led to significant changes in the civil-social environment (see Chapter 7). Not only has a differentiation of social classes occurred but also a meaningful change in the party itself has emerged. The 2000 survey data also confirms corresponding changes in the political-cultural orientations of the mass public towards liberal and pro-democratic values that are predicted by modernization theory. The data of the survey does not support the conventional view that the new bourgeoisie, private entrepreneurs, are pro-authoritarian and may become obstacles to democratization in China. Rather, the data suggests that these newly rich would prefer a democratic transition if the prospective democratic polity can provide more legal protection for their business and private properties.

These structural, social and value changes provide evidence for the suggestion that China's democratic reform of its authoritarian political system may proceed along the line of modernization theory; that is, following the footprints of the European first-wave democracies such as Britain, China is developing a capitalist economic system first in the name of socialism and under the guidance of the party state apparatus. In the context of China increasing integration with the world community, it would be less likely that China may take centuries to develop its democracy as the first-wave democracies did. Evidence of the institutional case studies suggests that the closer China moves, along the continuum of regime change (see Figure 2.1), towards democracy in terms of institution building in the civil-social, economic and constitutional arenas or environments, the more likely and sooner is democratic transition in China.

Added to the changing domestic institutional environments, China's increasing integration with the world community has created a pro-liberal and pro-democratic international institutional environment that may constrain, on the one hand, the authoritarian tendency of the ruling elite, and on other hand, promote liberal and pro-democratic values in the Chinese society.

Patterns of Institutionalization Behavior of the Ruling Elite

The institutional case studies suggest some meaningful changes in the institutionalization behavior of Mao and his successors. The most obvious is that the post-Mao ruling elite tend to be more responsive to changes in institutional environments and more concerned about achieving economic development than about the purity of socialist ideology. This change in the institutionalization behavior of the ruling elite was in fact initiated by Mao in late 1969 and early 1970 when Mao sensed China's security was in serious danger. The strategy to look towards the West for advanced technology and investment was endorsed by Mao and his colleagues (see Chapter 3). However, it may have been too late or too difficult for Mao to make sufficient adjustments to the changing environments. It is Deng Xiaoping who has made possible this change in the ruling elite's institutionalization behavior.

Deng achieved this through three measures: (1) supporting the discussion on the 'criteria of truth' that ideologically prepared the party and the mass public for economic reform and opening up to the rest of the world (see Chapter 4), (2) encouraging policy innovations from the periphery (see Chapter 5), and (3) offering a grand period of time for the reluctant colleagues to follow up along the reform line (see Chapter 5). The first measure was to find something from Mao's ideological legacy to justify economic reform and the open-door policy. The second one was to avoid direct confrontation with the conservative forces within the ruling elite. The third was to win over as many colleagues – chief actors, decision-makers, agents and players – as possible from the conservative forces.

Deng was a rational and calculated politician. When he sensed his power base was slipping away from him, he sided with the conservatives against his reformist colleagues in the spring of 1989. When he saw economic reform and the open-door policy in danger of being discredited by the conservatives, he made the southern coastal tour in early 1992, directly appealing to the local leaders and the mass public who had benefited by the reform and opening up processes.

The age of an all-powerful charismatic leader ended with the death of Mao. Deng's successor, Jiang Zeming, has less charismatic charm and no military background. The institutional case studies suggest that the post-Mao leaders of the CPC seem to rely more on the support of their colleagues and provincial leaders – state and provincial decision-makers – for new policy institutionalization. These characteristics of the CPC leadership also help to make them less authoritarian, more pragmatic, and more responsive to the institutional environments.

Besides the role of the leadership in changing the patterns of the ruling elite's institutionalization behavior, those changes in the institutional environments, discussed in the previous section, have exerted significant influence and constraints over the ruling elite's institutionalization behavior, leaving them few alternative policy options.

The changed patterns of institutionalization behavior of the ruling elite suggest that they are flexible, less authoritarian and prepared to make changes in the party ideology to maintain a sustainable economic growth, to keep the general public happy and to keep themselves in power. Deng's policy institutionalization criteria[3] and Jiang Zemin's 'Three Represents' and 'Three Innovations' will certainly reinforce the new patterns of institutionalization behavior. These institutionalization behavior patterns seem conducive to China's move towards the rule of law and eventually towards a democratic polity.

Prospects for a Democratic Transition

Prospects for a democratic transition in China needs to be considered within an international context in general and the transitional experience and lessons of the former Soviet Union and Taiwan in particular. The international influence has been discussed in Chapter Five (see Chapter 5) and the focus of discussion here is on the potential impact of the democratic transitional experience and lessons of the former Soviet Union and Taiwan.

In the late 1980s and early 1990s a wave of democratization swept through the Soviet camp, the former Soviet Union and Eastern European countries. Although the CPC was independent of the Soviet camp at that time, the Chinese revolution and the establishment of the CPC were modeled on the Russian Bolshevik revolution. The impact of the end of communism in the former Soviet Union and Eastern Europe on China, therefore, must have been tremendous. However, the CPC ruling elite managed to divert the impact by convincing its members and the general public that the communist failure in the former Soviet Union and Eastern

Europe had mainly derived from their economic failure. Therefore, to further promote market-oriented economic reforms was justified if the CPC ruling elite wanted to avoid a similar fate in China.

In the middle of 1990s the CPC ruling elite faced another political challenge from their old antagonists, the KMT, who began to democratize Taiwan's political system and to end the one-party regime. Taiwan's democratization should have a greater enduring impact on China's political development owing to the two sides' cultural heritage, political legacy, economic links, and similar economic-first transitional route.

Culturally speaking, the Taiwan residents share a common cultural heritage with the mainland people, including racial characteristics, linguistic features, and religious belief.[4] The success of a peaceful democratic transition in Taiwan has demonstrated that Chinese political culture is flexible enough to incorporate liberal and pro-democratic values. This common cultural heritage will facilitate the dissemination of liberal and democratic ideas and values and the experience of democratization into Mainland China with the broadening of cross-Strait cultural, academic, business, and official exchanges.

Politically, both sides share many common characteristics: one-party rule, the military under the control of the party, and little space for civil society. The political separation of Taiwan from Mainland China, in fact, is a legacy of the prolonged civil war between the two main political forces: the CPC and the KMT with the military victory of the former in Mainland China and the withdrawal of the latter to Taiwan in 1949. To distinguish the CPC rule from the dictatorship of the KMT rule, the CPC ruling elite set up a coalition government in 1949 that tolerated the autonomy of small parties and the independence of newspapers. However, the CPC ruling elite abandoned the coalition after the completion of the socialist transformation program by the end of 1956 and the launching of the 1957 Anti-Rightist Movement.[5] Since 1957 the CPC has exercised the one-party rule in Mainland China with a decade of Mao's personal rule over the party in 1966-76. Now the authoritarian regime in Taiwan, once criticized as a feudal and fascist dictatorship by the CPC ruling elite, has become democratic, and the transfer of the state power from one party to another in Taiwan is institutionalized, peaceful and in an orderly manner. Set in this historical context of the Chinese politics, Taiwan's democratization should both exert greater pressure on the CPC ruling elite and offer more hope to democrats in Mainland China than the democratization in Russia and the Eastern European countries.

Taiwan's democratization process and the peaceful transfer of the executive power from one political party to another may also offer the CPC ruling elite three precious lessons: (1) a well-prepared and well-crafted democratic transition may not generate repercussions to the former ruling elite if they lost an election to the opposition elite; (2) reconciliation has been achieved among the ruling and opposition elites and the general public without witch-hunting the former ruling elite for their party's historical coercive behavior; and (3) the former ruling elite may still have a chance to regain the state executive power in the next election. Taiwan's experience and lessons of democratization may provide some psychological comfort to China's ruling elite, intellectual elite, and business elite who may still harbor varying degrees of fear and apprehension about possible disorder and chaos that democratization may bring to China.

In terms of economic links across the Taiwan Strait, China's market-oriented economic reforms have opened new investment and market opportunities to Taiwanese entrepreneurs. By 1996 Mainland China has become Taiwan's third largest economic partner (after the United States and Japan) and first investment destination.[6] In 1998 Taiwan was Mainland China's fifth largest partner in trade and ranked fifth in terms of its investment in Mainland China.[7] If these mutually beneficiary economic links between Taiwan and Mainland China are to be continually promoted and strengthened, they will not only become the chief factor in dissolving the across-Strain tension[8] but also help to generate economic interests and forces in Mainland China supportive and conducive to democratization.

The peaceful transfer of power following the defeat of the ruling party, the KMT, in Taiwan's second presidential election in 2000, has demonstrated that Chinese traditional political culture did not pose serious obstacles to Taiwan's democratization, or, that Taiwan's political culture may have been shifted towards liberal and pro-democratic values during its modernization process and economic development. To a large extent, therefore, Taiwan's peaceful transition to democracy may be attributed to its economic-development-first transitional mode.

Considering its cultural, political and economic linkage with Mainland China discussed above, Taiwan's democratization should certainly bear a strong impact on the political development of the latter. The intensity of such an impact is growing daily with the completion of China's market-oriented economic reform, the further integration of China into the world community, and the magnitude of economic, social and political transformations generated through its economic reforms and integration with the world community.

The institutional case studies have produced evidence that China has also embarked on an economic-development-first transitional mode. The findings of the case studies also suggest a trend that China is moving away from its traditional one-party authoritarian rule, towards democracy on the continuum of regime change (see Figure 2.1), as institution building in the economic environment has been spreading into the ideological, civil-social, constitutional, and political environments (see Figure 2.2). It is conceivable that more institution building in these institutional environments may lead to more pressure on the ruling elite for a democratic transition.[9] Based on the 2000 survey of the public's political-cultural orientations, a number of possible sources of democratic transition may be identified.

The 2000 survey data has shown the majority of the general public are not happy with the government's handling of ten out of 20 issues. Four of the ten top-priority issues in the minds of the general public, opposing corruption, opposing bureaucratism, unemployment, and income distribution,[10] may develop into a public demand for a democratic transition. The multiple regression analysis of the 2000 survey data suggests that when corruption or bureaucratism develops into a crisis, those who are urban, male, young, better educated and party members are more likely to rise to demand a better government, and that when income distribution or unemployment becomes a crisis, those who are rural, female, young, less educated, and non-party members are more likely to challenge the government (see Table 7.10). The data analysis also suggests that if the government policy towards the private sector falters, especially in terms of protecting private property, private entrepreneurs are likely to revolt (see Figure 7.10).

These analyses suggest that different issues affect different groups of people. Public revolts against the government may not necessarily lead to a democratic transition. The multiple regression analysis of mass attitudes towards democratic, liberal and procedural values offers some clues about who may be most likely to initiate a democratic transition when such a crisis occurs (see Table 7.15). Those who are urban, male and better educated are more likely to demand both a democratic transition and the building of the rule of law. Those who are less privileged in the regime, less paid, non-party members, blue-collar and non-state workers, may also demand a democratic transition, but they tend to be less interested in the building of the rule of law. The result of their efforts may be another type of authoritarian rule. And those who are well-paid and party members may demand the building of the rule of law, but tend to be less interested in a democratic transition.

The above analysis of the possible reactions of people with different attributes only suggests the following possible scenarios. In reality, those who are less privileged in the regime may follow intellectuals in demanding the setting up of a democratic and procedural democracy, while the ruling elite may lead its members and the rich to a pre-emptive democratic reform, in an attempt to set up a democratic polity more favorable to the privileged, as did the ruling elites in Brazil and Bulgaria (Linz and Stepan, 1996; Munck and Leff, 1997).

The analysis of the survey findings confirms the tradition of Chinese intellectuals who value social justice and democratic principles very highly. In the 1990s many intellectuals published articles, arguing for the adoption of the Western style competitive free election, checks and balances on powers, and pluralism in the structure of political power.[11] It is conceivable that a crisis on one of these four issues may originate a demand for a more accountable government, and those who are urban and better educated may lead in the demand for a democratic transition based on the rule of law.

The 2000 survey data suggests that the mass public are expecting the ruling elite to deliver further economic and social welfare benefits. As the ruling elite's legitimacy to rule is based on its economic performance rather than on socialist or communist ideology, the ruling elite will lose its legitimacy to rule if it fails to keep on delivering benefits. When it fails to do so, the mass public with high levels of pro-liberal and pro-democratic attitudes may be more easily mobilized by political activists, reform-minded ruling elite, or intellectuals, to press for democratic reforms.

In sum, these social and economic transformations have led to the following structural and institutional transitions:

- A gradual diffusion of economic resources and a differentiation of social classes in the society;[12]

- A gradual shift from the charismatic, goal-rational, official nationalist, 'New' traditional, and/or eudemonic mode(s) of legitimation to the legal-rational mode of legitimation;[13]
- A gradual shift from the rule of man, to the rule of the party, and to the rule of law;
- A gradual shift in the public orientations towards less authoritarian, more liberal, and pro-democratic values.

Although the one-party regime in China is not heading towards a total collapse as predicted by Holmes (1993), it will become more and more difficult for the ruling elite to maintain their authoritarian rule within the domestic and international pro-democratic environments and to resist the growing pressure of democratization generated by the transformations discussed above.

To a certain degree, the pace and final form of China's democratization may depend on who will represent the general opinion of the mass public, initiate and control the process of a democratic transition. Postulated below are three possible types of democratic transition that may come to China: (1) it is initiated and implemented by the CPC ruling elite with limited or little involvement of the other elites; (2) it is initiated by the ruling elite or other elites and implemented jointly by the ruling and other elites; and (3) it is initiated by the defecting ruling elite or other elites and implemented without the CPC elite.

The first type is a pre-emptive political reform as happened in Brazil, Bulgaria, Romania and Taiwan, offering the ruling elite a high degree of control over the pace and process of democratization, which means little social and economic turmoil but a long process of gradually phasing the authoritarian features out of the newly-established democratic polity. The second type is a packed transition as occurred in Chile, Czechoslovakia, Hungary, and Poland, offering the ruling elite various degrees of control over the process of democratization, although the ruling elite cannot totally control the transition pace, which may limit the damages of social and economic turmoil but still means a relatively long process of squeezing authoritarian elements out of the new democratic polity.

The third type is a breakdown of the authoritarian regime and the crafting of a democratic policy without the participation of the old regime ruling elite as it took place in Russia, offering other elites a full control over the pace and process of democratization, which means lots of social and economic turmoil when the opposing elite are trying both to get recognized by the society for their democratic reforms and to discredit the legitimacy of the ruling elite. Since the opposing elite both initiate and implement the democratic transition, the new polity will have less authoritarian legacy.

The institutional case studies suggest that if the Chinese ruling elite can prevent these issues from developing into a crisis, it is more likely that China is heading towards the first type of democratic transition. If a crisis comes, the case studies also suggest, the second type of transition is more likely because the post-Mao ruling elite have become both flexible in their institutionalization behavior and more responsive to the institutional environments.

Cautions

The analysis in the previous sections suggests a reasonable probability that China is moving closer towards democracy. It does not rule out, however, a possible reversion to a Maoist authoritarian regime. The analysis of the 2000 survey data suggests two sources that may lead to such a reversion.

The first one is the growing disparity between the rich and poor, which is creating tensions between the rich and the poor. In 2000, the majority of the respondents (66.3 per cent) wish the government to do more to solve the problem, while in 1990, only 42.5 per cent of the respondents supported this position (see Table 7.7). If it develops into a crisis, the conservatives among the ruling elite may manipulate the anger of the less privileged to their own favor, that is, to increase the discretionary power of the regime in redistributing income, or to nationalize the private sector. Although to return to the former egalitarian distribution of income is less likely in the present institutional environments, the option is still at the disposal of the ruling elite.

The second danger is a growing feeling of nationalism among the Chinese public. The 2000 survey found a substantial increase in the number of respondents who consider the government has not done enough on the issues of Taiwan and foreign policy (see Table 7.7). Nearly half of the respondents want to see more government action on Taiwan, while in 1990 only 17 per cent of people said so. And 31.4 per cent of the respondents consider the government has not done enough on the issue of foreign policy, while in 1990, only 9.8 per cent said so. As the orthodox socialism is fading away in the face of 'getting rich' tide, nationalism may become a new ideology for the conservatives of the ruling elite.[14] The conservatives of the ruling elite may use the Taiwan issue to arouse nationalist feelings among the general public to support a return to a Maoist authoritarian regime. In both cases, a total restoration of a Maoist authoritarian rule is less likely but it may be more likely that the conservatives can temporarily postpone a democratic transition.

Concluding Remarks

The findings of the institutional case studies suggest a growing trend that China is moving on the continuum of regime change towards democracy (see Figure 2.1). The case studies have shown that changes in the policy institutional environments have exerted environmental pressures on the ruling elite to institutionalize the installment of a market economy and the restoration of private enterprises and property rights. The policy environmental pressures, which have been growing in intensity with China's reform and opening up spreading from the economic arena into the civil-social, constitutional, and political arenas, may eventually compel the ruling elite to institutionalize a pre-emptive democratic reform of the political system or may generate enough force from other power centers to demand a democratic transition. Although it may be too early to claim that China's economic-to-democratic transition is bound to happen, the findings of the three case studies suggest that China's economic reform and open-door policy may be the beginning of a traditional democratic transition that proceeds from economic and social arenas to constitutional and political arenas. China's democratic transition might have already been set in motion and China's democracy, therefore, may come much earlier than Deng Xiaoping predicted.[15]

Notes

1 For example, foreign-funded enterprises received 3 per cent of the total short-term loans in 1994 and 4.1 per cent in 1998, while Chinese domestic private enterprises only got less than 1 per cent share in both years.
2 Sullivan, 1999; Soto, 1999.
3 Namely, developing productivity, strengthening national capabilities, and raising people's living standards, against which a policy should be evaluated and tested.
4 In Taiwan the Han nationality accounts for 98 per cent of its 23 million population, much higher than in Mainland China (91.6 per cent, *The Fifth National Population Census*). For a discussion of the common cultural heritage, see 'On the Fallacy of De-sinicisation' 《去中国化的谬误》, *Central Daily News* 《中央日报》, Editorial, 1ˢᵗ July 2001 [http://www.cdn.com.tw/]. And also see Tu, 1998, pp.89-94.
5 Mao Zedong made it clear in 1945 that a coalition government was a new democratic political system based on the coalition of several democratic classes, including proletariat, peasants, intellectuals, petty bourgeois, and national bourgeois. It was different from the socialist system based on the dictatorship of the proletariat and the monopoly of power by one party as in the Soviet Union. Therefore, when China completed the socialist transformation and entered an era of socialism at the end of 1956, the coalition government become irrelevant and irritating to the CPC ruling elite; and its demise and the monopoly of power by the CPC seemed, therefore, quite logical to the CPC ruling elite. The 1957 Anti-Rightist Campaign paved the way for the monopoly of power by the CPC. See Mao Zedong, 1967, pp.930-1000.
6 Thirty thousand Taiwanese companies have business operation in Mainland China and over 100,000 Taiwanese live on a permanent basis there. For more discussion, see Cabestan, 1998, pp.228-9. Also see Howe, 1998, pp.143-4.
7 *China Statistical Yearbook 1999*, pp. 583-585; pp. 596-598.
8 For more discussion, see Clough, 1998, pp.10-27.
9 Harding (1987, p.201) observes that demands for fundamental political change are likely to grow in influence as economic development and social modernization proceed.
10 They were the major causes of the public anger and dissatisfaction with the government that led to student pro-democracy demonstrations both in early 1987 and in the spring of 1989.
11 For a detailed discussion of the increasing acceptance of democratic ideas by the intellectuals based on the emergence of a pluralistic society, see Ding, 1998.
12 According to the resource distribution theory of democratization (Vanhanen, 1997, p.5-6) further widely distributing economic resources in China will lead to democratization.
13 Holmes (1993) argues that there are seven internal legitimation modes in the communist world; they are:
   • 'Old' traditional – legitimacy is based on the long-established and widely accepted 'divine right of monarchs' or 'mandate of heaven';
   • Charismatic – legitimacy is based on the charisma of a leader;

- Goal-rational/teleological – legitimacy is based on the final goal of communism;
- Eudemonic – legitimacy is based on economic and social-welfare performance;
- Official nationalist – legitimacy is based on the glorification of national leaders or international status of the nation, etc.;
- 'New' traditional – legitimacy is based on the communist tradition of the leading role of the vanguard party, etc.;
- Legal-rational – legitimacy is based on 'the legality of patterns of normative rules'.

14 Freeden (1998, p.759) believes that nationalism is a thin-centered ideology, usually attached to the mainstream ideologies. However, in crises such as nation building, conquest, external threat, or disputed territory, nationalism may arise as a paramount issue. For more discussion, see Freeden, 1998.

15 When Deng Xiaoping was holding talks with members of the Drafting Committee of the Hong Kong Basic Law on 16 April 1987, he said that national free election on Mainland China could come after the first half of the 21st century (Deng, 1993, p.220).

Bibliography

Almond, Gabriel (1989), 'The Intellectual History of the Civic Culture Concept' in Gabriel Almond and Sidney Verba (eds.), *The Civic Culture Revisited*, Sage, Newbury Park, London and New Delhi.

Almond, Gabriel, and Verba, Sidney (1963), *The Civic Culture: Political Attitudes and Democracy in Five Nations*, Princeton University Press, Princeton.

Anderson, Kym and Chao, Yang Peng (1998), 'Feeding and Fuelling China in the 21st Century', *World Development*, Vol.26, No.8, pp.1413-29.

Andreosso-O'Callaghan, Bernadette and Qian, Wei (1999), 'Technology Transfer: A Mode of Collaboration between the European Union and China', *Europe-Asia Studies*, Vol. 51, No. 1 (1999), pp.123-42.

Armijo, Leslie Elliott, Biersteker, Thomas J. and Lowenthal, Abraham F. (1995), 'The Problems of Simultaneous Transitions', in Larry Diamond and Marc F. Plattner (eds.), *Economic Reform and Democracy*, The Johns Hopkins University Press, Baltimore and London.

Aslund, Anders (1994), 'The Case for Radical Reform', *Journal of Democracy*, Vol.5, No.4.

Assured, Erik and Bennett, W. Lance (1997), *Democracy and the Marketplace of Ideas: Communication and Government in Sweden and the United States*, Cambridge University Press, Cambridge.

Bai, Shazhou (1998), *The Illusion and Reality – Jiang Zemin's Political Reform* 《江泽民变法》, Mirror Books Ltd , Brampton, Ontario.

Balcerowicz, Leszek (1994), 'Understanding Postcommunist Transitions', *Journal of Democracy*, Vol.5, No.4 (October 1994).

Baum, R. (1986), 'Modernization and Legal Reform in Post-Mao China: the Rebirth of Socialist Legality', *Studies in Comparative Communism*, Vol. 19, No. 2, pp.69-103.

Baum, R. (1989), 'Introduction: Beyond Leninism? Economic Reform and Political Development in Post-Mao China', *Studies in Comparative Communism*, Vol. 22, No. 2/3, Summer/Autumn 1989, pp.111-23.

Bernstein, Richard and Munro, Ross H. (1997), 'The Coming Conflict with America', *Foreign Affairs*, (March / April 1997), pp.18-32.

Beyme, Klaus von (1996), *Transition to Democracy in Eastern Europe*, Macmillan, London.

Brown, Archie and Gray, Jack (1977), *Political Culture and Political Change in Communist States*, Holmes and Meier, New York.

Brzezinski, Zbigniew (1998), 'Disruption without Disintegration', *Journal of Democracy*, Vol. 9, No. 1, pp. 4-5.

Cabestan, Jean-Pierre (1998), 'Taiwan's Mainland Policy: Normalization, Yes; Reunification, Later', in David Shambaugh (ed.), *Contemporary Taiwan*, Clarendon Press, Oxford, pp.228-29.

Chan, A., Rosen, S. and Unger, J. (eds) (1985), *On Socialist Democracy and the Chinese Legal System*, Sharpe, Armonk, New York.

Chen, Changmao and Yu, Yaozhong (1999), 'Idiot Seeds and its Creator: Niang Guangjiu' 《傻子瓜子与创始人年广九》 in Zhang, Houyi and Ming, Lizhi (eds.), *Report on the Development of China's Private Enterprises (1978-1998)* 《中国私营企业发展报告 (1978-1998)》, Social Sciences Documentation Publishing House, Beijing.

Chen, Feng (1995), *Economic Transition and Political Legitimacy in Post-Mao China: Ideology and Reform*, State University of New York Press, Albany, New York.

Chen, Jie, Zhong, Yang and Hillard, Jan William (1997), 'The Level and Sources of Popular Support for China's Current Political Regime', *Communist and Post Communist Studies*, Vol. 30, No. 1, pp. 45-64.

Chen, Qingtai (2003), 'Actively Promoting the Healthy Development of the Private Sector' 《积极促进民营经济健康发展》, *China Economic Times* 《中国经济时报》, 6th January 2003, p.5.

Chen, Renliang (2000), 'The Opening up and Development of Shanghai Pudong New Area and the Role of the Legal Environment', a seminar paper at the *Symposium on China and Europe in the New Millennium*, Institute of European Affairs, Dublin, Friday 13 October 2000.

Chen, Xuewei (1987), *A Chronology of the NPC and Its Standing Committee, 1954 – 1987*' 《全国人大极其常委会大事记，1954-1987》, Legal Press, Beijing.

Chen, Xuewei (1990), *Remembrance of Forty Years* 《四十年回顾》, the Central Party School Press, Beijing.

Chen, Yizi (1998), 'The Road From Socialism', *Journal of Democracy*, Vol. 9, No. 1.

Cheng, Liaoyuan (1999), *From the Legal System to the Rule of law* 《从法制到法治》, Legal Press, Beijing.

Chhibber, Pradeep and Eldersveld, Samuel (2000), 'Local Elites And Popular Support for Economic Reform in China and India', *Comparative Political Studies*, Vol. 33, No. 3, pp. 350-73.

Chossudovsky, Michel (1986), *Towards Capitalist Restoration? Chinese Socialism after Mao*, Macmillan Education Ltd., Hampshire and London.

Clegg, Stewart R. (1989), *Frameworks of Power*, Sage, London.

Clough, Ralph N. (1998), 'The Enduring Influence of the Republic of China on Taiwan Today', in David Shambaugh (ed.), *Contemporary Taiwan*, Clarendon Press, Oxford, pp.10-27.

Cohen, Warren, I. (1980), *America's Response to China: An Interpretative History of Sino-American Relations*, second edition, John Wiley and Sons Inc, New York, Chichester, Brisbane, and Toronto.

Cook, Karen Schweer and Levi, Margaret (eds) (1990), *The Limits of Rationality*, University of Chicago Press, Chicago.

Craig, Stephen C., Niemi, Richard G. and Silver, Glenn E. (1990), 'Political Efficacy and Trust: A Report on the NES Pilot Study Items', *Political Behavior*, 12 (3).

Crowell, Todo and Mooney, Paul (1999), 'Right Down the Middle: On the economy, Jiang Zemin wants it fast and slow', *Asianweek*, Vol. 25, No. 40.

Dalton, Russell J. (1988), *Citizen Politics in Western Democracies*, Chatham House Publishers, Chatham, New Jersey.

Deng, Weizhi, Xu, Juezai, and Sheng, Yonglin (eds.), (1997), *Political Stability in a Transitional Society* 《变革社会中的政治稳定》, Shanghai People's Press, Shanghai:

Deng, Xiaoping (1983), *Selected Works of Deng Xiaoping, 1975-1982* 《邓小平文选，1975-1982》, Shanghai People's Press, Shanghai.

Deng, Xiaoping (1993), *Selected Works of Deng Xiaoping, Book Three* 《邓小平文选第三卷》, People's Press, Beijing.

Diamond, Larry (1992), 'Economic Development and Democracy Reconsidered', in G. Marks and L. Diamond (eds.), *Reexamining Democracy: Essays in Honor of Seymour Martin Lipset*, Sage, London.

Diamond, Larry (ed.) (1993), *Political Culture and Democracy in Developing Countries*, Lynne Reiner, Boulder.

Diamond, Larry and Plattner, M. (eds.) (1993), *The Global Resurgence of Democracy,* Johns Hopkins University Press, Baltimore and London.

Diamond, Larry, Linz, Juan J. and Lipset, Seymour Martin (1990), *Politics in Developing Countries: Comparing Experiences with Democracy: Asia Vol. 3,* Lynne Rienner, Boulder, Col.

Dickson, Bruce J. (2000), 'Membership has its Privileges, the Socioeconomic Characteristics of Communist Party Members in Urban China', *Comparative Political Studies,* Vol. 33, No. 1, pp.87-112.

Dimitrova, Antoaneta Lubomirova (1998), *The Role of the European Union in the process of Democratization in Central and Eastern Europe: Lessons from Bulgaria and Slovakia,* Ph.D. thesis, College of Humanities, University of Limerick, Limerick.

Ding, Yijiang (1998), 'Pre- and Post-Tiananmen Conceptual Evolution of Democracy in Intellectual Circles' Rethinking of State and Society', *Journal of Contemporary China,* 7 (18), pp.229-56.

Domes, Jurgen (ed.) (1979), *Chinese Politics After Mao,* University College Cardiff Press, Cardiff.

Dowd, Daniel V., Carlson, Allen and Shen, Mingming (1999), 'The Prospects for Democratization in China: evidence from the 1995 Beijing Area Study', *Journal of Contemporary China,* Vol. 8, No. 22, pp.365-80.

Duch, Raymond M. (1993), 'Tolerating Economic Reform: Popular Support for Transition to a Free Market in the Former Soviet Union', *American political Science Review,* Vol.87, No. 3, pp.590-608.

Elster, By Jon (1989), *The Cement of Society: A Study of Social Order,* Cambridge University Press, New York.

Esherick, J. W. (ed.) (1974), *Lost Chance in China,* Random House, New York.

Feng, Tianyu, Mao, Lai, et al. (1996), *History of China's Opening Up* 《中华开放史》, Hubai People's Press, Wuhan.

Feng, Yucheng and Hong, Lan. (eds.) (1999), *Reform of Investment Fund Raising, Revenue and Taxation* 《投资融资财税制度改革》, People's University of China Press, Beijing.

Flanagan, Scott C. and Lee, Aie-Rie (2000), 'Value Change and Democratic Reform in Japan and Korea', *Comparative Political Studies,* Vol. 33, No. 6, pp.626-59.

Francis, David R. (1999), 'Political freedom translates into economic freedom', *The Christian Science Monitor,* Thursday, 4 February 1999.

Freeden, Michael (1998), 'Is Nationalism a Distinct Ideology?' *Political Studies,* XLVI, pp.748-65.

Gibson, James L. (1992), 'The Political Consequences of Intolerance: Cultural Conformity and Political Freedom', *American Political Science Review,* 86 (2), pp.338-56.

Goldstein, Steven (1980), 'Chinese Communist Policy Toward the United States: Opportunities and Constraints, 1944-1950', in D. Borg and W. Heinrichs (eds.), *Uncertain Years,* Columbia University Press, New York.

Goldstein, Steven (1989), 'Sino-American Relations, 1948-1950: Lost Chance or No Chance?' in Harry Harding and Yuan Ming (eds.), *Sino-American Relations, 1945-1955,* Scholarly Resources, Wilmington.

Gong, Ting (1997), 'Forms and Characteristics of China's Corruption in the 1990s: Change with Continuity', *Communist and Post-Communist Studies,* Vol. 30, No. 3, pp.277-88.

Gray, Jack (1977), 'China: Communism and Confucianism', in Archie Brown and Jack Gray (eds.), *Political Culture and Political Change in Communist States,* Macmillan, London and New York, pp.197-230.

Gray, Jack (1998), 'Rethinking Chinese Economic Reform', *The Journal of Communist Studies and Transition Politics,* Vol.14, No.3, pp.134-54.

Greenberge, D., et al. (eds.) (1993), *Constitutionalism and Democracy: Transitions in the Contemporary World*, Oxford University Press, New York.

Grey, Robert D. (1997), 'Introduction: How to Understand the Probable Political Future of the Formerly Communist States', in Robert D. Grey (ed.), *Democratic Theory and Post-communist Change*, Prentice Hall, New Jersey.

Grossman, Peter Z. (1999), *Douglass North: Why Some Nations Can Sustain Growth*, The Center for International Private Enterprise, Washington, 25 September 1999, [http://www.cipe.org/ert/e19/desoto.html].

Gu, Changhao and Wang Songlin (1999), 'Innovation of Rules and Legislative Delegation', in Xu, Zhuxong and Zhu, Yanwen (eds.), *Democracy, Legal System, and the People's Congress System* 《民主法制与人大制度》, Fudan University Press, Shanghai.

Gu, Xin (1998), 'Plural Institutionalism and the Emergence of Intellectual Public Spaces in Contemporary China: four relational patterns and four organizational forms', *Journal of Contemporary China*, 1 (18), pp.271-301.

Gui, Shiyong (1998), 'Reform of the Planning and Investment System 《计划、投资体制改革》', in Zhang Zhuyuan, Huang Huanzhang and Li Guangan (eds.), *Twenty Years of Economic Reforms: in retrospect and prospect* 《20年经济改革回顾与展望》, Chinese Planning Press, Beijing.

Guo, Xuewang (1998), *Deng Xiaoping and Transformations of the Chinese Society* 《邓小平与中国社会的变迁》, the Yan Shi Press, Beijing.

Haggard, Stephan and Kaufman, Robert R. (1992), 'The Political Economy of Inflation and Stabilization in Middle–income Countries', in Haggard and Kaufman (eds.), *The Politics of Economic Adjustment*, Princeton University Press, Princeton.

Haggard, Stephan and Kaufman, Robert R. (1997), 'The Political Economy of Democratic Transitions', *Comparative Politics*, Vo.29, No.3, pp.263-83.

Haley, Usha V.V. and Low, Linda (1998), 'Crafted culture: governmental sculpting of modern Singapore and effects on business environments', *Journal of Organizational Change Management*, Vol. 11, No. 6, pp.533-53.

Hao, Yufan (1999), 'From Rule of Man to Rule of Law: an unintended consequence of corruption in China in the 1990s', Journal of Contemporary China, Vol. 8, No.22, pp.405-23.

Harding, Harry (1987), *China's Second Revolution: Reform after Mao*, The Brookings Institution, Washington D.C.

Harding, Harry (1998), 'The Halting Advance of Pluralism', *Journal of Democracy*, Vol. 9, No.1.

He, Baogang (1992), 'Democratization: Antidemocratic and Democratic Elements in the Political Culture of China', *Australian Journal of Political Science*, 27, pp.120-36.

He, Di (1995), 'From Cooperation to Confrontation: Chinese Communist Views on Sino-American Relations', in Thomas G. Paterson (ed.), *Major problems in American Foreign Relations, Volume II: Since 1914, Documents and Essays, Fourth Edition*, D. C. Heath and Company, Lexington, Massachusetts and Toronto.

He, Qinglian (1998), *Modernization's Pitfall – Economic and Social Problems in China Today* 《现代化的陷阱—当代中国的经济社会问题》, China Today Press, Beijing.

He, Qinglian (2000), 'China's Listing Social Structure', *New Left Review*, 5.

He, Qinglian (2000b), 'The 'New Rich' Wants to Maintain the Status Quo' 《'阔起来的'要维持现状》, *Minzhu Zhougguo*, No. 8.

Held, David (1987), *Models of Democracy*, Polity Press, Cambridge and Oxford.

Held, David (1995), *Democracy and the Global Order, from the Modern State to Cosmopolitan Governance*, Polity Press, Cambridge and Oxford.

Helliwell, John (1994), 'Empirical Linkages between Democracy and Economic Growth', *British Journal of Political Science*, Vol.24, No.2.

Holmes, Leslie (1993), *The End of Communist Power: Anti-corruption Campaigns and Legitimation Crisis*, Polity Press, Cambridge.

Howe, Christopher (1998), 'The Taiwan Economy: The Transition to Maturity and the Political Economy of its Changing International Status', in David Shambaugh (ed.), *Contemporary Taiwan*, Clarendon Press, Oxford, pp.143-4.

Hsiung, James Chieh (1970), *Ideology and Practice, the Evolution of Chinese Communism*, Pall Mall Press, London.

Hu, Xiaobo (1996), 'Decentralization Reform in Post-Mao China: A framework of Choice', *Issues & Studies*, Vol.32 No.9, pp.41-68.

Huang, Jen-the and Cheng, Wen-fa (1996), 'Mainland China's Tax Revenue and Extrabudgetary Funds', *Issues & Studies*, Vol.32 No.9, pp.69-86.

Huber, Evelyne, Rueschemeyer, Dietrich, and Stephens, John D. (1993), 'The Impact of Economic Development and Democracy' *Journal of Economic Perspectives*, Vol.7, No.3, pp.71-85.

Hunt, M. (1980), 'Mao Tse-tung and the Issue of Accommodation with the United States', in D. Borg and W. Heinrichs (eds.), *Uncertain Years*, Columbia University Press, New York.

Huntington, Samuel P. (1968), *Political Order in Changing Societies*, Yale University Press, New Haven.

Huntington, Samuel P. (1984), 'Will More Countries Become Democratic?' *Political Science Quarterly*, 99, 2, pp.193-218.

Huntington, Samuel P. (1991a), *The Third Wave: Democratization in the Late Twentieth Century*, University of Oklahoma Press, Norman and London.

Huntington, Samuel P. (1991b), 'After Twenty Years: the Future of the Third Wave', *Journal of Democracy*, Vol. 8, No. 4.

Inglehart, Ronald (1997), *Modernization and Postmodernization: Cultural, Economic and Political Change in 43 Societies*, Princeton University Press, Princeton, New Jersey and Chichester, West Sussex.

Jiang, Jianhua, Feng, Wanzhen, and Ji, Hong (eds.) (1999), *Handbook on People's Republic of China, 1949-1999* 《中华人民共和国资料手册》, Social Sciences and Documents Press, Beijing.

Jiang, Liu and Fu, Qingyuan (eds.) (1994), *Big Events of the Socialism with Chinese Characteristics*. 《有中国特色社会主义大事典》, People's Press, Beijing.

Jiang, Nanyang (1999), 'On Political Participation of the Owners of Private Enterprises 《论私营企业主的政治参与》', in Zhang, Houyi and Ming, Lizhi (eds.), *Report on the Development of China's Private Enterprises (1978-1998)* 《中国私营企业发展报告（1978-1998）》, Social Sciences Documentation Publishing House, Beijing.

Kaufman, Robert R. (1999), 'Approaches to the Study of State Reform in Latin American and Postsocialist Countries', *Comparative Politics*, Vol. 31, No. 3, pp.357-75.

Krasner, Stephen D. (1984), 'Approaches to the State: Alternative Conceptions and Historical Dynamics', *Comparative Politics*, 16, No. 2, pp.223-46.

Landman, Todd (1999), 'Economic Development and Democracy: the View from Latin America', *Political Studies*, Vol. 47, No.4 (September 1999).

Leffler, Melvyn P. (1992), *A Preponderance of Power: National Security, the Truman Administration, and the Cold War*, Stanford University Press, Stanford, California.

Li, Buyun (1996), 'Market Economy: System of Laws? Ruled by Law!' 《市场经济：法制？法治！》, *China Economic Times* 《中国经济时报》, 22 November 1996.

Li, Fan (1998), *Silent Revolution: Becoming Civil Society in China* 《静悄悄的革命——中国当代市民社会》, Mirror Books Ltd., Brampton, Ontario.

Li, Jian (ed.) (1998), *Personal Records of the Key Meetings at Historical Moments of the Communist Party of China* 《关键会议亲历实录》, the CPC Central Committee Party School Press, Beijing.

Li, Linda Chelan (1997), 'Towards a Non-zero-sum Interactive Framework of Spatial Politics: the Case of Center-province in Contemporary China', *Political Studies*, XLV, pp.49-65.

Li, Shantong and Hou, Yongzhi (2000), 'Characteristics of China's Economic Development and Major Tasks of Industrial Development during the "15th Five-year Plan" 《我国经济发展阶段特征与 "十五" 时期产业发展的主要任务》', *China Economic Times* 《中国经济时报》, 1st August 2000.

Linz, Juan J. And Stepan, Alfred (1996), *Problems of Democratic Consolidation: Southern Europe, South America, and Post-Communist Europe*, Johns Hopkins University Press, Baltimore.

Lipset, Seymour Martin (1959), 'Some Social Requisites of Democracy: economic development and political legitimacy', *American political Science Review*, 53, pp.69-105.

Lipset, Seymour Martin (1981), *Political Man: the Social Bases of Politics*, John Hopkins University Press, Baltimore.

Lipset, Seymour Martin (1993), 'Reflections on Capitalism, Socialism and Democracy', *Journal of Democracy*, 4 (2), pp.43-52.

Lipset, Seymour Martin (1994), 'The Social Requisites of Democracy Revisited', *American Sociological Review*, 59, pp.1-22.

Lipset, Seymour Martin, Seong, Kyoung-Ryung and Torres, John Charles (1993), 'A Comparative Analysis of the Social Requisites of Democracy', *International Social Science Journal*, 45, pp.155-75.

Liu Shaoqi (1969), *Collected Works of Liu Shao Ch'i: 1945-1957*, Union Research Institute, Hong Kong.

Liu Shaoqi (1981), *Selected Works of Liu Shaoqi, Book B* 《刘少奇选集下集》, Shanghai People's Press, Shanghai.

Liu, Zhifeng (ed.) (1999), *A Report on China's Political Reform* 《中国政治体制改革问题报告》, China Movies Printing House, Beijing.

Lu, Xiaobo (2000), 'Booty Socialism, Bureau-preneurs, and the State in Transition: Organizational Corruption in China', *Comparative Politics*, Vol.32, No. 3, pp.273-94.

Lu, Xueyi (ed.) (2002), *Report on the Research on Social Classes in China Today* 《当代中国社会阶层研究报告》, Social Sciences Documentation Publishing House, Beijing.

Lukes, Steven (1974), *A Radical View*, Macmillan, London.

Lukes, Steven (ed.) (1986), *Power*, Basil Blackwell, Oxford.

Ma, Licheng and Ling, Zhijun (1998), *Confrontations – Three Rounds of the Ideological Emancipation in Modern China* 《交锋——当代中国三次思想解放实录》, China Today Press, Beijing.

Maher, Kristern Hill (1997), 'The role of Mass Values', in Robert D. Grey (ed.), *Democratic Theory and Post-communist Change*, Prentice Hall, New Jersey.

Manning, Stephen Dale (1990), *Democratizing the Leninist Party-state: The Political Economy of Reform in China and the Soviet Union*, an unpublished PhD thesis, University of Wisconsin-Madison.

Mao, Zedong (1965), 'On New Democracy' 《新民主主义论》', in Mao Zedong, *Selected Works of Mao Zedong* 《毛泽东选集》, People's Press, Beijing, pp.623-70.

Mao, Zedong (1965), 'On Coalition Government' 《论联合政府》', in Mao Zedong, *Selected Works of Mao Zedong* 《毛泽东选集》, People's Press, Beijing, pp.930-1000.

Mao, Zedong (1977), *Selected Works of Mao Zedong, Book VI* 《毛泽东选集第五卷》, Shanghai People's Press, Shanghai.

March, James G and Olsen, Johan P. (1984), 'The New Institutionalism: Organizational Factors in Political life', *American political Science Review*, 78, pp.734-49.

March, James G and Olsen, Johan P. (1989), *Rediscovering Institutions*, Free Press, New York.

McGeary, Johanna (1999), 'The Next Cold War? The Cox report hypes the China danger, but the rivalry is real and growing, what should America do about it?' *Time*, Vol.153, No.22, 7 June 1999.

Migdal, Joel S., Kohli, Atul, and Shue, Vivienne (eds.) (1994), *State Power and Social Forces: Democratization and Transformation in the Third World*, Cambridge university Press, New York.

Milbrath, Lester and Goel, M. L. (1977), *Political Participation: How and Why Do People Get Involved in Politics?* 2d ed., Rand Macnally, Chicago.

Moore, Barrington (1950), *Soviet Politics, the Dilemma of Power, the Role of Ideas in Social Change*, Harvard University Press, Cambridge, Mass.

Moore, Barrington (1966), *Social Origins of Dictatorship and Democracy: Lord and Peasant in the Making of the Modern World*, Beacon Press, Boston.

Munck, Gerardo L. and Leff, Carol Skalnik (1997), 'Modes of Transition and Democratization: South America and Eastern Europe in Comparative Perspective', *Comparative Politics*, Vo. 29, No. 3, pp.343-62.

Nathan, Andrew J. (1986), *Chinese Democracy*, I. B. Tauris and Co. Ltd, London.

Nathan, Andrew J. (1990), *China's Crisis: Dilemmas of Reform and Prospects for Democracy*, Columbia University Press, New York.

Nathan, Andrew J. (1998a), *China's Transition*, Columbia University Press, New York.

Nathan, Andrew J. (1998b), 'Even Our Caution Must be Hedged', *Journal of Democracy*, Vol. 9, No. 1, pp.62-64.

Nathan, Andrew and Shi, Tianjian (1992), 'Cultural Requisites for Democracy in China: Findings from a Survey', *Daedalus*, Vol. 122, No. 2, pp.95-123.

Nathan, Andrew and Shi, Tianjian (1996), 'Left and Right with Chinese Characteristics, Issues and Alignments in Deng Xiaoping's China', *World Politics*, Vol. 48, No. 4, pp.522-50.

Naughton, Barry (1995), *Growing Out of the Plan: Chinese economic reform, 1978-1993*, Cambridge University Press, Cambridge.

Nelson, Joan M. (1994), 'Linkages between Politics and Economics', *Journal of Democracy*, Vol.5, No.4.

Nie, Norman H. G., Powell, Bingham Jr. and Prewitt, Kenneth (1961), 'Social Structure and Political Participation: Developmental Relationships', Parts I and II, *American Political Science Review*, 63 (2), pp.361-78; and 63 (3), pp.808-32.

North, Douglass C. (1990), *Institutions, Institutional Change, and Economic Performance*, Cambridge University Press, New York.

O'Brien, Kevin J. and Li, Lianjiang (1999), 'Selective Policy Implementation in Rural China', *Comparative Politics*, Vol. 31, No. 2, pp.167-86.

O'Donnell, Guillermo and Schmitter, Phillippe C. (1986), 'Tentative Conclusions about Uncertain Democracies', in Guillermo O'Donnell, Philippe C. Schmitter, and Laurence Whitehead (eds.), *Transitions from Authoritarian Rule*, The Johns Hopkins University Press, Baltimore.

Oksenberg, Michel (1998), 'Confronting A Classic Dilemma', *Journal of Democracy*, Vol.9, No.1.

Oksenberg, Michel (1999), 'The Long March Ahead', *South China Morning Post*, 1 October 1999.

Ostrom, E. (1991), 'Rational Choice Theory and Institutional Analysis: toward complementarity', *American Political Science Review*, 85, pp.237-43.

Pearson, Margaret M. (1997), *China's New Business Elite*, University of California Press, Berkeley, Los Angeles, and London.

Pei, Minxin (1995), 'The Puzzle of East Asian Exceptionalism', in Larry Diamond and Marc F. Plattner (eds.), *Economic Reform and Democracy*, The Johns Hopkins University Press, Baltimore and London.

Pei, Minxin (1997), 'Citizens v. Mandarins: Administrative Litigation in China', *the China Quarterly*, No. 152, pp.832-62.

Pellegrini, Frank (1999), 'China and the WTO', *Time, 15* April 1999.

Perry, Elizabeth J. (1995), 'Labor's Battle for Political Space: the role of worker association in contemporary China', in Deborah S. Davis, Richard Kraus, Barry Naughton, Elizabeth J. Perry (eds.), *Urban Spaces in Contemporary China: the Potential for Autonomy and Community in Post-Mao China*, Cambridge University Press, New York, 302-26.

Powell, Walter W. and Dimaggio, Paul J. (eds.) (1991), *The New Institutionalism in Organizational Analysis*, University of Chicago Press, Chicago.

Pridham, Geoffrey (1991), 'International influences and democratic transition: problems of theory and practice in linkage politics', in Geoffrey Pridham (ed.), *Encouraging Democracy: The International Context of Regime Transition in Southern Europe*, Leicester University Press, Leicester, London.

Przeworski, Adam (1991), *Democracy and the Market: Political and Economic Reforms in Eastern Europe and Latin America*, Cambridge University Press, Cambridge.

Przeworski, Adam and Limongi, Fernando (1993), 'Political Regimes and Economic Growth', *Journal of Economic Perspective*, Vol.7, No.3, pp.51-69.

Przeworski, Adam and Limongi, Fernando (1997), 'Modernization: Theories and Facts', *World Politics*, 49, pp.155-83.

Pu, Xingzu (1999), *The Political System of the People's Republic of China* 《中华人民共和国政治制度》, Shanghai People's Press, Shanghai.

Pye, Lucian and Verba, Sidney (1965), *Political Culture and Political Development*, Princeton University Press, Princeton.

Remmer, Karen L. (1997), 'Theoretical Decay and Theoretical Development: the Resurgence of Institutional Analysis', *World Politics*, 50, pp.34-61.

Rostow, W. W. (1971), *The Stages of Economic Growth: A Non-communist Manifesto*, Second Edition, Cambridge University Press, Cambridge.

Rueschemeyer, Dietrich, Stephens, Evelyne Huber, and Stephens, John D. (1992), *Capitalist Development and Democracy*, Polity Press, Cambridge.

Rustow, Dankwart A. (1970), 'Transitions to Democracy: Toward a Dynamic Model', *Comparative Politics*, 2, pp.337-63.

Scalapino, Robert A. (1998), 'Current Trends and Future Prospects', *Journal of Democracy*, Vol.9, No.1.

Schimitter, Philippe C. (1994), 'Dangers and Dilemmas of Democracy', *Journal of Democracy*, Vol.5, No.2.

Schimitter, Philippe C. (1996), 'The Influence of the International Context upon the Choice of National Institutions and Policies in Neo-Democracies', in Laurence Whitehead (ed.),

The International Dimensions of Democratization: Europe and the Americas, Oxford University Press, Oxford.

Schurmann, Franz (1968), *Ideology and Organization in Communist China*, University of California Press, Berkeley.

Segal, Gerald (1997), 'How Insecure is Pacific Asia?' *International Affairs*, Vol.73, No.2, pp.235-49.

Selden, Mark (ed.) (1979), *The People's Republic of China: A Documentary History of Revolutionary Change*, Monthly Review Press, New York and London.

Selden, Mark (1988), *The Political Economy of Chinese Socialism*, Sharpe, New York and London.

Seliger, Martin (1976), *Ideology and Politics*, The Free Press, New York.

Shi, Taifeng, et al. (1998), *Wade across the Swamp: Pondering over the Rule by Law* 《走出沼泽地－关于法治的思考》, The CPC Party School Press, Beijing.

Shirk, Susan L. (1993), *The Political Logic of Economic Reform in China*, University of California Press, Berkeley, California.

Sims, Holly (1999), 'One-fifth of the Sky: China's Environmental Stewardship', *World Development*, Vol.27, No.7, pp.1227-45.

Soto, Hernando de (1999), *Securing property Rights: the Foundation of Markets*, an interview with Hernando de Soto by the Center for International Private Enterprise, Washington, 25 September 1999.

Stueck, JR. William W. (1995), 'The American Failure to Negotiate', in Thomas G. Paterson (ed.), *Major problems in American Foreign Relations, Volume II: Since 1914, Documents and Essays*, 4th Edition, D. C. Heath and Company, Lexington, Massachusetts and Toronto.

Sullivan, John D. (1999), *Market Institutions and Democracy*, The Center for International Private Enterprise, Washington, 25th September 1999.

Sutter, Robert G. (1978), *China-Watch Toward Sino-American Reconciliation*, The Johns Hopkins University Press, Baltimore and London.

Tao, Kai (1999), 'Yang Xiguang's Role in the Discussion on the Criteria of Truth', in Kai Tao (ed.), *Guang Ming Daily and the Discussion on the Criteria of Truth*, Guang Ming Daily Press, Beijing.

Taylor, Mchael (1989), 'Structure, Culture and Actor in the Explanation of Social Change', *Politics and Society*, 17, pp.115-62.

Taylor, Robert (1996), *Greater China and Japan: Prospects for an economic partnership in East Asia*, Routledge, London and New York.

Taylor, Robert (1997), 'Chinese Macroeconomic Reforms and the Japanese Model: Implications for Japanese Companies', in Sam Dzever and Jacques Jaussaud (eds.), *Perspectives on Economic Integration and Business Strategy in the Asia-Pacific Region*, Macmillan, London.

Teiwes, Frederick C. (1993), *Politics and Purges in China: Rectification and the Decline of Party Norms, 1950-1965*, 2nd Edition, M. E. Sharpe, New York.

Thelen, Kathleen , Steinmo, Sven and Longstreth, Frank (1992), *Structuring Politics: Historical Institutionalism in Comparative Analysis*, Cambridge University Press, New York.

Thornton, Richard C. (1978), 'The Political Succession to Mao Tse-tun', *Issues and Studies*, XIV, 6, p.35.

Todavo, Mchael P. (1997), *Economic Development*, Longman, London.

Tu, Weiming (1998), 'Cultural Identity and the Politics of Recognition in Contemporary Taiwan', in David Shambaugh (ed.), *Contemporary Taiwan,* Clarendon Press, Oxford, pp.89-94.

Unger, Jonathan (1996), '"Bridges": Private Business, the Chinese Government and the Rise of New Associations', *The China Quarterly*, No. 147, pp.795-819.

Vanhanen, Tatu (1984), *The Emergence of Democracy: A Comparative Study of 119 States, 1985-1979*, The Finnish Society of Sciences and Letters, Helsinki.

Vanhanen, Tatu (1997), *Prospects of Democracy: A Study of 172 Countries*, Routledge, London and New York.

Waldron, Arthur (1998), 'The End of Communism', *Journal of Democracy*, Vol. 9, No.1, pp.41-7.

Wall, David (1996), 'China as a trade partner: threat or opportunity for OECD?' *International Affairs*, Vol.72, No.2.

Wan, Dianwu (1998), 'Reform of the Commodity Distribution 《商品流通体制改革》', in Zhang Zhuyuan, Huang Huanzhang and Li Guangan (eds.), *Twenty Years of Economic Reforms: in retrospect and prospect* 《20 年经济改革回顾与展望》, Chinese Planning Press, Beijing.

Wan, Li (1998) 'How the Agricultural Reform was Initiated 《农村改革是怎么搞起来的》', *China Economic Times* 《中国经济时报》, 30 April 1998.

Wang, Dongling (1998), *Patriotic Democrats in the Ten Years of Turmoil* 《十年风暴中的爱国民主人士》, China Cultural and Historical Press, Beijing.

Wang, Guixiu (1999), 'An Arduous and Prolonged Reform – Reflections on the Political Reform in the Last Twenty Years 《艰难而漫长的改革—政治改革二十年反思》', in Zhifeng Liu (ed.), *A Report on China's Political Reform* 《中国政治体制改革问题报告》, China Movies Printing House, Beijing.

Wang, Juntao (1998), 'A "Grey" Transformation', *Journal of Democracy*, Vol. 9, No.1.

Wang, Xiaolu (2000), 'China Will Bid Farewell to Poverty' 《二十年后中国将告别贫困》, *Economic Studies* 《经济研究》.

Weale, Albert (1999), *Democracy*, Palgrave, Hampshire and New York.

Weatherford, M. Stephen (1992), 'Measuring Political Legitimacy', *American Political Science Review,* 86 (1), pp.149-66.

Wei, Tongwu and Chen, Wenying (1998), *China's Successful Approach to Reforming its Ownership System* 《中国所有制改革成功之路》, Police Officer Education Press , Beijing.

White, Gordon (1993a), *Riding the Tiger: The Politics of Economic Reform in Post–Mao China*, Macmillan, London.

White, Gordon (1993b), 'Prospects for civil society in China: a case study of Xiaoshan city', The Australian Journal of Chinese Affairs, No. 29, pp.63-87.

White, Gordon (1996), 'Development and Democratization in China', in Adrian Leftwich (ed.), *Democracy and Development: Theory and Practice*, Polity Press, Cambridge.

Whitehead, Laurence (1986), 'International Aspects of Democratization', in O'Donnel, Guillermo, Schmitter, Philippe C. and Whitehead, Laurence (eds.), *Transitions from Authoritarian Rule: prospects for democracy*, 4, Johns Hopkins university Press, Baltimore.

Whitehead, Laurence (1991), 'Democracy by convergence and Southern Europe: a comparative politics perspective', in Geoffrey Pridham (ed.), *Encouraging Democracy: The International Context of Regime Transition in Southern Europe*, Leicester University Press, Leicester, London.

Whitehead, Laurence (1996), 'Three International Dimensions of Democratization', in Laurence Whitehead (ed.), *The International Dimensions of Democratization: Europe and the Americas*, Oxford University Press, Oxford.

Xiang, Chunyi (1991), 'The Party's Leadership and the Legal Construction 《党的领导与法制建设》', *Chinese Law* 《中国法学》, No.4, pp.3-12.

Xiao, Liang (1997), 'Theoretical Breakthrough and Reform Breakthrough 《理论的突破与改革的突破》', *Financial and Economic Studies* 《财经问题研究》, No.11.

Xiao, Liang (2000), 'Going Civil is not Privatization' 《民营化不等于私有化》, *Beijing Daily* 《北京日报》, 21st August 2000.

Xin, Chunying (1999), *Chinese Legal System and Current Legal Reform* 《中国法律制度及其改革》, Legal Press, Beijing.

Yang, Dali (1996a), 'Governing China's Transition to the Market', *World Politics*, 48, pp.424-52.

Yang, Dali (1996b), *Calamity and Reform in China: State, Rural Society, and Institutional Change since the Great Leap Famine*, Stanford University Press, Stanford.

Yang, Jisheng (1998), *The Era of Deng Xiaoping—a record of actual events of China's twenty years reform and opening* 《邓小平时代—中国改革开放二十年纪实》, Central Compilation and Translation Press, Beijing.

Yang, Yiyong, et al (eds.) (1997), *Fairness and Efficiency: problem of income distribution in China* 《公平与效率—当代中国的收入分配问题》, China Today Press, Beijing.

Zhang, Chunlin, Kong, Xiangzhi and Deng, Yihai (1993), *One Hundred Historic Events that Transformed China* 《改变中国的 100 件大事》, China Economics Press, Beijing.

Zhang, Houyi (1999), 'An Emerging Alien Force – Rebirth and Development of the Private Economy Since the Economic Reform 《又一支异军在突起—改革开放以来私营经济的再生与发展》', in Zhang, Houyi and Ming, Lizhi (eds.), Report *on the Development of China's Private Enterprises (1978-1998)* 《中国私营企业发展报告（1978-1998）》, Social Sciences Documentation Publishing House, Beijing.

Zhang, Houyi and Ming, Lizhi (eds.) (1999), *Report on the Development of China's Private Enterprises No.1 (1978-1998)* 《中国私营企业发展报告 N0.1》（1978-1998）, Social Sciences Documentation Publishing House, Beijing.

Zhang, Houyi, Ming, Lizhi and Liang, Chuanyun (eds.) (2002), *Report on the Development of China's Private Enterprises No.3* 《中国私营企业发展报告 No.3》, Social Sciences Documentation Publishing House, Beijing.

Zhang, Wei-wei (1996), *Ideology and Economic Reform under Deng Xiaoping 1978-1993*, Kegan Paul International, London and New York.

Zhang, Xiaowei (1998), 'Elite Transformation and Recruitment in Post-Mao China', *Journal of Political and Military Sociology*, Vol.26, pp.39-57.

Zhang, Zhonghou (1986), 'Checking on Power 《权力制约论》', *Science of Law* 《法学》, No.10.

Zhang, Zhuyuan (1998), 'Ownership Reform 《所有制改革》', in Zhang, Zhuyuan, Huang, Huanzhang, and Li, Guangan (eds.), *Twenty Years of Economic Reforms: in retrospect and prospect* 《20 年经济改革回顾与展望》, Chinese Planning Press, Beijing.

Zhang, Zhuyuan, Huang, Huanzhang, and Li, Guangan (eds.) (1998), *Twenty Years of Economic Reforms: in retrospect and prospect* 《20 年经济改革回顾与展望》, Chinese Planning Press, Beijing.

Zhao, Suishen (1998), 'Three Scenarios', *Journal of Democracy*, Vol.9, No.1.

Zheng, Shiping (1997), *Party vs. State in Post-1949 China*, Cambridge University Press, Cambridge.

Zhu, Fangmin, Yao, Shurong, Zou, Yi, and Hu, Shifa (1998), *The Private Economy in China* 《私有经济在中国》, China Urban Press, Beijing.

Documents and Reports

1. CPC and State Documents

Current Issues of the Rural Economic Policy 《当前农村经济政策的若干问题》 was approved and issued by the Politburo of the CPC Central Committee on 2nd January 1983.

Decision of the CPC Central Committee on Some Questions Concerning the Acceleration of Agricultural Development (Draft for Trial) 《中共中央关于加快农业发展若干问题的决定（草案）》 was issued by the CPC Central Committee in November 1978.

Instructions on the Development of Rural and Urban Retail Commercial and Service Industries 《关于发展城乡零售商业、服务业的指示》 was issued jointly by the CPC Central Committee and the State Council on 5th March 1983.

Provisional Regulations of the People's Republic of China on Private Enterprises 《中华人民共和国私营企业暂行条例》 was issued by the State Council on 25th June 1988.

Regulations on Several Issues Concerning the Transporting of Goods for sale by Co-operative Commercial Enterprises and Individuals 《关于合作商业组织和个人贩运农副产品若干问题》 was issued by the State Council on 25th February 1984.

Regulations on the Special Economic Zones (SEZ) in Guangdong Province 《广东省经济特区条例》 was adopted by the Standing Committee of the National People's Congress on 26th August 1980.

Regulations on the Work in Rural People's Communes (Draft for Trial) 《农村人民公社条例（试行草案）》 was issued by the CPC Central Committee in December 1978.

Ten Policies of the CPC Central Committee and the State Council on Further Revitalising the Rural Economy 《中共中央、国务院关于进一步活跃农村经济的十项政策》 was issued jointly by the CPC Central Committee and the State Council on 1st January 1985.

Ten Years' Planning Outlines 《十年规划纲要》 was adopted by the First Session of the Fifth National People's Congress in February 1978.

The Circular on Several Issues Concerning the Strengthening and Improving of the Rural Contracted Production Responsibility 《关于进一步加强和完善农业生产责任制的几个问题》 was issued by the CPC Central Committee on 27th September 1980.

The CPC Central Committee Decision on the Reform of the Economic System 《中共中央关于经济体制改革的决定》 was adopted at the Third Plenum of the CPC Central Committee on 20th October 1984.

The CPC Central Committee Resolution on the Cultural Revolution 《中共中央关于无产阶级文化大革命的决定》 was adopted at the 11th Plenary Session of the CPC Eighth Central Committee on 8th August 1966.

The CPC Central Committee's Circular on the 1984 Rural Work 《中共中央关于一九八四年农村工作的通知》 was issued by the CPC Central Committee on 1st January 1984.

The Summary of the National Rural Work Conference (December 1981) 《全国农村工作会议纪要（一九八一年十二月）》 was endorsed and issued by the CPC Central Committee on 1st January 1982.

2. Statistical Reports

China Financial Yearbook 《中国财政年鉴》1996, compiled by National Bureau of Statistics, People's Republic of China（中华人民共和国国家统计局）. Beijing: China Statistics Press, 1996.

China Statistical Yearbook 《中国统计年鉴》1996, 1997, 1999 and 2002, compiled by National Bureau of Statistics, People's Republic of China（中华人民共和国国家统计局）. Beijing: China Statistics Press, 1996, 1997, 1999 and 2002.

Communiqué of PRC on the Key Data of the Fifth National Population Census (No. One) 《第五次全国人口普查主要数据公报（第一号）》, issued by National Bureau of Statistics, People's Republic of China（中华人民共和国国家统计局）on 28th March 2001.

Communiqué of PRC on the Key Data of the Fifth National Population Census (No. Two) 《第五次全国人口普查主要数据公报（第二号）》, issued by National Bureau of Statistics, People's Republic of China （中华人民共和国国家统计局）on 2nd April 2001.

Jiangsu Statistical Yearbook 《江苏省统计年鉴》*1996*, compiled by Jiangsu Bureau of Statistics（江苏省统计局）, Beijing: China Statistics Press (1996).

Semi Annual Survey Report on Internet Development in China 《中国互联网络发展状况统计报告》, issued by China Internet Network Information Centre（中国互联网络信息中心）in January 2002.

Shanghai Statistical Yearbook 《上海市统计年鉴》*1996*, compiled by Shanghai Bureau of Statistics（上海市统计局）. Beijing: China Statistics Press (1996).

Statistical Communiqué of the People's Republic of China on the 1999 National Economic and Social Development 《中华人民共和国 1999 年国民经济和社会发展统计公报》, issued by National Bureau of Statistics, People's Republic of China（中华人民共和国国家统计局）on 28th February 2000.

Statistical Communiqué of the People's Republic of China on the 2000 National Economic and Social Development 《中华人民共和国 2000 年国民经济和社会发展统计公报》, issued by National Bureau of Statistics, People's Republic of China （中华人民共和国国家统计局）on 26th March 2001.

Statistical Communiqué of the People's Republic of China on the 2001 National Economic and Social Development 《中华人民共和国 2001 年国民经济和社会发展统计公报》, issued by National Bureau of Statistics, People's Republic of China （中华人民共和国国家统计局）on 28th February 2002.

Statistical Communiqué of Jiangsu on the 2000 Provincial Economic and Social Development 《江苏省 2000 年国民经济和社会发展统计公报》, issued by Jiangsu Bureau of Statistics（江苏省统计局）on 9th March 2001.

Statistical Communiqué of Shanghai on the 2000 Municipal Economic and Social Development 《上海市 2000 年国民经济和社会发展统计公报》, issued by Shanghai Bureau of Statistics（上海市统计局）on 9th March 2001.

World Development Indicators, World Bank, 1998-2002.

Zhejiang People's Government Report on the 2000 Provincial Economy 《2000 年浙江省经济运行情况》, issued by Zhejiang People's Government（浙江省人民政府）in March 2001. http://www.zhejiang.gov.cn/jjzk/jjzk.htm.

3. Others

Comprehensive Understanding of "State Innovation System" and Building an Overall "China (State) Innovation System" 《全面理解"国家创新体系"含义，构建完整"中国（国家）创新体系"》, a report presented by "State Innovation System" Research Unit, Institute of Philosophy, Chinese Academy of Social Sciences（中国社会科学院哲学研究所"国家创新体系"研究小组）, in 2000, (http://www.cass.net.cn/.).

The Case of Peng The-Huai 《彭德怀案件专辑》1959-1968. Hong Kong: Union Research Institute, 1968.

Index

For Product Safety Concerns and Information please contact our EU
representative GPSR@taylorandfrancis.com Taylor & Francis Verlag GmbH,
Kaufingerstraße 24, 80331 München, Germany

Printed and bound by CPI Group (UK) Ltd, Croydon, CR0 4YY
01/05/2025
01858334-0002